RABELAIS

A CRITICAL STUDY IN
PROSE FICTION

COMPANION STUDIES

HERTFORDSHIRE LIBRARY SERVICE

Hertfordshire
COUNTY COUNCIL
Community Information

Please renew/return this item by the last date shown.

So that your telephone call is charged at local rate, please call the numbers as set out below:

	From Area codes 01923 or 020:	From the rest of Herts:
Renewals:	01923 471373	01438 737373
Enquiries:	01923 471333	01438 737333
Minicom:	01923 471599	01438 737599

L32   www.hertsdirect.org

Rabelais

A CRITICAL STUDY IN PROSE FICTION

DOROTHY GABE COLEMAN

Fellow of New Hall and Lecturer in French,
University of Cambridge

CAMBRIDGE
AT THE UNIVERSITY PRESS
1971

Published by the Syndics of the Cambridge University Press
Bentley House, 200 Euston Road, London N.W.1
American Branch: 32 East 57th Street, New York, N.Y.10022

© Cambridge University Press 1971

ISBN: 0 521 08125 4

Printed in Great Britain by
Alden & Mowbray Ltd
at the Alden Press, Oxford

CONTENTS

i'r teulu

PREFACE

The *Cinquiesme Livre* was not published until 1564 when Rabelais had been dead eleven years. The problem of its authenticity has been discussed for almost 400 years; short of external evidence – an autograph or contemporary documentation – the problem cannot be solved. It is not discussed in this work at all.

The English version used throughout is that of Sir Thomas Urquhart of Cromarty (1611–60) for the first three books and that of Peter le Motteux for the fourth book. It is a very free interpretation, and occasionally I have indicated Urquhart's additions to the original by placing them in square brackets. Where it has been necessary to supply a more accurate rendering, this is followed by the initials 'D.C.' Passages from Rabelais in French are quoted from the Garnier edition, *Œuvres complètes*, ed. P. Jourda (2 vols, Paris, 1962).

May I thank Dr Alison Fairlie for her faith in me; Dr Grahame Castor, for having willingly submitted himself to reading a draft of this book; Dr Odette de Mourgues, who through wit, warmth and vigour has kept me on the Rabelaisian path; Professor Edward Wilson and Mr Michael Black, whose criticisms of the work have brought many improvements and would no doubt have brought even more but for the author's stubbornness, and finally my husband, without whom this book would not have been written.

D.G.C.

March 1971

ABBREVIATIONS

BHR	*Bibliothèque d'Humanisme et Renaissance*
THR	*Travaux d'Humanisme et Renaissance*
THR, ER	*Travaux d'Humanisme et Renaissance. Études Rabelaisiennes*

1

INTRODUCTION

Rabelais, like Shakespeare, is 'all things to all men'. In France the mere mention of Gargantua and Pantagruel, of *andouilles* or *fouaces*, of Chinon or La Devinière, prompts people to indulge in spoonerisms or burst into side-splitting laughter. In Britain the word Rabelaisian has become synonymous with ribaldry and one of his giants is enshrined in the language – in the phrase a Gargantuan feast – as a symbol of gluttony. As early as 1554 – a year after Rabelais had died – his 'merry jester' legend had taken root: a fat, wine-swilling, fun-loving, women-shunning, obscene and witty monk. This 400-year-old legend is a compliment to the breadth of his appeal, even if it conveys little of the shape of his fictional universe which encompasses the author, his characters, his language and his comic vision of the world he lived in. The legend creates a sympathy between audience and author built on fantasy, constant word-mongering, parodies, puns, intoxicated ridicule, scoffing and scurrilous remarks, and seals them in a comic interpretation of life. But the legend clouds the fact that he was a monk – first a Franciscan and later a Benedictine – in the age of the Reformation, a physician who loved to give anatomy demonstrations including dissections of the human body, and a scholar of vast erudition who also wrote a major work of fiction in his mother tongue.

As a monk, Rabelais was aware of the fundamentals of Christian belief. His own acquaintance with theology was deep, and all the assumptions he made about man and God were derived from it. He never gave up believing in an omniscient and omnipotent God, nor did he give up the ideal of man loving man. As a medical man, he edited the Latin letters of an Italian doctor, prepared an edition of Hippocrates' *Aphorisms* and Galen's *Ars medicinalis* and was in contact with the leading scholars in France in the 1520s and 1530s: people like Budé, Tiraqueau, Marguerite de Navarre and Dolet. As a literary man, he started writing in the vernacular rather late in life, if we accept 1494 as the probable date of his birth. For in the Lyons November fair in 1532 a small quarto volume of sixty-four leaves was on sale, called *Pantagruel. Les horribles et espoventables faictz et prouesses du tresrenommé Pantagruel Roy des Dipsodes filz du grand geant Gargantua. Composez nouvellement par maistre Alcofrybas Nasier.* There was no indication as to its authorship, beyond the anagrammatic pseudonym 'Alcofrybas Nasier', and it is not until the *Tiers Livre*, published in 1546, that we have the signature *M. Fran. Rabelais, Docteur en Medicine.*

We have no external evidence of Rabelais's literary talent before 1532; no contemporary indication that he was a good *raconteur*; his circle of friends in Fontenay-le-Comte or in Lyons testify to his learning and his skill as a physician; they congratulate him on his editions of medical classical texts but never even allude to his sense of humour or to his enjoyment of puns and spoonerisms. But Rabelais was aware of a wider public than the humanists; the success in the Lyons summer fair of 1532 of a little chap-book on Gargantua the giant by an anonymous author – not to be identified with Rabelais himself – was a reflection of this public. And Rabelais, who had hitherto allied himself with the humanists in restoring medicine to its ancient splendour, now wrote a book destined for more than the élite of the time. The Sorbonne condemned it in 1533 for its obscenity, but Rabelais had sufficient faith in his comic book to publish a sequel in 1534 entitled *La vie inestimable du grand Gargantua, pere de Pantagruel.* After this there is silence from his humanist friends – proof that the book had ceased to be regarded as simply clownish and was now considered dangerous and compromising. The atmosphere in France had deteriorated rapidly after 1534, and the freedom and ideals of the Erasmian era were snuffed out by persecution and the hardening of polemical attitudes. When the fabric of the church is safe, parody, satire and obscenity are given free rein, but between 1534 and 1550 both sides in the Reformation dispute became increasingly sensitive to irreverence and gaulois obscenity.

In the sermon tradition, particularly the Franciscan sermons – which Rabelais had been brought up on – there had been violent satire and invective against the clergy; attacking their lechery, simony, hypocrisy, their lack of devotion in church and their negligence of official duties as well as the perennial complaint of their illiteracy. The sermons were not meant to be ammunition for the Reformation, though in fact they were used as such by both Luther and Calvin. The works of Menot, Raulin and Maillard give a picture of the church from within, and *before* the Reformation; and they depict too the audience at which Rabelais was aiming, beyond the circle of his humanist friends. But fiction-writing stands abruptly at right angles to the sermonist's condemnation of this world or to erudite commentaries on the Bible. It would be an easy task for a humanist scholar to sit down in a well-stocked reference library, stuff his head with learned quotations and allusions, and with no more than a moderate talent turn out an encyclopaedic tome. But Rabelais did not do this. At which point the twentieth-century reader feels bound to ask such questions as 'Of what then does his greatness consist? Why is he worth reading? Is the tremendous joy in playing with reality, the mood of excitement and adventure, consonant with the ideas expressed? Is religion meant to be taken seriously?'

A book is in some ways a pact between author and readers and the best way to acquire a 'feel' for Rabelais's work is to examine at the outset a particular passage that can illustrate his richness as a writer in concrete terms. The passage that I have selected comes from the fourth and fifth chapters of *Gargantua* (pp. 21-4).[1] It describes how the pregnant Gargamelle devoured an enormous amount of tripe at a feast, how Grandgousier her husband lavished good fare on all his neighbours and how everyone present talked and talked.

L'occasion et maniere comment Gargamelle enfanta fut telle, et, si ne le croyez, le fondement vous escappe!

Le fondement luy escappoit une après dinée, le iij^e jour de febvrier, par trop avoir mangé de gaudebillaux. Gaudebilleaux sont grasses tripes de coiraux. Coiraux sont beufz engressez à la creche et prez guimaulx. Prez guimaulx sont qui portent herbe deux fois l'an. D'iceulx graz beufz avoient faict tuer troys cens soixante sept mille et quatorze, pour estre à mardy gras sallez, affin qu'en la prime vere ilz eussent beuf de saison à tas pour, au commencement des re-pastz, faire commemoration de saleures et mieulx entrer en vin.

Les tripes furent copieuses, comme entendez, et tant friandes estoient que chascun en leichoit ses doigtz. Mais la grande diablerie à quatre personnaiges estoit bien en ce que possible n'estoit longuement les reserver, car elles feussent pourries. Ce que sembloit indecent. Dont fut conclud qu'ils les bauffreroient sans rien y perdre. A ce faire convierent tous les citadins de Sainnais, de Suillé, de la Roche Clermaud, de Vaugaudray, sans laisser arrieres le Coudray Montpensier, le Gué de Vede et aultres voisins, tous bons beveurs, bons compaignons, et beaulx joueurs de quille là.

Le bon homme Grandgousier y prenoit plaisir bien grand et commendoit que tout allast par escuelles. Disoit toutesfoys à sa femme qu'elle en mangeast le moins, veu qu'elle aprochoit de son terme et que ceste tripaille n'estoit viande moult louable: 'Celluy (disoit il) a grande envie de mascher merde, qui d'icelle le sac mangeue.' Non obstant ces remonstrances, elle en mangea seze muiz, deux bussars et six tupins. O belle matiere fecale que doivoit boursouffler en elle!

Après disner, tous allerent pelle melle à la Saulsaie, et là, sus l'herbe drue, dancerent au son des joyeux flageolletz et doulces cornemuses tant baudement que c'estoit passetemps celeste les veoir ainsi soy rigouller.

Puis entrerent en propos de resieuner on propre lieu. Lors flaccons d'aller, jambons de troter, goubeletz de voler, breusses de tinter:

— Tire!

— Baille!

— Tourne!

— Brouille!

— Boutte à moy sans eau; ainsi, mon amy.

— Fouette moy ce verre gualentement;

— Produiz moy du clairet, verre pleurant.

— Treves de soif!

— Ha, faulse fievre, ne t'en iras tu pas?

— Par ma fy, me commere, je ne peuz entrer en bette.

— Vous estez morfondue, m'amie?

— Voire.

— Ventre sainct Quenet! parlons de boire.

— Je ne boy que à mes heures, comme la mulle du pape.

— Je ne boy que en mon breviaire, comme un beau pere guardian.

— Qui feut premier, soif ou beuverye?

— Soif, car qui eust beu sans soif durant le temps de innocence?

— Beuverye, car *privatio presupponit habitum*. Je suis clerc.

Foecundi calices quem non fecere disertum?

— Nous aultres innocens ne beuvons que trop sans soif.

— Non moy, pecheur, sans soif, et, si non presente, pour le moins future, la prevenent comme entendez. Je boy pour la soif advenir. Je boy eternellement. Ce m'est eternité de beuverye, et beuverye de eternité.

— Chantons, beuvons, un motet entonnons!

4

The occasion and manner how Gargamelle was brought to bed, and delivered of her childe, was thus: and, if you do not beleeve it, I wish your bum-gut fall out, and make an escapade. Her bum-gut, indeed, or fundament escaped her in an afternoone, on the third day of February, with having eaten at dinner too many godebillios. Godebillios are the fat tripes of coiros, coiros are beeves fatned at the cratch in Oxe stalls, or in the fresh guimo meadows, guimo meadows are those, that for their fruitfulnesse may be mowed twice a yeare, and of those fat beeves they had killed three hundred sixty seven thousand and fourteen, to be salted at Shrovetide, that in the entring of the Spring they might have plenty of poudred beef, wherewith to season their mouths at the beginning of their meales, and to taste their wine the better.

They had abundance of tripes, as you have heard, and they were so delicious, that every one licked his fingers, but the mischiefe was this, that for all men could do, there was no possibility to keep them long in that relish; for in a very short while they would have stunk, which had been an undecent thing: it was therefore concluded, that they should be all of them gulched up, without losing any thing; to this effect they invited all the Burguers of Sainais, of Suille, of the Rocheclermand, of Vaugaudry, without omitting the Boudray, Monpensier, the Guedevede, and other their neighbours, all stiffe drinkers, brave fellows, and good players at the kyles. The good man Grangousier took great pleasure in their company, and commanded there should be no want nor pinching for any thing: neverthelesse he bade his wife eate sparingly, because she was near her time, and that these tripes were no very commendable meat: they would faine (said he) be at the chewing of ordure, that would eat the case wherein it was. Notwithstanding these admonitions, she did eate sixteen quarters, two bushels, three pecks and a pipkin full: O the fair fecality, wherewith she swelled by the ingrediency of such shitten stuffe!

After dinner they all went out in a hurle, to the grove of the willows, where on the green grasse, to the sound of the merry Flutes and pleasant Bagpipes they danced so gallantly, that it was a sweet and heavenly sport to see them so frolick.

Then did they fall upon the chat of victuals and some belly furniture to be snatched at in the very same place, which purpose was no sooner mentioned, but forthwith began flaggons to go, gammons to trot, goblets to fly, great bowles to ting, glasses to ring, draw, reach, fill, mixe, give it me without water, so my friend, so whip me off this glasse neatly, bring me hither some claret, a full weeping glasse till it run over, a cessation and truce with thirst. Ha, thou false Fever, wilt thou not be gone? by my figgins, godmother, I cannot as yet enter in the humour of being merry, nor drink so currantly as I would. You have catch'd a cold, gamer, yea forsooth, Sir; by the belly of Sanct Buf, let us talk of our drink, I never drink but at my hours, like the Pope's Mule, and I never drink but in my breviary, like a faire father Gardien. Which was first, thirst or drinking? Thirst, for who in the time of innocence would have drunk without being athirst? nay, Sir, it was drinking; for *privatio praesupponit habitum*. I am learned you see: *Fecundi calices quem non fecere disertum*? we poor innocents drink but too much without thirst: not I truly, who am a sinner, for I never drink without thirst, either present or future, to prevent it, as you know, I drink for the thirst to come; I drink eternally, this is to me an eternity of drinking, and drinking of eternity; let us sing, let us drink, and tune up our round-lays.

Our first impression is of a pattern akin to a Rubens *kermis*, with all the enthusiasm, the energy, the dynamism and joy of a spectacle. Our eye moves from Gargamelle to a vast quantity of tripe, then to a thronging multitude of neighbours assembled in the willow-grove, rubbing shoulders with each other and exchanging jokes as they weave to and fro enjoying the tripe and wine. But the visual painting is, as it were, in the middle ground; the foreground is oral. The exuberant noise of language radiates through the scene, language which is crammed with popular idiom, with crude and vulgar expressions, with scholastic syllogisms, and with a pseudo-comic precision through superfluity of detail. We note the constant picking up of phrases (*'le fondement vous escappe/Le fondement luy escappoit'*), the long sentences alternating with crisp statements (*'Gaudebilleaux sont grasses tripes de coiraux'*), the continual references back which catch up with the immediate sense (*'tourne/brouille'* associated by the action of turning). There is a complex criss-cross and overlay of ideas throughout the whole passage, with poetic devices like the rhyming schema (*'Voire/boire'*), the onomatopoeia (*'breusses de tinter'*) and *jeux de mots* (*'entonnons'*). Our own participation in the scene is established by the use of the pronoun *vous*. A fascinating new range of patterns, forms, textures and perspectives has been revealed. At one moment our attention is held by the over-magnified texture of the tripe, at another by the perspective of a whole rural scene, where the fattening of beef for slaughter is enlarged into a pattern in which the primitive forces of hunger, appetite and the allaying of them are dovetailed with suggestions of fertility, pregnancy, ritual food-growing and hunting. Rabelais seems to possess the magic quality of making anything alive, intensely and joyfully alive, through his linguistic talent. Let us look more closely at the passage and its two distinct halves.

The first half is narrative and the second dialogue. In the first is a gigantic epic framework; in the second, a more human one of conversation. The first is a burlesque treatment of the earthy Gargamelle and the mock-heroic exit of all the '*citadins*' (a word used ironically so that every hamlet around becomes enlarged to the size of a fortified city) and Grandgousier's humorously lavish provision for his neighbours of all the good things there are for man to eat and drink. The second half of the passage brings the rhythm of narration to a standstill and offers instead a master-piece of dialogue. The whole passage serves to place the enormous pregnant Gargamelle in a vast setting of poetic drunkenness.

The first sentence is disorientating: a voice speaks which is entirely different from the one that the reader would expect, particularly if he was familiar with the chap-book on Gargantua which had come out in 1532. This voice is not the anonymous chronicler who recounts a tale of giants; it is an authorial *I*. Rabelais in saying 'si ne le croyez, le fondement vous escappe!' adopts a voice which is more intimate, closer to his readers. A scatalogical note is heard in the spluttering exclamation. It is not Franciscus Rabelaesus speaking but Alcofrybas, and they are two different persons. They are writing in different languages and they do not combine to form a single identity. Before this point, it seems that we are reading a popular book. Yet the shape of the sentence, with its matter-of-fact beginning followed by the emotive, authorial, obscene exclamation is disorientating. Is Rabelais saying to us, his readers: 'I am on your side. You are on my side'? Is this an invitation to participate in the game of fiction? We look at his whole narration now with spectacles provided by the author. We enter into the fictional theatre where Gargantua is to be born. The birth of a son is normally a serious topic, but here the view of it is unconventional. For the childbirth is isolated from its usual paraphernalia – midwives, pails, brown paper and so on. The human body is seen with the detachment of a physician; and that detachment is the first essential ingredient for comedy. The phrase '*le fondement vous escappe!*' – in the sense 'may your anal prolapsus take place' – punishes the readers' disbelief with the threat of a technical medical event. Addressed as it is to possibly sceptical readers, it makes us laugh. At the beginning of the next sentence, when it is repeated, it is applied to Gargamelle and takes on a literal sense. Her advanced pregnancy together with the indigestion caused by eating all that tripe will provide a double case of prolapsus: the falling down of the uterus in child-birth and of the rectum in diarrhoea. There is thus a play on the two uses: the figurative one – 'may your bum-gut fall down 'applied to the reader – and the literal anatomical one applied to Gargamelle.

From that point on we realize that any subject can be viewed from a comic angle provided we have the detachment to suspend both emotion and moral judgement. This first sentence in fact gives us a view of the coherence of Rabelais's vision throughout the books: we laugh at the discrepancy between the normal human and emotional attitude to childbirth and the abnormal or medical one given here. The violent distancing of pregnancy and childbirth is comic in the same way as the allusion to the sexual act in the phrase *'beaulx joueurs de quille'* later on in the passage, where there is a play on the two meanings, 'good skittle-players' and 'good copulators'. Words such as *baudouiner* (*Quart Livre*, chapter 52), *beliner* (*Tiers Livre*, chapter 12), *chevaucher* (*Pantagruel*, chapter 21), *faire la beste à deux doz* (*Gargantua*, chapter 3), *se frotans leur lard* (*Gargantua*, chapter 3) and *jouer du serrecropiere* are all descriptions of the sexual act but are not inserted merely for their obscenity; they all exemplify the comic and ebullient way in which Rabelais depicts events. Similarly, one looks at all the names for a penis (*Gargantua*, chapter 11) with the detached, somewhat startled eye of an amused spectator. This coherence of Rabelais's comic vision brings us to the unity of his technique in general, and we can now briefly look at some of the relevant details in the present passage.

First, the epic treatment of appetite: Grandgousier, his friends and Gargamelle have prodigious eating capacities. This enlarge-ment of all normal proportions is a comic device and is a pointer towards the treatment in the *Quart Livre* of messere Gaster where the *Venter Deus* is exploited in a ruthless manner. Within this epic treatment there is a delicious appeal to all the senses. Consider the adjectives used to describe the tripe: *'grasses, copieuses'* and *'fri-*

andes' all evoke the appetizing sight and smell of a luscious meal. Then there are the colloquial verbs describing a human being's capacity to eat – '*bauffreroient*' – 'eat voraciously' – is a dialect word from Anjou; '*boursouffler*' literally means 'to increase in bulk, distend and swell'; and the sentence enclosing the latter verb, 'O belle matiere fecale que doivoit boursouffler en elle!' shows Rabelais's command of rhetoric and comedy in applying a grandiloquent linguistic form to something that is low and coarse. Look too at the way the tripe is defined: with a parody of scholastic argumentation, which employs low terms within the structure which suggests the syllogism. Both the chain of reasoning and the way in which it is expressed reveal an almost metaphoric way of composing prose. '*Gaudebilleaux* (from *gode* – a popular dialect word for an old cow; *beillas* – another dialect word for the intestines of a cow) *sont grasses tripes de coiraux*' (again a dialect term from Anjou, meaning beef fattened from birth for slaughter): the form of a syllogism is hinted at; it is as if the first premiss is given, then comes the common term '*coiraux*' and the second premiss – 'Coiraux sont beufz engressez à la creche et prez guimaulx.' But it is only the form that is kept; the reasoning itself is a calculated travesty of scholastic discourse. A twentieth-century reader may know that '*gaudebilleaux*' are the modern *tripes à la mode de Caen* and so be able to savour in imagination this succulent dish, which has been simmering for twelve hours in an hermetically-sealed brown earthenware pot, with the aroma of onions, carrots, garlic, leeks, spices and a final dash of calvados.

The salty tripe must first be washed down with wine and so, at the beginning of the repast, one has to 'faire commemoration de saleures et mieulx entrer en vin'. But the phrase has a double meaning: 'to nibble at hors d'œuvres' and, in liturgical usage 'to offer a short prayer', as, for instance, at the beginning of mass, commemorating the lesser of two feasts that fall on the same date. Rabelais the monk can borrow the technical term and apply it to something totally disconnected with its liturgical meaning, relying on his audience's knowing the term and so catching the humour of the expression.[2] Later on, in the same paragraph, he uses as a periphrasis the phrase '*diablerie à quatre personnaiges*' to mean 'but the trouble was'. Here he is evoking for his readers the world of medieval farce: for a *diablerie* was a play acted by imps or devils, sometimes Satan and his followers, and played by four different characters. It was notoriously difficult both for the players to act and for the spectators to understand. Already we see what kind of difficulties of language and allusion we are up against: the vocabulary is rich, ranging from popular speech and dialect terms through Latin ecclesiastical terms to sixteenth-century features like *la prime vere* and *saleures*, and with allusions drawn from the church, and from medieval and classical literature.

Secondly, his characters are grotesquely comic: with a few brush strokes he delineates Gargamelle – as greedy as a sow – and we see her as the pivot around whom the whole comic framework turns. Grandgousier is childlike, smiling, earthily coarse (for instance in his chiding of Gargamelle – 'Celluy ... a grande envie de mascher merde, qui d'icelle le sac mangeue') and combining gluttony with a *joie de boire*. His love of fine wines from the Loire valley is natural (the vineyards had been established since about the fourth century AD); they belong to his native countryside and besides, they are excellent! His benevolence is apparent when he invites all his neighbours from all the villages and hamlets around his court to the *kermis*. Grandgousier's love of food and drink not only characterizes the giants but also introduces Rabelais's leitmotif of culinary terms. For instance, the entry of Panurge (*Pantagruel*, chapter 9) and of frere Jan (*Gargantua*, chapter 27) and the counterpoint between them in the third and fourth books has gastronomy as its ground bass.

Thirdly, the intrusion of a comic precision is a way of 'disrupting' the epic framework of the narration. Thus the precise number of cows slaughtered to produce this quantity of tripe, 'faict tuer troys cens soixante sept mille et quatorze', and the precise amount of tripe consumed by Gargamelle, 'elle en mangea seze muiz, deux bussars et six tupins', both serve to enhance the fantasy. Within this comic fantasy, Rabelais can describe crude objects sometimes in an enlarged close-up, so that the most repulsive aspects of familiar things (for instance, in this passage man's defecatory functions) shock our complacent view of reality. In this first half both the detached and the close-up views occur in quick proximity and we view Rabelais as if he were a photographer with a movie camera. Furthermore, the accumulation and enumeration bring with them a lengthening of the sentences: for instance, the sentence beginning 'D'iceulx graz beufz …' has to be read as if it had no real breaks; in the repetition of '*beufz*', in the echo of *sallez* in '*saleures*', and in the breathless panting rhythm, content and form drive us on to the triumphant conclusion – one must have some wine. Everything demands a re-orientation on our part: the fantastic and the real, the gigantic and the human, jostle with one another; the reader is hurried from one plane to the next with no time or breathing space to become accustomed to Rabelais's world. The intrusion of a self-conscious author is a pointer to Rabelais's presence throughout his work; the *vous* are ourselves, his intended readers. He hints that extempore and 'natural' ways of composing make it impossible for him to give a meaningful account of the world except through these burlesque purple-coloured spectacles. The world here is muscular, sinewy and fictive and the comic vision cuts out any emotion, appealing only to our intellect.

Turning to the second half of the passage, we find first of all that the whole of the last part, from 'Je ne boy que à mes heures' to the end, was not added until the 1542 edition published by François Juste. Two comments can be made on this: first, that the apparent spontaneity of this discourse is belied by the further enumeration of the gossip. This confirms an impression gained in the first half: like all authors of the sixteenth century, Rabelais added rather than suppressed in his corrections. For instance, he augments a phrase until it becomes an ebullient enumeration as in chapter 11 of *Gargantua:*

First edition	*Second edition*
et patrouilloit partout. Les petitz chiens de son pere mengeoyent en son escuelle.	et patroilloit par tout, et beuvoyt en sa pantophle, et se frottoyt ordinerement le ventre d'un panier. Ses dens aguysoit d'un sabot, ses mains lavoyt de potaige, se pignoyt d'un guoubelet. Les petitz chiens de son pere mengoyent en son escuelle.*

*and dabled, padled and slabbered every where: He would drink in his slipper, and

Secondly, it is a monk's joke that is added here. It is interesting that several of his other corrections in *Gargantua* were obviously motivated by prudence: for instance, in chapter 18, the hood, the *lyripipion* of Janotus de Bragmardo which was *theologal* until 1542, became *à l'antique* in François Juste's edition. Janotus himself instead of being a *theologien* is called a *sophiste*. Thus, Rabelais moderated his attacks on the Sorbonne, treading gently in matters where a compromising stance would expose him to the danger of being called a heretic. However, this whole complex of jokes about thirst on the analogy of 'Which comes first, the hen or the egg?' is judged by Rabelais to be uncompromising and so it is safe to insert it at this point.

The dialogue here is masterly. Questions and answers interweave in a series of subtle chains. The transition from one word to another makes the ideas follow on, more by free association with one another than as part of a logical sequence. The absence of a logical link between ideas means that the words lose one of their essential functions – that of communicating – and become instead the starting point for his mythical fantasy. The distinction between what language expresses and the meanings it creates by its patterning is one of the main features of Rabelais's comic style. He can play on double or often triple meanings, as for instance in '*Ventre sainct Quenet!*' where the first meaning is a swearword, and the second a diminutive referring to an indecent part of woman's anatomy. He can employ Latinisms, nicknames and spoonerisms to entertain his readers, who like him have forgotten about any story. The whole conversation has two themes: food and drink. The speed of the repartee, the exchange of words, liberally sprinkled with interjection and exclamation, the answers relying on *jeux de mots* or on verbal similarities, and the sheer number of characters talking produce the effect of a verbal tempest which makes it impossible for the reader to know whether he is in a real world or in a world of fantasy created by Rabelais.

Let us look briefly at some of the detail. First of all, Rabelais

ordinarily rub his belly against a Panier: He sharpened his teeth with a top, washed his hands with his broth, and combed his head with a bole ... his fathers little dogs eat out of the dish with him, and he with them.

opens the scene in a fast, buoyant way, 'Lors flaccons d'aller,
jambons de troter, goubeletz de voler, breusses de tinter ...'
The infinitives immediately catch our attention, giving a racy
start to the passage. The verbs remain a dominant feature of his
style: the rhythm of the phrases when read aloud and the way in
which each reinforces the others make us aware that it is the
spoken word, with all its ebullience and vitality, that is respon-
sible for the dynamics of Rabelais's style. The combination of
symmetry and apparent spontaneity gives us an aesthetic satisfac-
tion and we are able to share something of the author's great
delight in manipulating language, a delight which reflects the
joie de vivre that is so characteristic of Rabelais's four books. The
interspersion of Latin with French is also amusing: a twentieth-
century reader who enjoys *Comic and Curious Verse* – for example:

> Prope ripam fluvii solus
> A senex silently sat;
> Super capitem ecce his wig,
> Et wig super, ecce his hat.

> Blew Zephyrus alte, acerbus
> Dum elderly gentleman sat;
> Et a capite took up quite torve
> Et in rivum projecit his hat.

– is ready for, 'Je ne boy que à mes heures, comme la mulle du
pape.' 'Je ne boy que en mon breviaire, comme un beau pere
guardian.' This series of jokes comes from Rabelais's own background: as a Franciscan he knew that monastic life was dominated
by *heures;* day was divided up into 'canonical hours', matins,
vespers and other fixed hours of worship, periods of meditation
and prayer, interspersed with concrete realities of eating, drinking,
urinating or defecating. '*Comme la mulle du pape*' plays on two
meanings of *mulle:* a mule and a slipper; the first meaning had
already been used by Rabelais in *Pantagruel,* chapter 7, 'Apologie
d'icelluy, contre ceulx qui disent que la Mule du Pape ne mange
qu'à ces heures.' Mules are a stubborn yet gentle race and the
honour of carrying the pope gives rise to an almost proverbial
expression for anything done fantastically. The second meaning
is the white slipper embroidered with a cross of gold which people

kissed in religious reverence when given audience by the pope. Thus the sentence has the meaning 'I only drink at my own times'; the double-play on *'heures'* is followed by the pun on mule/slipper in *'mulle'*. The *'breviaire'* of the second sentence is a prayer-book and also a flask; the association of ideas from *heures* to *livre d'heures*, to breviaries and then to drink is a hint that *matiere de breviaire*, which will be the leitmotif of frere Jan later on in *Gargantua*, already contains the double meaning of the technical contents of a breviary juxtaposed with a major theme of the whole book – drinking. The last comparison is ironic: *'comme un beau pere guardian'* is an allusion to the superior in a monastery of Franciscans, and the addition of *'beau'* to *'pere'* is a comic and endearing term.

The variety of people present in this discourse is indicated by means of little touches in the dialogue like *'Produiz moy du clairet'* where the legalistic term *'produiz'* – 'bring me or show me' – shows that a lawyer is speaking; or *'me commere ... m'amie'* which reveals the presence of women among the crowd. The qualities of poetic prose are already exhibited here: for instance, in the long reply on the contrast between *'innocent'* and *'pecheur'*: 'Non moy, pecheur, sans soif, et, si non presente, pour le moins future, la prevenent comme entendez. Je boy pour la soif advenir. Je boy eternellement. Ce m'est eternité de beuverye, et beuverye de eternité.' The words, which could have been the serious start to an argument of Christian doctrine, are in fact a reply to the question asked a few lines back –'Qui feut premier, soif ou beuverye?' The pivot of this phrase is *'soif'* but the intervening suggestion that no one would have drunk in the age of innocence except to satisfy the body's needs, has made innocence the centre of interest. The conversation meanders through the Latin maxim that 'A lack of something can only be defined if there has been previous possession', to the Horatian line, 'Whom has the flowing bowl not made eloquent?' and finally to *'soif'* from which it had started. This apparent incoherence aptly portrays the rambling nature of a conversation between people who are sipping and talking at the same time. The quoted reply goes through a logic-chopping analysis of something that would be trivial to an outsider. The elliptical form is deliberately obscure, as it moves abruptly from drinking in the past, present and future; and the splendid conclusion is expressed in a poetic form – 'Ce m'est eternité de beuverye, et beuverye de eternité' which forces drinking and the incongruous metaphysical concept of eternity into a comically intimate relationship. Rabelais savours the delight of playing with words, rolling them around in his mouth as his characters drink wine: they are earthy, they are good and they give an intoxicating aesthetic pleasure. The world does not exist once and for all in a set form; every glance the author gives renews and rediscovers its freshness. External reality loses its constraining power and we are made ready to step inside Rabelais's fictional world. Novel juxtapositions of words hurl the things they signify into new relationships, the perception of which gives us both a mental and a physical exhilaration. What this passage reveals above all is that we must participate fully: we need to see the author's irony, parody and sheer *bouffonnerie* before coming to grips with his serious content.

Having discovered the *ondoyants et divers* aspects of Rabelais's world, the richness of his vocabulary and the galvanizing dynamics of his style, we can now consider some of the general orientations of his work.

2
ORIENTATIONS: 'ARTFUL RAB'LAIS'

'Artful Rab'lais' is a pregnant phrase. It comes from J. Mitchell's poem printed in 1694 at the beginning of Peter le Motteux's translation of the fourth and fifth books of the voyage of Pantagruel. The verse runs thus:

> Motteux has now unscreen'd the Mystic Veil,
> Which Artful Rab'lais o're the Treasure drew:
> To him who gives what th'other did conceal,
> An equal Praise, but greater thanks are due.

Mitchell's admiration for the translation may not be ours, nor indeed ours the view of Rabelais shrinking in glory beside the giant-like Motteux, but his choice of words to characterize Rabelais is extremely apt. For the *Oxford English Dictionary* gives several meanings to *artful* – an adjective which orientates our study.

The first meaning given is that of *learned* or *wise*, a meaning that is obsolete today but made perfect sense to the seventeenth-century British public for whom the translation was intended. It turns our attention to the Renaissance, in which Rabelais's learning was embedded. For the first half of the sixteenth century in France is a focal point for the bilingual – Latin and French – Renaissance. As twentieth-century students of European literature we take it for granted that we are dealing with vernacular literatures; perhaps we feel that we cannot adequately assess Latin work and perhaps we tend to think of the Latin verses written by present-day classical scholars as academic exercises or *divertissements*; perhaps too, we are unsympathetic to imitation, seeing it as a purely sterile form of composition. Even the upper *échelons* of critics often treat the Latin works of, for instance, Erasmus merely as source books. Yet we would be wrong to dismiss Latin works in this way, forgetting that from them the learning or wisdom of

Rabelais was derived. For there were writers in the Renaissance who by their re-discovery of the Golden Age, through their experimentation with forms like mock-praises and dialogues, through their translation of Greek and Latin books, and through their attempt to synthesize antiquity and Christianity were the most influential men of their time. One tradition was being rejuvenated by other older traditions and the historical sense which, 'compels a man to write not merely with his own generation in his bones, but with a feeling that the whole of literature of Europe from Homer ... has a simultaneous order ...'¹ was being born anew. And imitation had an important rôle to play in this blending of ancient literature with modern European aesthetics.

But this first meaning of *artful* goes even deeper, and we shall have to delve further into the kind of learning and wisdom that a sixteenth-century man possessed. We do not live today in an age of absolutes as regards ethics, metaphysical beliefs or even literary judgements. If we were to ask a modern philosopher or poet questions like 'What is truth?' or 'What is beauty?' we would be likely to be told that these are badly formulated questions and cannot be answered, since they assume an entity which we know does not exist. Yet, these questions would have struck philosophers, painters, architects and writers in the sixteenth century as natural and valid. They would mould very precisely a society's attitude to education, to literature, to culture, indeed to all humane activities.

France, in the first third of the sixteenth century, was passionately concerned about religion; about the 'restoration of letters' that occupied the minds of men from Francis I down to journeyman printers; and about moral philosophy. Rabelais, writing in Latin to his legal friend Tiraqueau in 1532, speaks thus about the re-flowering of the Golden Age:

Comment expliquer, très docte Tiraqueau, que dans notre siècle si plein de lumière, où une faveur singulière des Dieux nous donne de voir la restauration des plus hautes sciences, on rencontre çà et là des hommes ainsi faits qu'ils ne veulent ni ne peuvent se dégager du brouillard épais et presque cimmérien de l'époque gothique, ni lever leurs yeux vers le flambeau éclatant du soleil?²

Why did the years around 1532 seem like the birth of a new period or a precise stage in a new culture; why did it bring an awareness to many writers that they could follow what Rome had done after she had vanquished the Greeks: imitate the best literature and the best philosophy that the Greek world had produced, assimilate and digest it and then creatively re-shape it in her own conditions? Since Petrarch, the *studia humanitatis* had been recognized pre-eminently as studies befitting a human being; they were humaneness, civilization. The editing of Latin and Greek texts, teaching them professionally – these were the primary interests of the *umanisti*, that is, classical scholars. And among humanists the learned Rabelais was at home. Studying rhetoric, grammar, poetry, moral philosophy and history was their chief aim, for in these books eloquence and wisdom seemed to be united. Out of the reading of the classics as a central element in education there grew in Italy a new kind of syncretic philosophy, Neo-Platonism, which combined Platonism with Christianity. And it is in the hands of Italians like Ficino or Pico that the emphasis on man as the centre of the world attains to its most famous expression. In Pico's *Oration* man becomes the creator of his own life and destiny; he can act at will, choose for himself a sphere of activity, and his moral actions – be they bad or good, bestial or angelic – are his own responsibility.

Humanism as such, however, is a thoroughly secular movement; for example, its writings might deal with jurisprudence, mathematics or logic; they would not be specifically either for or against Christian belief; they were matters of strictly professional expertise, as they are today. Nevertheless, in the problem of assessing man as a whole there is indeed a line of thinkers who form and influence opinion in France and who may properly be called Christian humanists, not so much because they were Christians while other humanists were not, as because the fusion of classics and Christianity, the assumptions and evaluations of humanity, the educational, cultural and religious programme which they promoted were all stamped with a confidence in man. And it is to these, in particular to Erasmus, that the thought of Rabelais leads us. For again in 1532, Rabelais wrote to Erasmus with boundless gratitude, 'Father have I called you, nay mother I would name you . . .'; and as if to justify his calling Erasmus a mother, he develops the parallel with women carrying children in the womb, nourishing and protecting them from the air around them, without having seen them until they are born. Erasmus was looked on by Rabelais as the master of culture: he had edited numerous classical texts and he had translated several dialogues of Lucian into Latin. He had used the same methods for editing and commenting on the New Testament in Greek as he had used for Latin or Greek works. Both the classics and Christianity were supported by a belief in the worth of divine revelation and the perfectibility of human reason. Erasmus, like Thomas More and Colet in England, took for granted the freedom of the human will and sought worthy human life via religion, true happiness and true piety coupled with human reason. But when Erasmus uses terms like 'nature', 'reason' or 'virtue' are the assumptions underlying them the ones Rabelais had? What did sixteenth-century Christian humanists mean by *suivre la nature, vivre selon la raison* or *vera religio*? Categories like Stoic, Sceptic, Platonic, and Epicurean are almost meaningless in this century which was so syncretic in philosophy and in religion. The terminology and the vocabulary of both French and Latin were so non-static and so erratic within the same writer that it is with great caution that one starts feeling one's way to the norm.

Nature and reason, in the sixteenth century, were the two aspects of man: the Neo-Platonists in Italy and Erasmus in Northern Europe both focus attention on the rational quality of man in a generic sense – as contrasted with animals, who live according to *their* nature. That there was a particle of the divine in man was an idea current in antiquity, re-shaped by the Christian fathers and coupled in the sixteenth century with the maxim *suivre la nature* which carried implications about value judgements. Living a life which was in agreement with nature has a strong Stoic flavour: indeed in the very terminology of 'living consistently with one's nature' one is pushed back to Cicero's *de natura deorum* or *de finibus*. *Naturae convenienter vivere*, is the pass-word amongst ancient Stoics like Seneca or Renaissance ones like Budé. For the individual, the ethical problem is to bring himself as one part of nature into harmony with the whole. For instance, Cicero can say that virtue is a state of mind, a disposition of the soul; it is not an act; it is the bent of mind or its aim, and its desire is everything.[3] And so Rabelais's famous passage in *Gargantua* (chapter 57) is concerned with a commonplace idea: 'parce que gens liberes, bien nez, bien instruictz, conversans en compaignies honnestes, ont par nature un instinct et aguillon, qui tousjours les poulse à faictz vertueux et retire de vice, lequel ilz nommoient honneur'.* Man's reason causes him to be in harmony with nature, since in obeying his reason he is living in accordance not only with his own true nature but also with nature as the rational principle governing the world. What is natural in this sense is therefore morally good; so only the reasonable man can follow the path of goodness, and a man can only be free and good when in harmony with himself. So it is a sixteenth-century commonplace to link man's rational faculty with that which is good.

The interdependence of moral and intellectual traits is basic for the whole century: it is an educational assumption in Rabelais and a theological one in Erasmus.[4] But one can equally well see in the opposition that Montaigne makes between *boni* and *docti* in *Du Pédantisme* (I. 25) a clear-cut distinction between *sagesse* and mere *science*: good men have judgement within them in so far as they are *natures belles et fortes*, whilst men relying on pedantic knowledge have nothing within them. In Stoic terms virtue is willing cooperation with the deity: the individual can only have peace of mind when his will is directed in harmony with Divine Will. Thus does Rabelais's Hippothadée reason in the *Tiers Livre* and thus does Pantagruel move reasonably and naturally through the whole book. His tranquillity and independence depend on the fact that he serves men but does not get worried (i.e. *scandalizé*) by them; he engages in action without desire; he will sacrifice anything but his own internal calm.

Pantagruel's own attitude to life corresponds closely to the

---

* because men that are free, well-borne, well-bred, and conversant in honest companies, have naturally an instinct and spurre that prompteth them unto vertuous actions, and withdraws them from vice, which is called honour.

theory of indifference which the Roman Stoics had worked out, and which had also become a commonplace of Renaissance thinking. The question of the value of things was advanced in terms of what is reasonable; things are indifferent in themselves, rather it is the attitude of mind that endows them with value. Erasmus in his *Colloquies* returns again and again to this theory, as it is pronounced by Saint Paul, that Christian obedience to the external divinity, itself a form of freedom, is all that a Christian should aim at, and all trivial activities like eating, drinking, making love are indifferent because their value depends solely on the individual's attitude to them. We shall see how crucial this theory is to the understanding of the *Tiers Livre* in particular, but at this stage it is enough to point out how the aim of the whole century, ethically, was to fuse together the Stoic strain of 'choosing those things which are in accordance with nature, and avoiding those things which are against nature'[5] with a new form of Christianity.

From the metaphysical Christian viewpoint, from the recognition of the limitations of man, there comes a point where the logical has to cede to the non-logical: the freedom of the human will must submit to Divine Providence, predetermined from all eternity. Neither Erasmus nor Rabelais wasted time in abstract argument, but the paradox is there: they both subscribe to the doctrine of the Fall, they both subscribe to the faultiness of man's perverted nature and yet, at the same time, they both stress man's potential for good. It is almost as if they aimed at bringing man back to his pristine state of goodness while knowing that this was by definition impossible.

There is a fundamental break between this moral attitude and the line of thought pursued by Luther: that since the Fall, man can no longer participate in the divine; the Fall itself was a free act which separated man from God. So the perfectibility of man through a combination of his own efforts and divine revelation, as taught by Erasmus and Rabelais, is to Luther impossible by definition. For him man can only be personally lifted out of the *condition humaine*, seen as unstable and discontinuous, by a divine illumination, and the doctrine of predestination is implicit from the beginning as it is a logical outcome of the negation of free-will. But one must stress that the whole sixteenth century was *un siècle qui croit*: it offered no standpoint in metaphysics or science from which to combat the religious framework. However sharp the differences were between the Lutheran and the Erasmian evaluation of man, one must not move outside the then existing metaphysical framework.

Where Luther demanded an utter commitment to God and the knowledge that man was nothing, Erasmus and Rabelais posit man as simultaneously everything and nothing: '*Rien n'est, sinon Dieu, perfaict*', says Rabelais in the prologue to the *Tiers Livre*. Rabelais is free to mock man and the forms of religion without being for that reason fundamentally irreligious. Professor Busson says 'L'ironie, le lucianisme qui persiffle les choses de la religion sont ce qui est le plus contraire au génie de Calvin',[6] and indeed the very fact of being aware of an older tradition and the consciousness that the world is paradoxical make Rabelais and Erasmus create work which is ambiguous and equivocal. In an age of fierce religious commitment Rabelais might have been misunderstood: he was made a target of assault by conservative catholics who saw Lutheran theses beneath the *bouffonnerie*, but equally Calvin and his followers could write of him: 'Or voici un rustre qui aura des brocards vilains contre l'Escriture saincte: comme ce diable qui s'est nommé Pantagruel, et toutes ces ordures et vilenies...'[7] Obviously, we shall be able to see rather more clearly where Rabelais places himself in relation to religion later in this work; but it is not enough here to 'follow the book' since we often cannot understand the book without a knowledge of the general intellectual, metaphysical and moral assumptions that the author had. Therefore, the background will be present always, ready to guide us as to what precise meaning the author seems to want.

We appear to have let slip from our memory the meanings of *artful* and the rôle of the *OED* as their midwife. In exploring the sense of *learned*, however, we have already slightly touched upon another meaning of *artful* – 'produced by art, artificial as opposed to natural'. The non-pejorative sense of *artifex* (which as an adjective comes very close to *artful*) is, of course, a prime feature of all the literature of the Graeco–Roman civilization, and when we are looking at Rabelais as a writer we are in no way expecting him to be natural in the sense of 'spontaneous'. Fashioning impressions of the real world into the shape of an artifact recalls to our mind the controlled texture, the organization of structure and the exploitation of form that Vergil, for instance, used in writing an epic. *Artful* in the sense of *produced by art* is one of the meanings that will direct our study. But there are other senses offered by the *OED*: 'clever, artistic, skilful in adapting means to ends' and the rather pejorative meaning of 'crafty, wily and cunning'. And it is these meanings that give a particular focus to our study. In the last two decades, scholars from France, America and Great Britain have put us tremendously in their debt: we can begin to read Rabelais with some of the puzzlements and obscurities smoothed out. The probing into the contemporary climate of ideas and the reading of Rabelais in their light means that we are trying to read his works as a contemporary might have read them. (This incidentally should have enormous qualifications written into it, for his readers were as diverse as they are today and to piece together an 'interpretation of Rabelais' for the average reader of any century is impossible.) But there are two different ways of looking at him: *in* time, vertically, alongside Erasmus, Luther, Marguerite de Navarre, Calvin and Montaigne; and *out of* time, horizontally, alongside Balzac, Cervantes or Joyce. The first approach is concerned with explaining and describing him in context, and the second with asking specific questions about his fictional work. It is with the second point of view that our study will be primarily concerned: *artful, produced by art, skilful* and perhaps *wily*. The former viewpoint will, however, be enriched by examining the latter. From the next chapter onwards we shall be asking questions about the fictional nature of the prologues, the point of view that Rabelais took as a writer, the form he chose to present his work in, what kind of characterization he opted for and what kind of linguistic talent he possessed. These questions will be presented in literary terms but we shall not always expect purely literary answers to them.

We shall look at Rabelais primarily as a comic artist, not as a moralist nor as a Stoic Christian of the first half of the sixteenth century. If he had been aiming at a religious exposition of his views he would have joined the company of people like Lefèvre d'Étaples and published commentaries to texts, so achieving his aim in a less ambiguous way. But he chose to write in a fictional framework, and this choice in itself means that we cannot be content with a simple summary of his views. The swift and ironical humour which dominates the work suggests a sceptical and artistic detachment from life. His work is not a philosophical treatise but rather a perceptive prose fiction, which uses all the threads of thought of his time yet, while making imaginative use of this or that doctrine, never enunciates any. The value of any literature lies not in the soundness or originality of its philosophical doctrines nor in the moral earnestness of its intention. The medieval tradition was didactic, and Rabelais is on new ground; on this new ground we must not step with heavy moral weight. Rabelais like Proteus can change his shape and personality at will – he will be a *bouffon*, *réformateur*, Erasmian, philosopher, Menippean satirist, an *abstracteur de quintessence*; and he invites us to share his fun in each of the guises he chooses. Étienne Pasquier, at the end of the sixteenth century said, 'combien qu'il ait escrit en prose des faits heroïques de Gargantua et Pantagruel si estoit-il mis au rang des poëtes ...' It is in this light that we shall look at him.

THE PROLOGUES

It is important to catch the parody and irony in Rabelais's whole work, for otherwise one fails to note the subtle nuances as well as the direct allusions which make the work not just another medieval book but a synthesis of medieval and Renaissance ways of thinking, ways of writing and ways of composing literature. One can use, for example, the first prologue to Cervantes's *Don Quixote* as a way of putting the satire and irony of Rabelais in the right perspective. There is a delightful conversation with an intelligent friend who listens to Cervantes's moans about the absence of anything to say in a prologue. The friend says roughly: 'To gain respectability as a writer, you simply add a list of Latin and Greek sources in every conceivable place so that the readers will find such a weighty tome that they will immediately think you are a scholar!' Cervantes as a fully conscious artist is here gently satirizing the sixteenth century and it is these qualities of his which determine how readers will take *Don Quixote*. Rabelais too starts with parody and irony and the best way of savouring him is to look at the way he sells his wares in the prologues to the four books.

The prologues establish an immediate relationship between author and reader. For the reader this introduction is more dis-orientating than the passage on which we commented in the first chapter. Irony, parody, *bouffonnerie*, apparent seriousness, erudition and crudity succeed each other with such rapidity that one is left with no steadying vision or norm which would bring into focus the patterns of the kaleidoscope. The prologues are as poly-valent as the books they serve to present, so facing us with the problem of how to interpret Rabelais. They are not an ingenuous tissue of disconnected and enigmatic statements and avowed in-tentions, but a public platform where we witness again the *mask* or *persona* assumed by Rabelais in his work. It is not the real author's voice that is heard – that is, the real Rabelais talking in real life – but the created author's voice; for Rabelais adopts a conscious, indeed self-conscious rôle of literary creator. In one way, this is nothing new – for Lucian, Seneca in his *Apocolocyntosis*, or Erasmus in his *Praise of Folly*, use this device of the authorial *I* which is not identified with themselves as real persons but is part of the genre they are writing in – Menippean satire or fool literature or satirical eulogy. Thus Erasmus says 'Mine is not the first of this kind . . . Homer . . . with the battle of frogs and mice; Virgil, with the gnat and puddings; Ovid with the nut...'; and there follows a long list of satirical inventors, among whom Erasmus would place himself.[1]

So they can all expect that in a satirical piece of fiction the mask assumed by the author will be accepted by the readers. In another way, this is quite novel; for as long as critics of Rabelais take what he says in his prologues seriously they show that they have not yet distinguished between the mask and the real Rabelais. An intensely debated example of this is the prologue to *Gargantua*, with its central crux of the *sustantificque mouelle*.[2] This apparent invitation to the reader to search beneath the surface frivolity for the hidden essence of Rabelais's work has been the signal for scholars to catch and systematize Rabelais the thinker at the expense of Rabelais the artist. The prologues rather raise certain basic questions: 'What is the relationship between the author and reader? between the author and his characters? between the author and the contents of his fictional world?' – questions that we will be asking in the context of Rabelais's whole work.

The immediate predecessor of *Pantagruel* on the literary market was the *Grandes et Inestimables Cronicques du grant et enorme geant Gargantua*, by an unknown author, on sale at the Lyons summer fair of 1532. The book has a splendid woodcut as a frontispiece, showing a peddlar selling his wares – bootlaces and popular books as well as dangerous works from abroad like Lutheran tracts. The story is of the giant Gargantua, with lashings of miraculous events and a great emphasis on gigantic size. It opens with an address to its readers, 'Tous bons chevalliers et gentilz hommes vous debvez sçavoir que au temps du bon roy Artus . . .' whereupon the author launches into the story, assumes the rôle of omniscient narrator and recounts the giant's adventures. Rabelais's formula in the prologue to *Pantagruel*, 'Très illustres et très chevaleureux champions, gentilz hommes et aultres, qui voluntiers vous adonnez à toutes gentillesses et honnestetez ...'* though ostensibly addressing the same category of readers, gently mocks them and parodies the very tales of chivalry they read. Note the epithets which he adds to the nouns: '*chevaleureux*' has already an archaic flavour in the sixteenth century and the excessive use of '*très, bien, beaucoup*' is a feature of earlier narrative writing. Rabelais's formula, of the *Gargantua* prologue, 'Beuveurs tres illustres, et vous, Verolez tres precieux ...' is a parody of the gently ironic cliché of *Pantagruel*, with its repetition of '*tres illustres*', and the substitution of '*tres precieux*' for the previous '*très chevaleureux*' – which enables Rabelais to ensure a clear echo between the two. Furthermore, it characterizes the readers 'à vous, non à aultres, sont dediez mes escriptz', echoing the elaborations on the gouty, pox-ridden readers of the *Pantagruel* prologue, and it issues a warning that the readers are stepping into a burlesque world. In the prologue to the *Tiers Livre* Rabelais develops again the address to the *beuveurs*, who are now well-known to us as his readers, as in the *Gargantua* formula, and gives us yet another characteristic – *bonnes gens*. It is almost as though this formula is establishing a fictitious dialogue between the author and his readers – as if the latter were sitting at the author's feet merely listening to a story. But it is the opening of the *Quart Livre* that displays the character of Rabelais's *captatio benevolentiae* to the full: 'Gens de bien, Dieu vous saulve et guard! Où estez vous? Je ne vous peuz veoir. Attendez que je chausse mes lunettes! Ha, Ha!'† The strikingly oral character of the whole paragraph, the highly artistic inconsequence of the developments and digressions, indicate the intimacy and familiarity that Rabelais has by now established with his readers. The greater degree of particularization achieved with each opening address marks the progression from parody to a highly personal way of talking to his readers, so that in the *Quart Livre* he seems to recall his readers

---

* Most Illustrious and thrice valourous Champions, Gentlemen and others, who willingly apply your mindes to the entertainment of pretty conceits, and honest harmlesse knacks of wit ...

† Good People, God save and keep you: Where are you? I can't see you; stay – I'll saddle my Nose with Spectacles – Oh, Oh!

in a familiar way, asks after their health and that of their families. Let us now look at each prologue chronologically and consider its character and organization.

The prologue to *Pantagruel* is comparatively simple in structure: praise of the *Chronicques* and their reading public takes up the largest section, followed by Rabelais's reasons for offering *Pantagruel* and his protestation of its truthfulness. Within each section, however, the marks of the author's *persona* and the complex attitude to his readers are evident. For example, the praise of the *Chronicques* is highly charged with mockery, calculated bathos and a sustained rhetorical tone which uncovers the basic irony. Apparent praise is suffused throughout with jest and censure: firstly through a deliberate confusion of contexts, of the *galant* and the religious, and secondly through a grotesque inflation of the importance of the chap-book. Thus, for example the public has 'n'a gueres veu, leu et sceu ... comme vrays fideles, les avez creues gualantement', the mockery being pointed by the juxtaposition of the inappropriate adverb with the religious analogy. Again the *gentilz hommes* who have used the book as a stop-gap in amorous conversations are *bien dignes de grande louange*, a phrase whose ironic intent is intensified in the 1537–42 editions by the addition of *et memoire sempiternelle*. Then too Rabelais mockingly wishes every one to devote all his time to the *Chronicques*, learn them off by heart and transmit them to his children 'et à ses successeurs et survivens bailler comme de main en main, ainsy que une religieuse Caballe'* – another phrase added in later editions and reinforcing the earlier religious analogy. The religious leit-motif is finally used as a double-edged mockery in the statement 'car il en a esté plus vendu par les imprimeurs en deux moys qu'il ne sera acheté de Bibles en neuf ans'.†

The actual praise of the utility of the *Chronicques* is both a parody of the prologues to tales of chivalry and also a rhetorical development which follows the line from reality to fantasy that

---

* and deliver them over to his successors and survivors from hand to hand, as a religious Cabal.

† for the Printers have sold more of them in two moneths time, then there will be bought of Bibles in nine years.

Rabelais is to trace so often later on in his work. The old *chansons de geste* and tales of chivalry almost always announced the utility of their contents in their prologues, which became longer in the fifteenth- and sixteenth-century printed editions than in the earlier manuscript versions. Rabelais turns claims of truthfulness into untruthfulness, firstly by means of absurd concrete proofs, whose improbability is heightened by the formulae adopted: 'J'en ay congneu de haultz et puissans seigneurs en bon nombre', where the device of the authorial *I* is used to 'support' the truth of the tale, or 'Aultres sont par le Monde (ce ne sont fariboles)' where the author anticipates incredulity by a 'tongue-in-cheek' amused protestation of veracity. Secondly he reports wildly grotesque evidence in a matter-of-fact manner: the disappointed hunter can find comfort in reading the *gestes* of Gargantua and the book will cure even a physical ailment like toothache. Rabelais treats the book as a pharmaceutical product and precisely describes the farcical procedure with a mixture of technical and familiar vocabulary: one can wrap the book between 'deux beaulx linges bien chaulx et les appliquer au lieu de la douleur', then 'les sinapizand aveques un peu de pouldre d'oribus';* here the juxtaposition of the technical term *'sinapizand'* (mustard poultice) with the mock-pharmaceutical pseudonym for human excrement points the burlesque. Then with the rhetorical question 'Mais que diray je des pauvres verolez et goutteux?' comes a rise in tone, introducing the long exclamatory lyrical description of the miraculous properties of the *Chronicques*. Within this section there are clear instances of one of Rabelais's comic devices, namely the way in which he will skirt cruelty and the macabre by analogies which transform them into comedy. The smallpoxed and gouty are compared in their horrific physical condition to animals and musical instruments, and so the reader's emotional involvement is suppressed: 'le visaige leur reluysoit comme la claveure d'un charnier' and their teeth 'leur tressailloyent comme font les marchettes d'un clavier d'orgues ou d'espinette quand on joue des-

---

* to put the said Chronicles betwixt two pieces of linnen cloth made somewhat hot, and so apply them to the place that smarteth, synapising them with a little powder of projection, otherwayes called doribus.

sus'* and the discrepancy between the two terms of comparison produces a shock of comic reaction.

The final section of the prologue, consisting of Rabelais's presentation of his own book to the public, is interesting in several ways: first, for the attitude of the author towards his readers, second for the tone adopted and last for the thumb-nail sketch of the author, as he will appear in the books. The author qualifies himself as *vostre humble esclave* merely wishing to *accroistre vos passetemps dadvantaige* – which could have come out of any narrative writing – but adds that it is a book 'de mesme billon, sinon qu'il est un peu plus equitable et digne de foy que n'estoit l'aultre'† which counteracts the effect of the *humble esclave* and adds a dimension of self-consciousness. The tone adopted in the protestations and justifications is clearly popular, as revealed by the affective and intensive level of the style, full of oaths, curses, exaggerations and puns or spoonerisms. The grotesque exaggeration and fantastical playing with letters and words reveal the conscious parody in this popular style. The author emerges as one who will indulge in wild fantasy, supported by protestations of veracity, which only serve to intensify it by comic juxtaposition. Now this is quite different from Erasmus in his dedicatory letter to Thomas More, who says of his *Praise of Folly*, 'such toys are not without their serious matter ... For my own part, let other men judge of what I have written ... I have praised folly, but not altogether foolishly ...'[3] – where there is a serious note – and different too from that of Lucian who satirizes the customary protestations of truthfulness from story-tellers:

Be it understood then that I am writing about things which I have neither seen nor had to do with nor learned from others – which, in fact, do not exist at all and in the nature of things cannot exist. Therefore my readers should on no account believe in them.[4]

Rabelais grotesquely parodies the narratives in vogue and as

---

* till their faces did glister like the Keyhole of a powdering tub, their teeth dance like the jacks of a paire of little Organs or Virginals, when they are played upon.
† do offer you for a Present another book of the same stamp, only that it is a little more reasonable and worthy of credit then the other was.

guarantee of his own veracity offers the fact that he has served the giant Pantagruel:

C'est des horribles faictz et prouesses de Pantagruel, lequel j'ay servy à gaiges dès ce que je fuz hors de page jusques à present, que par son congié je m'en suis venu visiter mon païs de vache, et sçavoir si en vie estoyt parent mien aulcun.*

The second part of this statement, with its apparent hints of realism and biographical detail, has occupied commentators; but far more interesting from a literary point of view is that Rabelais uses a narrative device here which suggests that we are already inside the fictional world and are alerted to the possible rôle of the author participating in the events. Already this first prologue suggests to the reader the disruptive presence of the author's *persona*, and displays the narrative technique with its editorial commentary and rhetorical elaborations, the mixture of styles and the absence of any stable level from which the reader can view the story.

The *Gargantua* prologue is more complex in that it not only exhibits a different structure and a greater variety of tones and levels; it also poses more problems. It is dominated by the opening description of Socrates, which leads to the editorial commentary around the theme of 'appearances are deceptive'. This in turn leads to a discussion by the author of his own book and his mode of composition, with suggestions to readers as to how they may interpret the work. It is important to see in its proper perspective Rabelais's announcement that he is writing first and foremost a comic book. He indicates a burlesque framework immediately with the formula '*Beuveurs* ... *et Verolez*' and this seems to indicate his imitation of the Italian monk Folengo (1496?–1544), who wrote a long burlesque–heroic work in macaronic verses where Latin and Italian were mingled together. For in Folengo's work the whole theme of drink is all-pervading and Rabelais uses it as a leitmotif in this prologue in order to sketch in further aspects of

* It is of the horrible and dreadful feats and prowesses of Pantagruel, whose menial servant I have been ever since I was a page, till this houre that by his leave I am permitted to visit my Cow-countrey, and to know if any of my kindred there be alive.

his *persona*. For example it is brought in abruptly with the question 'Crochetastes vous oncques bouteilles?' in the Socratic section, and more importantly as part of a highly contrived scholarly disclaimer in the final section. The claim that he has written the book in spare moments, 'Car, à la composition de ce livre seigneurial, je ne perdiz ne emploiay oncques plus, ny aultre temps que celluy qui estoit estably à prendre ma refection corporelle, sçavoir est beuvant et mangeant',* is part of the game he is playing with his readers, and later he states, 'A moy n'est que honneur et gloire d'estre dict et reputé bon gaultier et bon compaignon, et en ce nom suis bien venu en toutes bonnes compaignies de Pantagruelistes',† thereby reasserting and rounding off the *persona* he has chosen to assume as author. Other distinct echoes of Folengo's tone and vocabulary occur in Rabelais's description of his own books as *ces beaulx livres de haulte gresse* and in the paragraph where he promises every kind of revelation in his book, 'vous revelera de très haultz sacremens et mysteres horrificques, tant en ce que concerne nostre religion que aussi l'estat politicq et vie oeconomicque'.‡ This seems inspired by Folengo's bizarre prefaces (in macaronic untranslatable Latin) to his *Baldus* written under the fictitious name of Aquario Lodola and printed in the 1521 Tusculan edition with which Rabelais must have been familiar. One of these, the *Laudes Merlini eiusdem Magistri Aquarii Lodolae*, indulges in burlesque lyrical ecstasy at the wondrous contents of the book:

Singula tamen brancatissime ad ultimum attaccavi, tantam philosophiae, astronomiae, cosmographiae, musicae, nigromantiae, phisicae, alchimiae, sparpagnationem et doctrinam maravigliatus ut nihil Pytagoram, nihil Platonem, Ptolomeum, Boëtium, Zoroastrum, Avicennam, Geber fuisse iudicatum est.

---

* For in the composing of this lordly book, I never lost nor bestowed any more, nor any other time then what was appointed to serve me for taking of my bodily refection, that is, whil'st I was eating and drinking.

† I truly hold it for an honour and praise to be called and reputed a Frolick Gualter, and a Robin goodfellow; for under this name am I welcome in all choise companies of Pantagruelists.

‡ which will disclose unto you the most glorious Sacraments, and dreadful mysteries, as well in what concerneth [our] Religion, as matters of the publike State, and Life œconomical.

Praeterea grandiloquacitationem sermonisque pinguedinem masticantes, Ciceroni Vergilioque incagare praesumimus.[5]

The Plautine grotesqueness of the Latin compounds – for instance, *'grandiloquacitationem'* – the disproportion of the language as a whole and the parodied metaphors of *'sermonis pinguedinem masticantes'* are all elements of the world Folengo is creating where things are not themselves and where the burlesque is dominant.

Now if we look at Rabelais's prologue there are possible hints scattered thickly through it as to its apparent seriousness. First, Rabelais seems to have borrowed from Erasmus's adage on Socrates. In 1515 Erasmus had produced *Sileni Alcibiadis* in which, taking up Alcibiades' comparison of Socrates to Silenus in Plato's *Symposium*, he glosses a Silenus as 'a thing which in appearance (at first blush, as they say) seems ridiculous and contemptible, but on closer and deeper examination proves to be admirable, or else with reference to a person whose looks and dress do not correspond at all to what he conceals in his soul'.[6] The Sileni, on the first level of interpretation are figurines with, on the outside, grotesque sculptured images of musicians or artists and on the inside, by touching a spring, so to speak, figures of gods come into view. On the second level of interpretation the central theme of the adage, 'appearances are deceptive', may seem to us supremely appropriate to describe the rich complexity of Rabelais's own work. Secondly, Rabelais's discussion of allegorical modes of interpretating works of art invites the modern reader to take the actual promise of a *sustantificque mouelle* at its face value. It may seem to us that we are being induced by 'frequent meditation [to] break the bone and suck out the marrow' (Urquhart) and to think of Rabelais's books as ones, in Bacon's famous phrase, 'to be chewed and digested'. But when we start 'chewing' – for instance the Socratic theme – it becomes clear that Rabelais has converted the serious Erasmian description into something more ambiguous. Yet the first sentence does not contain unmistakable clues as to the ambivalence: it reads like a translation, 'Alcibiades, ou dialoge de Platon intitulé *Le Bancquet*, louant son precepteur Socrates, sans controverse prince des philosophes, entre aultres parolles le

dit estre semblable es Silenes',* where Erasmus speaks thus: 'And
in the Symposium of Plato, Alcibiades starts his speech in praise of
Socrates by drawing a comparison between him and the Sileni.'[7]
But at the beginning of the next sentence we notice that Rabelais
changes the Sileni of Erasmus and Plato from ornamental
statuettes to apothecaries' boxes filled with drugs, spices and preserves. He elaborates the description of these boxes, 'pinctes au
dessus de figures joyeuses et frivoles, comme de harpies, satyres,
oysons bridez, lievres cornuz, canes bastées, boucqs volans, cerfz
limonniers',† which contain, 'les fines drogues comme baulme,
ambre gris, amomon, musc, zivette, pierreries et aultres choses
precieuses'.‡ This suggests that the purely functional description
given by Erasmus,

For it seems that the Sileni were small images divided in half, and so constructed
that they could be opened out and displayed: when closed they represented
some ridiculous, ugly flute-player, but when opened they suddenly revealed
the figure of a god, so that the amusing deception would show off the art of the
carver ...

is not what really interests Rabelais. The picturesqueness of his
description, the homely familiarity of certain allusions, the delight
in sound and symmetry (e.g. *pauvre de fortune, infortuné en femmes*),
the periodic construction at the end of the paragraph consisting of
lists of nouns with qualifying adjectives leading to the verbs describing human activity, all indicate a rhetorical level which puts
the reader on the alert as regards Rabelais's style. The suspicions
aroused by this rhetoric are turned into certainties when Rabelais
gives us the reason for his portrait of Socrates. The very listing of
the books, '*Gargantua, Pantagruel, Fessepinte, La Dignité des Braguettes, Des Poys au lard cum commento*', with invented titles alongside his own, the vulgarity and obscenity, warn the reader that

* Alcibiades, in that Dialogue of Plato's, which is entituled *The Banquet*, whil'st he was
setting forth the praises of his Schoolmaster Socrates (without all question the Prince of
Philosophers) amongst other discourses to that purpose said, that he resembled the
Silenes.

† painted on the outside with wanton toyish figures, as Harpyes, Satyrs, bridled Geese,
horned Hares, saddled Ducks, flying Goats, Thiller Harts ...

‡ fine drugs, such as Balme, Ambergreece, Amamon, Musk, Civet, with several kindes of
precious stones, and other things of great price.

Rabelais is mocking violently. When he then proceeds to play mock-seriously with the vocabulary of allegorical interpretation: 'Et, posé le cas qu'au sens literal', the reader is again alerted by the irrelevant analogy with the *chant de Sirenes*, prompted no doubt by the play on *Silene - Sirene*, and by the switch to 'Crochetastes vous oncques bouteilles?' We can savour the tone here by contrasting it with the straightforward method of Erasmus when he gives many examples of deceptive appearances: 'The very Scriptures themselves have their own Sileni. If you remain on the surface, a thing may sometimes appear absurd; if you pierce through to the spiritual meaning, you will adore the divine wisdom', and after approving allegorical interpretations of Homer, compares his own fables to the Gospel parables: 'The parables of the Gospel, if you take them at face value – who would not think that they came from a simple ignorant man? And yet if you crack the nut, you find inside that profound wisdom, truly divine, a touch of something which is clearly like Christ himself.' The tone is perfectly in accordance with the seriousness of Erasmus's purpose: after all, the whole description of Socrates in this adage is to culminate in an exposition of Erasmus's eclectic Christianity. Rabelais on the other hand explicitly mocks at the habit of looking for the allegorical message of ancient authors and disclaims any such intention.

In spite of the great variety of tones in this prologue and the constant shifts in perspective and style, it is clear that mockery, sustained irony and parody underlie the major sections – the Socratic theme, the *os medullare* discussion, the promise of revelations in his work, the jesting on allegory and the scholarly disclaimers built on the wine theme – and these make it impossible to take a *simpliste* view of the promise of a *sustantificque mouelle*. Whether or not there is an underlying seriousness in Rabelais's books can be fully revealed only by the books themselves. More interesting in this prologue are the very distinct features of Rabelais the artist. The *persona* of the author is more complex than in the *Pantagruel* prologue, in that the self-consciousness has increased: the comments on his own work such as *ces beaulx livres de haulte gresse*, the ironic '*ce livre seigneurial*', and the *ces haultes* *matieres et sciences profundes* suggest the further dimension of self-parody and self-mockery by the author. This is borne out too by the comment on his readers as *mes bons disciples* with the added phrase *et quelques aultres foulz de sejour* and by the books he chooses to invent and ascribe to himself 'les joyeulx tiltres d'aulcuns livres de nostre invention' like '*La Dignité des Braguettes*'. The author's *persona* is a combination of the paternal, jovial, wine-bibbing story-teller and the bullying, cajoling, mesmerizing word-spinner, who will hurl the reader into an unfamiliar world of burlesque and fantasy. The quizzical mock-oracular injunction to the reader at the end confirms the hints of conspiracy between author and reader, so that the latter can share in the creative fun: 'Pour tant, interpretez tous mes faictz et mes dictz en la perfectissime partie; ayez en reverence le cerveau caseiforme qui vous paist de ces belles billes vezées.'* For the first time too we have a descriptive label for such readers: they are *pantagruelistes*.

The need for close contact between reader and author is reinforced by the prologue to the *Tiers Livre*, a highly complex overture in which the main theme – that of Diogenes and his barrel – is linked to a number of subsidiary themes through its associations and variations.[8] The story itself was borrowed from Lucian's *The way to write History* and was well-known in the Renaissance: when Corinth was about to be besieged by Philip, King of Macedon, all the inhabitants set to work, some fortifying their walls, some polishing their armour and some keeping guard over the city. Diogenes, a fellow Corinthian, in order not to be chastised for idleness, went out of town and vehemently rolled his barrel – as his contribution to the war-game. The texture of this prologue is dense and allusive and yet its framework is much more markedly oral in character than that of the first two. The author tells his stories in the atmosphere of a friendly gathering. In the early sections he plays with his readers, whose complicity he seems confident of, before finally getting to the point of narrating the story of Diogenes: 'Si n'en avez ouy parler, de luy vous veulx presentement une histoire narrer, pour entrer en vin (beuvez

---

* For this cause interpret you all my deeds and sayings in the perfectest sense; reverence the cheese-like brain that feeds you with these faire billevezees.

doncques) et propous (escoutez doncques).'* The delaying tactics
and the oral presentation of the story are very different from the
explicit and (from the narrative point of view) straightforward
introduction of Socrates in the *Gargantua* prologue. The atmosphere of complicity between author and readers is strengthened
by the variations on the main theme of the prologue. From the
first bantering paragraph, where the initiative is given to the
words themselves, where puns and associations of ideas play
around *veoir*, *bien* and particularly *vin*, the basic metaphor is the
barrel of Diogenes, transformed into Rabelais's wine barrel containing the precious liquor of his works. The prologue is loosely
constructed, full of apparent digressions and connected only by
the story-telling manner of the author. In all this it is richly
reminiscent of Lucian's manner of establishing contact with a
familiar audience in a piece such as the *Dionysus*, which may have
been written as an introduction to the second book of the *True
History*.[9] Lucian's tone is extremely casual: for example he starts
'When Dionysus led his host against the men of Ind (surely there is
nothing to prevent my telling you a tale of Bacchus!) ...' The
transitions in Lucian's piece are managed in a markedly oral
manner: for example ' "But what has your Dionysus to do with
Dionysus?" someone may say. This much ...' Or again 'As we
are still in India I want to tell you another tale of that country
which "has to do with Dionysus".' What is even more interesting
is that the basic structure of the piece relies on the narration of
a story and then its application to his own work: the first term of
comparison is the fable and the second the work of his own that
he is introducing. This corresponds closely, as we shall see, to the
structure of the prologue to the *Tiers Livre*.

The supporting links in Rabelais's prologue are also presented
in a casual oral manner. For example, the personal analogy
between Diogenes and the author is worked out by way of personal biographical details and topical allusions, and within this
framework the further illustrative anecdote of the camel and the
slave is introduced with the phrase *Me souvient toutesfoys avoir leu*

---

* If you have not heard of him, I will presently tell you a Story to make your Wine relish:
  Drink then, so, to the purpose.

que ... The central metaphor gathered from the tale of Diogenes is taken, in the manner of Lucian, as a particularly appropriate vehicle of comparison to his own work. The metaphor itself is a rich indication of the extended self-consciousness of the author and it is worked out at great length. Rabelais builds it into a complete tableau of his own art, drawing from the barrel *sentences Pantagruelicques* or *Diogenicques*, and orchestrating the analogy with a range of comparisons from classical mythology such as the *couppe de Tantalus*, the *cornucopie*, the *bouteille de Pandora*. Furthermore the actual technique of recounting Diogenes' activity is in itself a kind of commentary on or a demonstration of his own art. This last point emerges clearly from the variants and additions of the 1552 edition *reveu et corrigé par l'Autheur*: they are almost all additions to the already exuberant verbal accumulations in the 1546 edition. For example, in the second paragraph *propriété, faculté, vertus* are added to the long list of qualities *du benoist et desiré piot*: to the list of verbs recounting the activity of Diogenes are added *nattoit, grattoit, flattoit, barattoit* and many others. Professor Tétel has recently analysed the order, rhythmic patterns, rhyme and other sound-associations and metaphoric leaps that underlie the apparently chaotic verbal exuberance of such lists, and shows the whole figure of Diogenes and his barrel to be suggestive of the gratuitous fun Rabelais finds in this linguistic revel.[10]

The self-consciousness of the author and the familiarity between author and reader are confirmed in the leisurely pace of the last section of the prologue, which sets the seal on the special relationship with the reader: 'Je recongnois en eulx tous une forme specificque et propriété individuale, laquelle nos majeurs nommoient Pantagruelisme, moienant laquelle jamais en maulvaise partie ne prendront choses quelconques ilz congnoistront sourdre de bon, franc et loyal couraige.'* The threads of the drinking theme that runs through the whole prologue emphasize this intimacy between author and reader, and in the last section the exhortations to readers to drink their fill of his works echo the closing words of

---

* So I perceive in them all one and the same specifical Form, and the like individual Proprieties, which our Ancestors call'd Pantagruelism; by virtue whereof, they will bear with any thing that floweth from a good, free and loyal Heart.

Lucian's *Dionysus*. In addition there are echoes here of the formulae of address to readers in previous prologues: 'je ne l'ay persé que pour vous, *Gens de bien*, *Beuveurs* de la prime cuvée, et *Goutteux* de franc alleu' (my italics) and the embroidery of oaths and curses against those outside the magic circle of the author's listeners is reminiscent of the closing paragraphs of the *Pantagruel* prologue.

The actual significance of the figure and fable of Diogenes informs the viewpoint adopted by the created author. On the one hand the serious associations of Diogenes for an author like Erasmus seem to offer a parallel with the Socratic theme of the *Gargantua* prologue. Rabelais could indeed have borrowed some of the material on Diogenes from the same Erasmian adage on Socrates. Thus, for example, the anecdote in which Alexander the Great wishes he were Diogenes is related by Erasmus specifically to the Silenus analogy:

Another Silenus was Diogenes, whom the mob considered a dog. But it was about this dog that a divine observation was made by Alexander the Great, the fine flower of princes, it seems, when in his admiration for so great a soul he said 'If I were not Alexander, I would wish to be Diogenes' though he ought all the more to have wished for the soul of Diogenes, for the very reason that he was Alexander.[11]

The cumulative evidence of the prologues to *Gargantua* and the *Tiers Livre* thus seems to reveal a Rabelais who has adopted the *personae* of two historical characters, both reinforcing the Silenus-theme of 'appearances are deceptive', with Diogenes mocking the Corinthians in the futile absurdity of their war-like activities and displaying the superiority of his own balanced view of human events. But this interpretation takes account only of the skeletal idea-content of the two prologues, without allowing for the author's manner, his burlesque framework, the treatment of his themes and the variety of tones, particularly his sharp irony. It seems more likely that in the prologue to the *Tiers Livre*, by aligning himself with the activities of Diogenes, whose contempt for public affairs and refusal to involve himself must have been well known to him, Rabelais is indicating his unwillingness to be committed at the political and religious level and declaring instead his unique commitment to his writing. The hints to the reader that his work is like a Silenus jar are delivered more in the manner of Lucian in the *Dionysus* than of Erasmus in his adage: that is, cryptically and non-committally, in the style of a satiric writer. Lucian says:

But I promise confidently that if they are willing this time as they were before to look often upon the mystic rites and if my boon-companions of old remember 'the revels we shared in the days that are gone' and do not despise my Satyrs and Sileni, but drink their fill of this bowl, they too will know the Bacchic frenzy once again, and will often join me in the 'Evoe'. But let them do as they think fit: a man's ears are his own.

The art of Rabelais is at its fullest in this prologue, both in the verbal control and in the mixture of styles – from the sober classical paragraph of 'Puys doncques que telle est ou ma sort ou ma destinée' to the vulgar exaggerated curses of 'Jamais ne puissiez vous fianter que à sanglades d'estrivieres.' The self-consciousness of the author is fully extended and includes in the anecdote of the slave and the camel a hint of *nouveauté*, which may again be inspired by Lucian's treatment of this theme in his prefatory pieces.[12]

The prologue to the *Quart Livre* is not only much longer than the other three but different in character and structure. The colloquial atmosphere created by the extensive fictitious dialogue between author and reader at the beginning, and reintroduced at the end with specific exhortations to the reader, is this time the frame for a complete fiction, itself told in an oral manner – Aesop's fable of the woodcutter and his axe. There are a number of features in Rabelais's technique here which bear witness to the development of his art. The dialogue between author and reader relies on the conspiratorial devices noticed in previous prologues but this time it also introduces two serious leitmotifs which together form the substance of the prologue: health and moderation. The two themes are handled in an oral manner, and are loosely knit: in the opening 'exchange of news' between author and reader the former describes the state of his own health in what is the fullest and most Stoic definition of Pantagruelism to be found anywhere in his works: 'Je suys, moiennant un peu de Pantagruelisme (vous entendez que c'est certaine gayeté d'esprit conficte en mespris des choses fortuites), sain et degourt.'* Later the health motif shades into the theme of moderation by way of the wish that God will grant all men good health 'et accomplira cestuy nostre soubhayt, attendu qu'il est mediocre'.† The transition from this to the actual fable is again achieved in a Lucianic manner: 'A propos de soubhaictz mediocres en matiere de coingnée (advisez quand sera temps de boire), je vous raconteray ...'‡ In the actual narration a certain nonchalance over details enhances the atmosphere of a conversation among friends: thus for example, 'Aelian escript qu'il feut Thracian; Agathias, après Herodote, qu'il estoit Samien: ce m'est tout un';§ or again 'et lors opinoit la vieille Cybele, ou bien le jeune et clair Phoebus, si voulez'.¶ The author chooses to tell the tale in a particularly complicated way, in that the main fable serves as a framework for several anecdotes and leads into a full-scale tableau of the gods in council. Both the creation of an oral atmosphere, with its leisurely pace and opportunities for digression, and the actual telling of the story reveal another dimension of the author's *persona* in these prologues. For we have here for the first time all the elements of a sophisticated narrator: dramatization, characterization, control of pace and timing, concern for verisimilitude, little editorial commentary, with the initiative given to the characters and story, which are thus allowed to develop a convincing life of their own.

The world of the gods is vividly dramatized with liberal use of dialogue, speech and telling details. From the first moment when Couillatris' cry is heard and Jupiter stops short in his deliberations

---

* For my part I am thereabouts, thanks to his blessed Goodness; and by the means of a little Pantagruelism, (which you know is a certain Jollity of Mind pickled in the scorn of Fortune).
† and that he will grant this our Wish, because 'tis moderate and mean.
‡ Now I talk of moderate Wishes in point of Hatchet (But hark'e me, be sure you don't forget when we ought to drink) I'll tell you ...
§ Aelian writes that he was of Thrace, and Agathias after Herodotus, that he was of Samos; 'tis all one to Frank.
¶ and old Gammer Cybele was just giving her Opinion, or if you had rather have it so, it was Young Phoebus the Beau.

to bellow at the mission of Mercure 'Quel diable ... est là bas qui hurle si horrifiquement?'* the reader is inside the assembly of the gods. The character of Priapus dominates the assembly and he is portrayed both in physical detail – 'la teste levée, rouge, flamboyante et asseurée'† and in character – for example his obsession with the physical and the obscene, his talent for making the other gods and goddesses laugh and his gift for telling a story. His interventions come naturally and plausibly. For instance when Mercure reports that Couillatris has lost his axe, 'Priapus restoit debout au coing de la cheminée. Il, entendent le rapport de Mercure, dist en toute courtoysie et joviale honesteté ...'‡ Other gods are sketched in, with their appropriate attributes and characteristics: Vulcan with his 'jambe torte, en feist pour l'amour de s'amye, trois ou quatre beaulx petitz saulx en plate forme';§ Mercure 'avecques son chapeau poinctu, sa capeline, talonnieres et caducée';¶ and Jupiter 'contournant la teste comme un cinge qui avalle pillules, fit une morgue tant espouvantable que tout le grand Olympe trembla'.‖ The pace of the gods' council is leisurely and the whole situation is used in a Lucianic way to include fantasy and satire on human affairs: thus the past history of Jupiter's settlements of men's petty squabbles, which forms an integral part of the council, provides an opportunity for topical allusion and derision. The case of Ramus and Galland is introduced wittily: 'Mais que ferons nous de ce Rameau et de ce Galland, qui, capparassonnez de leurs marmitons, suppous et astipulateurs, brouillent toute ceste Academie de Paris?'** As in Lucian's *Icaro-*

* What a Devil have we below ... that howls so horridly?
† standing up and taking off his Cowle, his Snout uncas'd and rear'd up, fiery and stifly propt.
‡ Priapus was standing in the Chimney-corner, and having heard what Mercury had reported, said in a most courteous and jovial manner ...
§ and even set limping Vulcan a hopping and jumping smoothly three or four times for the sake of his Dear.
¶ Heaven's Foot-messenger, thanks to his low crown'd narrow-brim'd Hat, and plume of Feathers, Heel pieces, and running Stick with Pigeon Wings.
‖ Jupiter, with an awkward turn of his Head, like a Jackanapes swallowing of Pills, made so dreadful a Phyz, that all the vast Olympus quak'd again.
** But what shall we do with this same Ramus and this Galland with a Pox to 'em, who surrounded with a swarm of their Scullions, Blackguard Ragamuffins, Sizers, Vouchers and Stipulators, set together by the Ears, the whole University of Paris?

menippus the affairs of men are seen from the viewpoint of the gods and thus appear ridiculously small, while their squabbling provides fun and pastime for the gods.

Rabelais's control of pace and timing is demonstrated in the course of the prologue: thus at the beginning, when he is setting his readers at ease with banter and exchange of views, the pace is leisurely; but the introduction of the story of Couillatris is swift and only the necessary minimum of detail is given: 'De son temps, estoit un pauvre villageois natif de Gravot, nommé Couillatris, abateur et fendeur de bois, et, en cestuy bas estat, guaingnant cahin caha sa paouvre vie. Advint qu'il perdit sa coingnée.'* The tableau of the gods in council forms a large interlude in the actual story and is conducted in a slow 'naturalistic' way, while the narrative sequel, recounting the fate of Couillatris and his imitators, is handled speedily but with full details of Couillatris' rise and prosperity.

The last section of the prologue resumes the dialogue with the readers which had formed the framework to the story. And this time the fable is commented on and its implications drawn out in an almost didactic way. The tone is set with a number of imperatives, such as *Prenez y tous exemple, Soubhaitez doncques mediocrité* and *Humiliez vous*, interlarded with examples and anecdotes to illustrate the theme of moderation. The intrusion of religious themes and satire on Genevan ethics at the end suggests that the now intimate bond between author and readers is sufficiently strong and wide to embrace communal viewpoints on topical matters, though the author is careful to close on the burlesque note so integral to the prologues, and to resume the story-telling *persona*: 'Or, en bonne santé toussez un bon coup, beuvez en trois, secouez dehait vos aureilles, et vous oyrez dire merveilles du noble et bon Pantagruel.'†

In this prologue as a whole we are less aware of the *persona* of the self-conscious artist than of the self-effacing author, allowing

---

* In his time liv'd a poor honest Country Fellow of Gravot, Tom Wellhung by Name, a Wood-cleaver by Trade, who in that low Drudgery made shift so, to pick up a sorry Lively-hood. It happen'd that he lost his Hatchet.

† Now, my Lads, as you hope for good Health, cough once aloud with Lungs of Leather;

his story to move forward, and to reveal itself through the characters, dialogue and description. This feature foreshadows the narrative technique of the *Quart Livre* itself, where the finest results of the oral manner are to be found, with all the characters allowed on occasion to tell their own stories, often in a familiar, wine-bibbing atmosphere.

The characteristics of the four prologues are interesting hints towards Rabelais's technique in general. The most marked features are the development of the complicity between author and readers and the *persona* of the author. The familiarity and the conspiracy between author and readers may be seen as an anticipation of Rabelais's comic technique, where the author needs to take his readers into his confidence and make them feel superior to the characters whose discomfiture they are laughing at. The self-conscious, self-mocking *persona* adopted by the author is essential in a book where irony and parody play a large rôle. For this dramatized author can stand above and apart from his created world and manipulate it playfully and ambivalently. The sharp irony of *ces tant veritables contes, ce livre seigneurial*, prepares the reader for the multiplicity of dimensions in Rabelais's handling of reality and fiction in the books themselves, and the disruptive presence of the author who is *amused* at the very improbability of the tales he tells is already amply foreshadowed in the prologues.

Finally, the prologues suggest in miniature the technique of the books: their jerky, rambling, violently shifting tempo and style already suggest the technique of disintegration. And their loose, disjointed form will be sufficiently flexible to allow attitudes and ideas, theories and people to be questioned and ridiculed, thrown into reverse and often reaffirmed.[13]

Take me off three swinging Bumpers; Prick up your Ears; and you shall hear me tell Wonders of the noble and good Pantagruel.

4

THE OLYMPIAN AUTHOR

In the prologues Rabelais had created a mask through which he could speak: a fictitious personage who talks to and sometimes at his readers, in the same way as Folly does in Erasmus's *Praise of Folly*. This mask, the *persona* of the author, is a second self created by Rabelais much as Proust creates his narrator Marcel: it is a self who can be made to choose his standpoint irrespective of the real Rabelais's ideas or views. In other words, this *persona* or mask that the author creates for himself should in no way be identified with the real Rabelais whom biographers try to elucidate for us; the mask cannot be used directly as part of the biographical data. Thus, whenever in this chapter we are dealing with Rabelais the author of a prose fiction as opposed to Rabelais the real man, who lived between 1494 and 1553, we are going to call him 'the created author'.

It is essential for the reader to recognize that an author puts himself at a distance from his fictional world; for unless we are able to recognize that a love lyric, for example, may have nothing to do with the real man's passion, but rather with the created author who has chosen a situation and a main character – in this case a plaintive lover with an *I* who sings of his love – and has adopted a style appropriate to this created set of circumstances, we are in danger of confusing questions of sincerity and authenticity with the business of criticism. Furthermore, the twentieth-century taste in fiction and in criticism is for the story to tell itself dramatically rather than be merely told. And this distaste for the omniscient narrator, who creates his setting in time and place, who makes his characters speak and who controls their exits and entrances as if he were a god playing with human puppets, leads us to look backwards with Jamesian eyes and affix labels consonant with twentieth-century criticism. Nathalie Sarraute, discussing the omniscient narrator in Balzac, calls the relationship between created author and envisaged reader a pact between the *outrecuidance* of the former and the *docilité* of the latter: the envisaged reader is forced to accept that the truth of Balzac's fictional world can only be reached by submissively following every particle of the physical and mental description and every facet of the generalization offered by the omniscient narrator.[1]

This docility of the envisaged reader is important for sixteenth-century tales, but where you have intrusions by the created author, using the authorial *I* form, there is in addition the presence in the work of a fully self-conscious author. This presence of the author is the conscious adoption of a point of view through which a created author sees his story and directs his envisaged readers to view the story in the same light. In a work of irony, satire or comedy we expect a degree of detachment to come from the created author's prevailing note of intellect playing on the narrative. Thus, if the created author wishes to mock supernatural characters he may produce monstrous hyperboles in describing their behaviour in order that the envisaged reader should laugh at the impossibility of taking such acts seriously.

In Rabelais's comic work the question of focus must ultimately be explained by the work in its entirety, by the created author's attitude to the characters and to the fictional world he has created as well as his commentary on the topics, events and incidents which he includes in his vast transmogrifying canvas. In this chapter we shall be concerned only with the various ways the created author works. At the outset, let us define our terminology. The 'created author', whom we have already defined (p. 45), will eventually become, as the argument progresses, the 'Olympian author'. There is no difference in degree or quality between the created author and the Olympian author: the second term is merely a sharper definition (in optical terms). This Olympian author is a fully conscious narrator who organizes and unifies each chapter, and his qualities determine the quality of the work. The Olympian author uses two techniques. The first is the *I* technique – a conscious intrusion, which may indeed stop the narrating of the story to give us rhetorical commentary of great fullness on the events. This disruptive technique is the one most dominant in all the four books, and it raises the question whether or not the envisaged reader is docile or impatient, and also from what position the created author regards the story. Does he look from above at the fictional world he depicts, using the *I* technique to bring his readers to the same level? When the *I* technique is crucial – after a dangerous religious or philosophical allusion – we shall have to consider where the envisaged reader is set. The omniscient technique is seen in comic scenes where there is no authorial intrusion, and in editorial scenes where the story is being related. The other technique that we shall be looking at is the relationship *moi esclave/mon maistre Pantagruel*, hinted at in the prologue to *Pantagruel*: this is the pseudonymous Alcofribas Nasier speaking. In the first two books he is present; he is absent in the *Tiers Livre*; and he has an enlarged rôle in the *Quart Livre*, where Alcofribas speaks as a member of the company sailing in the ship, observing the behaviour and joining in the fun. This is, however, a fairly limited rôle, with narrower channels of information, but when it occurs it is giving its own story from the centre of the picture.

We shall sometimes find serious issues manipulated by one of these techniques, and it will be important in this chapter to be aware of how the device works before we can evaluate Rabelais's thought. Examination of these techniques will depend on the variants in the different editions, and on the differences between the two versions of the beginning of the *Quart Livre*, published in 1548 and 1552. If to quote Professor Lloyd Austin on Mallarmé, 'Au fond, lettres et premiers états des poèmes donnent accès à la biographie essentielle du poète, sinon à la seule valable',[2] this is even truer for a sixteenth-century writer than for Mallarmé since the biographical documents are considerably scarcer and we are of necessity thrown back on textual variants as a way of tracing the growth of the author's mind.

In the prologues, one gradually becomes aware of a highly self-conscious author, who is constantly slipping in rather dangerous comments and then blandly stepping aside so that the envisaged reader can make up his own mind on certain issues. Before one has even started to read Rabelais's work, there is an artistic sense in which the created author's mask has been firmly donned: the editorial commentary is salvaging order out of the seeming chaos of each prologue. We may think of other authors like Swift where we can see the author's created self at work: the superior, self-controlled, ironical, sometimes malicious and sometimes gentle narrator of *Gulliver's Travels*. Swift protests that his 'style is very plain and simple' and indeed it can be read in the nursery without awareness of the ambiguity, irony and lacerating satire. When the reader comes to the last chapter in 'A Voyage to the Houyhnhnms':

Thus, gentle reader, I have given thee a faithful history of my travels for sixteen years, and above seven months, wherein I have not been so studious of ornament as of truth. I could perhaps like others have astonished thee with strange improbable tales; but I rather chose to relate plain matter of fact in the simplest manner and style, because my principal design was to inform, and not to amuse thee ...

does he accept this claim of utter veracity at its face value? Or rather is he not left, as he has been throughout the tales, in two minds about meaning? The created author is there all the time, sometimes amusing the readers, sometimes mocking them for their credulity and simplicity, sometimes persuading them to suspend their disbelief as he narrates the story of the Yahoos. The created author is given, indeed assumes for himself, boundless freedom as the narrative proceeds. The envisaged reader is forced to make his own judgement on everything: Swift and Lemuel Gulliver are indeed two persons and nothing that Gulliver describes is automatically ascribed to Swift.

But it is Cervantes, the other great fiction writer of the sixteenth century, who gives us our best clue: for in *Don Quixote*, we soon perceive that he is building up multiple perspectives through which to project the narrative. The most obvious one is the pretence of using the Arabic chronicler Cide Hamete Benengeli, to suggest that the fiction is a real historical narrative which can be vouched for: 'At this critical point our delightful history stopped short ... This caused me great annoyance for my pleasure from the little I had read turned to displeasure at the thought of the small chance there was of finding the rest of this delightful story.'[3] This play with 'history', 'fiction' or 'story' is ironical in Cervantes, as his prefaces show well enough; he is gently satirizing all the romances of chivalry and handsome knights whose adventures had found many narrators. But, more important, it is a neat technique to introduce the main intermediary – the pseudo-chronicler – through whom the created author can be at once inside and outside the story. By this device another layer is erected between the created author and his characters.

One immediately recalls *Gargantua*, where the whole genealogy of the giants is said to have been found in a delightful little book:

Et fut trouvée par Jean Audeau en un pré ... un grand tombeau de bronze ... Icelluy ouvrans ... trouverent ... un gros, gras, grand, gris, joly, petit, moisy livret, plus, mais non mieulx sentent que roses. En icelluy fut ladicte geneallogie trouvée, escripte au long de lettres cancelleresques ... Je (combien que indigne) y fuz appelé.* (chapter 1)

The 'translator' of this genealogy adds that rats and other beasts have nibbled away the beginning of the genealogy and gives the conundrums in the next chapter with the first five letters of five lines obscured. This is the same technique that the created author in *Don Quixote* used: the unworthy *je* in *Gargantua* is created in the same way as the pseudo-chronicler Cide Hamete Benengeli. Furthermore, the created author of *Don Quixote* can allude to the real Cervantes: for instance, in the captive's tale, he refers to the slavery of Cervantes in this way:

The only one who held his own with him was a Spanish soldier called something de Saavedra ... And if it were not for lack of time I would tell you something about that soldier's deeds, which you would find much more entertaining and surprising than this story of mine.[4]

Rabelais uses the same trick of perspective several times: for example, in the *Quart Livre*, chapter 27 – he refers to the 'real' person as 'Rabelays' along with other 'real' people whose existence can be established in archives. In other words, in both *Don Quixote* and in Rabelais's books, the use of real life or of real incidents is yet another perspective on the fiction which both

* This Genealogy was found by John Andrew in a meadow ... [in] a great brazen tomb ... opening this Tomb ... [found] a big, fat, great, gray, pretty, small, mouldy, little pamphlet, smelling stronger, but no better than roses. In that book the said Genealogy was found written all at length, in a Chancery hand ... I (though unworthy) was sent for thither.

Rabelais and Cervantes are creating. Cervantes winds his story around a knight who is himself constantly moving to and fro between fiction and reality while the created author stands back, and, as it were, abdicates responsibility for the various tricks of perspective he has used. The subtle and *nuancé* counterpoint of Sancho Panza and Don Quixote uses a number of techniques of this kind and so does Rabelais.

From the first chapter in *Pantagruel* we can see the self-conscious, dramatized narrator at work in this 'disruptive' rôle: the technique, although at first zigzagging in an erratic way, yet finally unifies the shape of the chapter. This narrator often uses *vous* to mean the envisaged readers, *nous* to mean created author and envisaged readers, and *je* to mean the created author alone: for instance, he gives us a certain amount of information about Pantagruel while suggesting that we have heard it before, 'Ce ne sera chose inutile ne oysifve, veu que *sommes* de sejour, *vous* ramentevoir la premiere source et origine d'ont *nous* est né le bon Pantagruel: car *je* voy que ...'* (The italics are mine.) The casualness of the reporting, the self-controlled use of the authorial *I* form and the comic aura achieved, these are very different from fifteenth-century narratives. The rôle of the created author in earlier *chroniques* or *nouvelles* was limited. There was, of course, the authorial *I* technique: for instance, all the formulae of reporting and of telling the tale in a quasi-oral setting had become clichés; phrases like *Que vous diray-je?, comme vous orrez, Or nous fault ici laissier le nom, Et atant laisseray cy aucun peu a parler, ne demandez pas se fut joyeuse* and *Or escoutez, s'il vous plaist* were commonplaces of expression. But what had not yet been exploited very much was an ironic or comic attitude in the narrative where there is a constant play between the objective meaning and the intention of the created author. For example, there is a distinct contrast between *Pantagruel* and a *chronique* like *La vie [de] robert le diable* (as it appeared in prose *c.* 1520). The *chronique* relates the marvellous events of Robert's life and his terrible and wicked

---

* It will not be an idle nor unprofitable thing, seeing we are at leisure, to put you in minde of the Fountain and Original Source, whence is derived unto us the good Pantagruel; for I see that ...

deeds with an alternation between the omniscient technique and the authorial *I* form. The prologue has already shown us that 'listoire cy apres escripte et laquelle ientens narrer a esté par le merite de la glorieuse vierge marie miraculeusement conduite', so that the final conversion to Christianity, with Robert becoming a doer-of-good-deeds does not cause the narrative to move beyond one level. The envisaged reader accepts the *miraculeux*, since he has been prepared for it; the expression has not been double-edged in the *chronique*; the framework is vast but willingly received; and there has been no interference of levels. In fact, there is no juxtaposition of references at all. Whereas in these first words of *Pantagruel* (quoted above), the disruptive narrator is playing with the vast framework to induce comic reactions in his reader. For instance, the heroic adjective '*bon*' (like *pius* in the *Aeneid*) is turned to mock-heroic use immediately, since it is going to be used through all the books as a qualification for Pantagruel. In this first chapter this disruptiveness serves a number of functions. Sometimes the technique tells a story or makes an allusion to topical events or to familiar proverbial situations: for instance, in the account of the swelling of all the people on earth, some in the ear, some in the nose, some in the shoulder, there comes a break in the true narration, and a comment relates it to a piece of 'wisdom': the people have bequeathed this swelling of the ear to the Bourbonnais, a heritage which they have today – 'et dict on que en Bourbonnoys encores dure l'eraige, dont sont dictes aureilles de Bourbonnoys'. Sometimes the disruptiveness establishes a conspiracy between the created author and his male readers: for instance on women's insatiable demands in sexual matters, 'Et d'iceulx est perdue la race, ainsi comme disent les femmes, car elles lamentent continuellement qu'il n'en est plus de ces gros, etc. vous sçavez le reste de la chanson'.* Sometimes it turns the real world into a fanciful astronomic cosmos where even astrologers are awry, 'qui sont cas bien espoventables et matieres tant dures et difficiles que les Astrologues ne y peuvent

---

* Of these beleeve me the race is utterly lost and quite extinct, as the women say; for they do lament continually, that there are none extant now of those great, etc. you know the rest of the song.

mordre; aussy auroient ils les dens bien longues s'ilz povoient toucher jusques là!'* And sometimes it claims speciously a matter-of-fact truthfulness: for instance, 'On moys de octobre, ce me semble, ou bien de septembre (affin que je ne erre, car de cela me veulx je curieusement guarder).'†

All these examples are, as it were, breaks in transmission in narrating the actual origin of the giant, and establish the fantastic and grotesque point of view in which the envisaged readers are now settling themselves. We enjoy seeing how far the created author's fantasy reaches; we expect the topical allusions which he embroiders into the narrative; and we are at ease with the gigantic framework because it is interrupted constantly to bring in shafts of comic light by the 'disruptive' technique. In the last section of this first chapter, there is a quasi-dialogue between the created author and his envisaged readers: with tongue-in-cheek serious-ness, he says, 'J'entens bien que ... vous faictez ... un doubte bien raisonnable'. He then forestalls incredulity by giving an explanation to justify himself – 'La demande est bien faicte ... mais la responce vous contentera'. Now the speciousness of the rôle played by the created author here is equalled by that of the envisaged reader, who does not expect justifications. When they are produced, the reader is wholly amused at the way the created author lies his way out of the corner he has put himself in. This device of fictitious dialogue is important for two reasons: first, for its relevance to the question of what form Rabelais chose for his work[5] and secondly, because it enables him to veil dangerous comments with this cavalier-like tone. The attitude to the readers, which regards them as superior to those who lap up contemporary stories, is something like Lucian's:

[readers] will find it enticing not only for the novelty of its subject, for the humour of its plan and because I tell all kinds of lies in a plausible and specious way, but also because everything in my story is a more or less comical parody of

* which are cases very terrible, and matters so hard and difficult, that Astrologians cannot set their teeth in them; and indeed their teeth had been pretty long if they could have reached thither.
† In the moneth of October, as I take it, or at least September, (that I may not erre, for I will carefully take heed of that).

one or another of the poets, historians and philosophers of old, who have written much that smacks of miracles and fables.[6]

When Lucian says 'in a plausible and specious way' our created author uses various tricks of language to gain the same end: for instance in this first chapter, we have *tous bons hystoriographes* being mocked at, *faictes vostre compte* which Urquhart renders as 'however, account you it for a truth' – and at the end of the chapter we are in the same attitude as we are throughout *A True Story* – we do not believe a word of it.

In this first chapter then, we have another layer added on to the chronicling of the birth of the giant: yet, though 'disruptive' in the actual narrating, it imposes an organizing shape on the chapter as a whole. The created author – whether using *je* or *nous* – is clearly the dominating voice in the chapter. The way it ends, with a quasi-fictitious dialogue, suggests that this device will be an ambiguous one, particularly when Lucian and his *Icaromenippus* are mentioned at the conclusion. This can be shown by looking at this device – the fictitious dialogue – in another context. In the 1542 version of the prologue to *Pantagruel* we have one on a dangerous topic, namely religion: embedded in the quasi-fictitious dialogue is the claim that the book contains *telles vertus, proprietés et prerogatives*, the boast that it is the only one of its kind, and that anyone disbelieving that can be called *abuseurs, prestinateurs, emposteurs et seducteurs* – the two words *prestinateurs* and *emposteurs* coming for the first time in the 1542 edition. The dialogue still maintains a light note and the addition of those two words does not alter its structure. In other words, the created author here takes stand against the predestination of Calvin – a real issue – and works the allusion into a pre-existing comic form – the fictitious dialogue. The words make clear Rabelais's abhorrence of several important doctrines of Calvin but do not at all detract from the fictional form in which he as created author is writing. If we return to the fictitious dialogue at the end of the first chapter, we notice that the tone of the reply to the incredulous readers, worried by the sheer impossibility of taking the genealogy as truthful, is conveyed by the mixture of obscene language with apparently serious authorities. For example, to justify his wild interpretation of the flood in the Bible, he chooses to cite the Hebrew doctors in this way, 'je vous allegueray l'autorité des Massoretz, bons couillaux et beaux cornemuseurs Hebraïques',* destroying the seriousness with the nouns '*couillaux*' and '*cornemuseurs*'. In the last words of the chapter, 'Avés vous bien le tout entendu? Beuvez donc un bon coup sans eaue. Car, si ne le croiez, non foys je, fist elle …'† the created author places all his cards on the table: denying all credibility to the stories he tells. This pretext of simply telling tales for everyone's amusement is a device which he can use very often at the end of a chapter where the argument has been highly controversial and highly topical but the envisaged readers are assumed to be on the author's side.

This intrusive device, with rhetorical elaborations and justifications for giving the information sometimes, and with editorial asides, appears again and again in *Pantagruel*. In chapter 1 the time sequence is disrupted for the narrator to enter with a particular theme – wine tasting: here it is the fate of Noah, for planting the vine 'dont nous vient celle nectaricque, delicieuse, precieuse, celeste, joyeuse et deïficque liqueur qu'on nomme le piot'.‡ In chapter 2 another theme comes in within an intrusion – the physical condition of pock-marked people: with the nonchalance of the first person, he says, 'si vous voulez taster de la vostre propre, ou bien de celles des verollez quand on les faict suer; ce me est tout un'.§ Chapter 4 brings in another convention: that of the conspiratorial relationship between the created author and his envisaged readers, who are referred to as *bonnes gens*: 'Que fist-il? Qu'il fist, mes bonnes gens? Escoutez.'¶ At the end of chapter 20 he gives notice to all his readers that he could write a book to explain all the signs that Panurge and Thaumaste use, 'mais l'on

* I will bring unto you the authority of the Massorets, good honest fellows, true ballokeering blades, and exact Hebraical bagpipers.
† Have you understood all this well? drink then one good draught without water; for if you beleeve it not: no truly do I not, quoth she.
‡ from whence we have that nectarian, delicious, precious, heavenly, joyful and deifick liquour, which they call the piot or tiplage.
§ if you will taste of your own, or of those that have the pox, when they are put into sweating, it is all one to me.
¶ What did he? Heark what he did, good people.

m'a dict que Thaumaste en feist un grand livre, imprimé à Londres, auquel il declaire tout sans rien laisser. Par ce, je m'en deporte pour le present'.* Gradually, through devices such as this, one sketches in a portrait of the story-teller: the nonchalant maker-up of tales which he then elaborates while his envisaged readers sit docile, for they too are in the game; the fantasy is a two-way relationship between author and reader.

The last chapter of *Pantagruel* is almost an epilogue on the created author: he is tippling, his head is swimming with the new wine and he promises another book after this one, even adding a summary of what it will contain. This is a normal fifteenth-century convention for ending a book, but the created author gives the impression that we have been reading a piece of prose fiction with two main characters – Panurge and Pantagruel. To whet our appetites even further he promises more adventures on the same level: the giant and his companion are going to be involved in more exploits which will be both grotesque and comic. The created author's original intention is thus made quite clear. And the first edition ends there. In later editions, however, the created author has to justify himself against the criticism that the book had incurred, and so he furthers the conspiracy between the reader and himself: he dramatizes himself, he magnifies his replies, he uses sarcasm and finally oaths, curses and other highly emotive language. This use of popular language is another device of the created author: he will revert, under pressure, to a mixture of styles, but the reader, however much he may be disturbed, is intellectually engaged by all this on the author's side. For example, here he turns his language into a burlesque treatment of the Sorbonne, where '*escargotz*' is placed between '*cagotz*' and '*hypocrites*' to bring it out of satire into the purely comic: 'vous et moy sommes plus dignes de pardon q'un grand tas de sarrabovittes, cagotz, escargotz, hypocrites, caffars, frappars, botineurs'.†

---

* but I have been told that Thaumast made a great book of it imprinted at London, wherein he hath set down all without omitting any thing, and therefore at this time I do passe by it.

† you and I both are farre more worthy of pardon, then a great rabble of squint-minded fellowes, dissembling and counterfeit Saints, demure lookers, hypocrites, pretended zealots, tough Fryars, buskin-Monks.

This mixture of styles is important and will be looked at in further chapters, but it is not invented by Rabelais. As Auerbach pointed out, 'Paradoxically, it stems from late medieval preaching ... the humanists adopted this mixture of styles, especially for their anti-ecclesiastical, polemical and satiric writings.'[7] One can find it in the Latin works of Erasmus – for instance the colloquy called 'The Fish-Diet' – so vulgarity, obscenity and emotive language are not new to the highly cultured class that was reading Rabelais's works.

Thus in the first chapter and in the last we have the created author and the envisaged reader travelling along the same track: both are looking from above at the fictional world which is being created. From the envisaged reader's point of view there is a constant shifting of viewpoints because the created author does not allow him to settle down comfortably into a state of disbelief. The fiction-making is gigantic, *merveilleux*, fantastic, but both created author and his envisaged readers view it from afar: we can enjoy the satire and the make-believe because we are outside the created author's fictional theatre. Indeed, the intrusive *I* technique compels the reader to identify himself with the editorial commentary, whether by the straight authorial *I* form or through the use of the second person in addresses to the reader, or in the indirect conspiratorial form of *nous*. It is often boisterous, sometimes coarse and obscene and always delightful. We, the readers, are assumed to have the same culture as the created author and can look down on the characters he is creating. The coarse and obscene language, the different levels of style, the intermingling of dimensions, the comic behaviour and jests depend, to a large extent, on us, the envisaged readers; it is we who must perceive the created author's playing with phenomena; and when we have realized that, we know that we are in the game of fantasy.

This perspective holds good for the comic too. Take a comic episode like the death of the female giant Badebec in chapter 3. Gargantua is presented to us as someone who is very good at summoning arguments for and against a view, but helpless when it comes to resolving difficulties. This could be a serious matter. But in saying that Gargantua is 'empestré comme la souriz empeigée ou un milan prins au lasset',* the created author instantly arouses our mirth by the comic similes. The terms of comparison are animals, and anything suggesting the automatic or bestial reduces the giant to a lower level than the reader. Again we might take the list of terms of endearment for his dead wife, ending with the simile in which Gargantua 'pleuroit comme une vache. Mais tout soubdain rioit comme un veau'.† This is not only ridiculous in itself but manages to create a kind of balance between his desire to laugh and cry at the same time which is comic. This type of simile occurs very often in the four books and each time it evokes a comic reaction in the reader. We do not sympathize with the giant, since his grief is not registered at all, except in a comic light. Furthermore in the whole first paragraph, from the rather clumsy fifteenth-century device with which the character and his dilemma are introduced, 'Quand Pantagruel fut né, qui fut bien esbahy et perplex? Ce fut Gargantua son pere. Car, voyant ...'‡ to the similes at the end we are aware that the created author is taking pleasure in viewing the scene with an intellectual detachment which does not seek to arouse any emotional sympathy for Gargantua. If this were not enough, there are the quick asides from the created author, the perpetual seesaw of the argument and finally the epitaph composed by Gargantua for his wife. In the whole chapter we have a *reductio ad absurdum* of the rhetoric employed by the giant whose great stature is mentally diminished by the animal comparisons.

As for the story-telling: within the setting of the gigantic *merveilleux* there is an intertwining of the disruptive *I* technique and that of the omniscient narrator. Let us take chapter 4 and see how it works. It starts off with an *I* narrator, 'Je trouve par les anciens historiographes et poëtes que ...'§ This statement gives boundless scope for lavish use of the *merveilleux*, for in its ironical turn – saying seriously what is meant to be taken jocularly – it

---

* remaining pestered and entangled by this means, like a mouse catch't in a trap, or kite snared in a ginne.
† he did cry like a Cow, but on a sudden fell a laughing like a Calfe.
‡ When Pantagruel was borne, there was none more astonished and perplexed then was his father Gargantua; for of the one side, seeing ...
§ I finde by the ancient Historiographers and Poets, that ...

sets the tone, which is of fiction-making under the pseudo-chronicler's guise. The chronicler goes on with the story, full of the usual fifteenth-century devices – *Je laisse icy à dire comment* or *et vous prent ladicte vache* – while all the time the authorial *I* brings the story up to date with allusions like 'qui est encores de present à Bourges', or his reference to a real product 'comme sont ceulx que l'on faict à Tain pour le voyage du sel de Lyon' when he describes the cables that they tied around the baby Pantagruel. Every explanation is more fantastic than the previous one, and it is no surprise to find the authorial *I* constantly there. Similarly in the next chapter, the juxtaposition of the *merveilleux* with ordinary and witnessable reality is there: the *grosse roche* at Poitiers, on which students play, is described in the present tense, though just before Pantagruel has moved it and set it up on four gigantic pillars. Real persons like the 'docte Tiraqueau' are saluted in the middle of a fabulous journey Pantagruel is making to see the 'grand pere du beau cousin de la sœur aisnée de la tante du gendre de l'oncle de la bruz de sa belle mere, [qui] estoit enterré à Maille-zays'.*

Between chapter 6 – which is the very comic one on the *escholier Limousin* – and chapter 9 – which is the entry of Panurge on the stage – comes the famous letter from Gargantua to Panta-gruel on education. Taken out of its context it is most often quoted as a hymn of praise to the progress of knowledge in the French Renaissance, with the images of spring, re-birth and re-flowering conveying the fresh enthusiasm of letters and humanism of the time. But it is rather puzzling from the narrative point of view. To recover its full flavour we need to examine its context. The beginning of the chapter shows no change from the previous narrative of the *merveilleux*. The tone is the same when we learn how well Pantagruel studies, 'Pantagruel estudioit fort bien, comme assez entendez' (note how this phrase – 'as you may well conceive' – occurs every time the marvellous prowess, the physical activity, and the size of Pantagruel and Gargantua are in question), and he *proufitoit de mesmes*, and there follows a simile which is

* grandfather to the Cousin in law of the eldest Sister of the Aunt of the Son in law of the Uncle of the good daughter of his Stepmother, was interred at Maillezais.

fantastic and earthy at the same time, and again provides a grotesque illustration of the size of the giant, 'car il avoit l'entendement à double rebras, et capacité de memoire à la mesure de douze oyres et botes d'olif'.* The end of the chapter is in the same tone;

Ces lettres receues et veues, Pantagruel print nouveau courage, et feut enflambé à proffiter plus que jamais; en sorte que, le voyant estudier et proffiter, eussiez dict que tel estoit son esperit entre les livres comme est le feu parmy les brandes, tant il l'avoit infatigable et strident.†

Everything is in the same tone as the previous chapters: the marvellous way Pantagruel can do a thing is like a fire running through dry wood, once his fire and ardour have been aroused, for he has memory and understanding far above our own. What then do we make of the letter, which is inserted in this *merveilleux* background, but which is a piece of scholastic reasoning on immortality, as Gilson has shown us?[8] There is no hint of parody,[9] no note of irony, no sign of the 'disruptive' technique and no tinge of the *merveilleux* in the style of the letter. The vast programme of education coexists on the same plane as the grotesque style of the framework. There is a certain unease in the juxtaposition of two literary devices here: the technique of letter-writing and the narrative *merveilleux*. There is the same stylistic unease in the introduction of all the letters and speeches in the four books and it will be looked at in chapter 8 below.

On being introduced to Panurge in chapter 9, Pantagruel takes an instant liking to his appearance and character. We wonder whether the created author will from this point on put himself in Pantagruel's place and give us Pantagruel's own view and his own attitude to Panurge – love, sympathy, tolerance and a high degree of fun – or whether the created author will remain in the background, intervening only as a dramatized narrator. The

---

* for he had an excellent understanding, and notable wit, together with a capacity in memory, equal to the measure of twelve oyle budgets, or butts of Olives.
† These letters being received and read, Pantagruel pluck't up his heart, took a fresh courage to him, and was inflamed with a desire to profit in his studies more then ever, so that if you had seen him, how he took paines, and how he advanced in learning, you would have said that the vivacity of his spirit amidst the books, was like a great fire amongst dry wood, so active it was, vigorous and indefatigable.

answer partly comes in chapter 17 where we hear the voice of the *moi esclave* quite clearly and we are in no doubt that he is a character in the story who will, every now and again, intervene to relate something that he sees or feels strongly about. The *esclave* takes over the narrative and gives some details about himself: for example, 'je gaigné les pardons au premier tronc seulement, car je me contente de peu en ces matières',* a detail which by contrast heightens our impression of the way Panurge steals the money in every church he goes into. Towards the end of this chapter the *esclave* is caught up in a quick and racy dialogue with Panurge, and the two cap each other's remarks with gusto. The *esclave* says 'car tu seras une foys pendu', and Panurge jumps in with 'Et toy . . . tu seras une foys enterré. Lequel est plus honorablement, ou l'air, ou la terre?'† This is another element of dramatic technique: by giving the *esclave* this episode in the church with Panurge, the created author has given us another view of Panurge's character. This little episode, where we hear neither Pantagruel nor the persistent *I* voice of the created author, is lively reporting, and it offers us, the envisaged readers, the chance of seeing Panurge from outside the god-like vantage point of the created author. But there is again a certain incoherence in the *esclave's* rôle in this first book, as he only makes one more appearance, in chapter 32 – 'ce que l'auteur veit dedans sa bouche'. Pantagruel covers the army with his tongue, *comme une geline faict ses poulletz* – a simile which is at once fantastic and animal-based – and so prepares the way for the *esclave* to see all sorts of unexpected things in the giant's mouth.[10] But before he does enter, we have a plea not to take the story too seriously, 'Ce pendent, je, qui vous fais ces tant veritables contes, m'estois caché dessoubz une fueille de bardane . . .'‡ and a little later, the *esclave* calls upon the gods of mythology in the same way as Folengo does in his *Baldus* to support his account, 'Mais, ô dieux et déesses, que veiz ja là?

* and I got the pardons at the first boxe only, for in those matters very little contenteth me.
† for thou wilt be hanged one time or another . . . And thou wilt be interred sometime or other; now which is most honourable, the aire or the earth?
‡ In the mean time I, who relate to you these so veritable stories, hid myself under a burdock-leafe . . .

Juppiter me confonde de sa fouldre trisulque si j'en mens.'* The *esclave* is in other words the created author: for he speaks with the same speciousness and the same detachment from the story as we have known from the created author. The readers are not expected to believe a word of it. In the ensuing dialogue between the *esclave* and a cabbage planter whom the *esclave* finds in the strange new world, we are in a nonsense situation, similar to a Welsh nursery rhyme:

> Ar y ffordd wrth fynd i'r Bettws
> Gwelais ddyn yn plannu tatws;
> Gof'nais iddo beth o'n wneud,
> Plannu tatws, paid a deud.†

This is rustic humour, that of a crafty peasant turning his chores into a joke with the old saying *paid a deud*. In both situations – the nonsense rhyme and the cabbage planter's – the humour is achieved through the question being asked on one level and answered on a different level. The cabbage planter is clearly planting cabbages, but the *esclave* is *tout esbahy* and is forced to ask, 'Mon amy, que fais tu icy?' And gets the answer, 'Je plante, (dist-il), des choulx'. However, even here the personification is not consistent: we gradually become aware that the *esclave* is indeed the created author under his pseudonym Alcofribas, who has a delightful conversation with the giant on his way out of the body. But at the same time the created author's voice – in the use of the pronoun *nous*, for instance – is still heard: 'comme nous avons dict dessus', he says, when he catches the smell from Pantagruel's stomach after the garlic stew he had eaten in chapter 31. One can see here, in the ambivalence with which the pseudonymous Alcofribas functions, that essentially the created author, the *esclave* and Alcofribas are the same person. Yet one can also see what Rabelais is doing: Alcofribas creates a change of perspective. The mental picture of *Pantagruel* is now seen from a different angle; Alcofribas creates a level intermediate between us and the giants; he is our guide in this episode, and the created author, by

---

* But, oh gods and goddesses, what did I see there? Jupiter confound me with his trisulk lightning if I lie.
† On the way to Bettws, I saw a man planting potatoes: I asked him what he was doing, planting potatoes, but tell no one.

using Alcofribas, can seemingly abdicate his responsibility for tricks of changing perspective, as Cervantes does through his pseudo-chronicler.

In other words, the created author has indeed many 'novelistic' devices – like the personification of Alcofribas, the 'disruptive' technique, the omniscient narrator – but all these devices, intertwining with each other, detach the envisaged readers from the centre of the story – which is the account of a giant's adventures. They move us far enough away from our customary view of the world and make us share in creating a new and comic one. Fictionally, one feels an intellectual detachment from the story and from the characters and there is no emotional involvement at all. In this first book, we are always directed to like Pantagruel, but never to identify ourselves with him – 'Et le bon Pantagruel ryoit à tout'. Where there is satire guided by Pantagruel, as in the episode of Thaumaste (chapters 18, 19 and 20), we are constantly aware that we are looking down on the events and on the characters, even on Pantagruel. Each intervention from the created author reminds us of the distance between *us* and the fictional world, 'Messieurs, vous qui lisez ce present escript, ne pensez que jamais gens plus feussent eslevez et transportez en pensée que furent, toute celle nuict, tant Thaumaste que Pantagruel.'* We are seeing everything through a telescope which the created author is showing us how to use.

When we look at the Olympian author in the second book, *Gargantua*, we find again every technique we noticed in *Pantagruel*; the only difference is the greater sophistication in their handling. Thus, for example, in the quasi-dialogue between the created author and envisaged readers there is a racier and more impatient tone: in chapter 9, where the so-called symbolism of colours in Gargantua's livery is discussed, the created author can afford to be self-mocking. For instance, he reminds us of the prologue in his allusion to the theme of drink – '*vous mocquez du*

---

* Gentlemen, you that read this present discourse, think not that ever men were more elevated and transported in their thoughts, then all this night were both Thaumast and Pantagruel.

vieil beuveur';* he can preen himself and throw off with a light shrug things like – 'Qui vous meut? Qui vous poinct? Qui vous dict que blanc signifie foy et bleu fermeté? Un (dictes vous) livre trepelu ...'† He gives himself elbow-room to mock violently a book like the *Blason des couleurs* which all the people at court take seriously and which is fashionable. He will one day write a book which will be more worthy than this one, 'et monstrer, tant par raisons philosophicques que par auctoritez receues et approuvées de toute ancienneté, quelles et quantes couleurs sont en nature ...'‡ The envisaged readers are on the author's side throughout, and when one comes to the end of the chapter – 'c'est le pot au vin, comme disoit ma mere grand'§ – in the throw-away reference to his grandmother one can recognize the tone in which he has been conducting the whole chapter.

The *I* technique is sharper, more intellectual and more subtle in *Gargantua* than in *Pantagruel*, for example, in Gargantua's strange method of being born in chapter 6. The naturalistic dialogue between Grandgousier and Gargamelle with male and female viewpoints on giving birth is finely done.

GRANDGOUSIER —Je le prouve ... Dieu (c'est nostre Saulveur) dict en l'evangile Joan. 16: 'La femme qui est à l'heure de son enfantement a tristesse, mais lorsqu'elle a enfanté elle n'a soubvenir aulcun de son angoisse.'

GARGAMELLE — Ha ... vous dictes bien et ayme beaucoup mieulx ouyr telz propos de l'Evangile et mieulx m'en trouve que de ouyr la vie de saincte Marguerite ou quelque aultre capharderie.¶

(1534 version)

The satire here is directed against the apocryphal lives of saints which people read instead of the words of the Gospel, but after

* You laugh at the old drinker.
† What is it that induceth you? what stirs you up to believe, or who told you that white signifieth faith, and blew, constancy? An old paultry book, say you ...
‡ to shew both by Philosophical arguments and authorities, received and approved of by and from all antiquity, what, and how many colours there are in nature ...
§ which is my best Wine-pot, as my Grandame said.
¶ GRANDGOUSIER—I can prove it ... God (that is our Saviour) says in the gospel of St John, Chapter 16, verse 21, 'A woman when she is in travail hath sorrow, because her hour is come: but as soon as she is delivered of the child, she remembereth no more the anguish, for joy that a man is born into the world.'
GARGAMELLE—Ha! you say well, and I much prefer to hear such quotations from the Gospel and I feel better for it than to hear the life of St Margaret or some other rubbish. [D.C.]

1542 the whole dialogue was cut out. The omission of such a passage shows us how the conscious artist, even in a gigantic and fantastical situation, worked prudently. But there is a much clearer omission in this same chapter. This is the quasi-fictitious dialogue towards the end: it starts off in exactly the same tone as we have met before in *Pantagruel*: 'Je me doubte que ne croyez asseurement ceste estrange nativité. Si ne le croyez, je ne m'en soucie.'* This looks like the same take-it-or-leave-it attitude, the same nonchalant disclaimer of truth, but in 1534 he had gone on to make a subtle and profound satire against the theologians at the Sorbonne, saying,

Ne dict pas Solomon Proverbiorum 14: 'Innocens credit omni verbo etc.', et Sainct Paul, prime Corinthio. 13: 'Charitas omnia credit'. Pourquoy ne le croyriez vous? Pour ce (dictes vous) qu'il n'y a nulle apparence. Je vous dictz que pour ceste seule cause vous le debvez croyre en foy parfaicte. Car les Sorbonistes disent que foy est argument des choses de nulle apparence.†

Professor Screech's argument is apposite here.[11] It might seem as if the created author was aiming a shaft of satire against the Sorbonne's definition of faith – believing a lot of things which don't seem very likely – and was opposing to it a serious belief in the power of God through faith and trust. The tone of voice, however, and the fictional form of this two-way dialogue make it anything but a biting satire of the theology of the time. Rather, by quoting the Bible, he is surely using it in the same way as he uses for instance the Elder Pliny, 'Lisez le septiesme de sa *Naturelle Histoire, capi. iij*, et ne m'en tabustez plus l'entendement.'‡ However this allusion to a point of theological doctrine is too near the danger-mark and the conscious artist tones down subversive ideas that medieval artists could have got away with. Where in 1534 he had been fictionalizing religion in the same tone and in the same

---

* I doubt me, that you do not throughly beleeve the truth of this strange nativity; though you believe it not, I care not much.
† Does not Solomon say in Proverbs 14, 'Innocens credit omnia verbo'? and St Paul in I Corinthians 13, 'Charity believeth all things'. Why should you not believe it? For this reason (say you) that it does not seem likely at all. I tell you that this single reason should make it seem perfect faith to you. For the professors of Theology at the Sorbonne say that faith is just this: believing a lot of things which do not seem likely at all. [D.C.]
‡ Reade the seventh book of his *Natural History*, chapt. 3, and trouble not my head any more about this.

way as he fictionalized everything else, by 1542 a note of cautiousness, of prudence, made him reef his sails and move in the direction the wind was blowing.

The narrative technique as a whole is far more advanced than in *Pantagruel*. The events are tighter, the battles are more lively, frere Jan is given a much more developed character and the disruptive technique is much stronger. The created author dramatizes, satirizes and makes poetic and comic twists. There is a certain incoherence in the narrative, in the way for instance in which the omniscient narrator gets caught up with one of the characters' narrative. The most obvious example is in the Abbey of Thélème episode (chapters 52 to the end): it is Utopian and satirical. *Restoit seulement le moyne à pourvoir* starts the scene, with a dialogue between Gargantua and frere Jan about the requirements of an abbey that frere Jan is to have. It looks as though the whole thing will be carried on in the interchange of these two. But before long the omniscient narrator returns, and in parenthesis the *I* technique as well, with 'Davantaige, veu que en certains conventz de ce monde est en usance que, si femme aulcune y entre (j'entends des preudes et pudicques) ...'* and apart from an attempt in that same paragraph to continue the narrative in the mouth of Gargantua (*disoit Gargantua*) there is no coherence at all; with the result that one has to accept the ensuing chapters as being in the control of an omniscient narrator – with the architectural plans and the inscription on the gates, the manner of dwelling and the fine clothes of all the inhabitants – and the narrative is rather flat and lumpy.[12] The famous chapter 57 on *Fay ce que vouldras* is engineered by the omniscient narrator, and he switches to the present tense to explain the motto, 'car nous entreprenons tousjours choses defendues et convoitons ce que nous est denié'.† This is a serious speech, making use of what Erasmus had been saying on education, particularly in his book *De pueris* which came out in 1529. The narrator praises emulation and calls it honour, and behind it all suggests a firm belief in the perfectibility of man.

---

* Moreover, seeing there are certaine convents in the world, whereof the custome is, if any woman come in (I mean chaste and honest women) ...
† for it is agreable with the nature of man to long after things forbidden, and to desire what is denied us.

Whether or not the created author is speaking for the real man Rabelais on a topic that is both scriptural and educational will be looked at later: here we merely notice the lack of verisimilitude in the way the whole Abbey of Thélème is narrated.[13] At the end of chapter 57 we have the created author's *I* technique entering, 'Je ne veulx oublier vous descripre un enigme qui fut trouvé aux fondemens de l'abbaye en une grande lame de bronze. Tel estoit comme s'ensuyt.'* This puts the whole episode in perspective, and thus in the last chapter of *Gargantua* the giant gives one explanation whilst frere Jan gives a totally different one. The book ends with the words of frere Jan.

The conspiracy between the created author and envisaged readers has developed to a sophisticated degree in *Gargantua* and we can say that we are looking at things from a distance established for us by the Olympian author: he relies on the docility that he has created in *Pantagruel* as our only possible reaction fictionally, and furthermore, he knows that we have read his first book and so he can make allusions to it (e.g. chapter 1, chapter 3 – where he even calls the envisaged readers *vous aultres mes bons averlans*). Almost intentionally, he can drop into the Gascon dialect, 'Et sabez quey, hillotz? Que mau de pipe vous byre!'† (chapter 11) after the very rich comic paragraph on the childhood of Gargantua, in order to disrupt his readers, to make them aware that the created author and themselves are really enjoying words, the sound of them, the sense, literal and metaphorical, of words as they come in this marvellous book. His cavalier tone, his take-it-or-leave-it attitude, imply 'you know as well as I do what fiction-making is like, what the characters that are created are like. Why, the commentators who were present at the scene when Grandgousier welcomed back his fine warriors (chapter 37), can tell you much better than I can what really happened to his wife' but, 'jamais on ne veit gens plus joyeux, car *Supplementum Supplementi Chronicorum* dict que Gargamelle y mourut de joye. Je n'en sçay

---

* Here must not I forget to set down unto you a riddle, which was found under the ground, as they were laying the foundation of the Abbey, ingraven in a copper plate, and it was thus as followeth.

† But hearken, good fellows, the spigot ill betake you, and whirl round your braines, if you do not give eare.

rien de ma part, et bien peu me soucie ny d'elle ny d'aultre'.* A couldn't-care-less attitude to the whole fictional world he is creating is obvious here; and what is more important, he can make his envisaged readers feel that they too are not readers of *chansons de geste* or anything else: they are in the game of creating fiction. When he has to make an end of Picrochole (chapter 49), after the soothsayers' prediction that he will be returned to his kingdom *à la venue des cocquecigrues*, he does it in this way, 'Depuis ne sçait on qu'il est devenu. *Toutesfoys l'on m'a dict qu'il est de present* ...'† (my italics). The Olympian author is consciously being purely fantastic here and knows that his envisaged readers are only too eager not to seat themselves in a comfortable suspension of disbelief.

In the *Tiers Livre* the Olympian author is in complete control over the framework from the first chapter on colonization to the grand finale on the herb called Pantagruelion (chapters 49 to the end). It is an absurdly burlesque perspective controlled by the authorial *I* technique. Every time that the authorial *I* knows how the envisaged readers will react to such and such a situation, he makes asides, plays with words in two or three meanings and makes a small thing grow until it reaches monstrous proportions. For instance, in the first chapter he makes mock of Utopia because, *vous entendez assez*, this is how idealized societies behave, 'les Utopiens avoient les genitoires tant feconds et les Utopienes portoient matrices tant amples, gloutes, tenaces, et cellulées par bonne architecture, que ...'‡ Coarse language mingles with borrowings from Plutarch, Pliny, Sir Thomas More and Erasmus to produce almost a continuation of the prologue. For instance, the same forms of expression are used – *Noterez doncques icy, Beuveurs*, or *Notez aussi, Goutteux fieffez* to continue the leitmotif of drinking, and the whole chapter is one delightful farce. The

---

* never was seen a more joyful company; for *supplementum supplementi Chronicorum* saith, that Gargamelle died there with joy; for my part, truly I cannot tell, neither do I care very much for her, nor for anybody else.

† What is become of him since we cannot certainly tell, yet was I told that he is now ...

‡ that the Utopian Men had so rank and fruitful Genitories, and that the Utopian Women carried Matrixes so ample, so glutonous, so tenaciously retentive, and so Architectonically cellulated, that ...

second chapter extends the created author's summing up of Pantagruel, previously given in *Pantagruel* (chapter 31): 'Je vous ay ja dict et encores rediz, que c'estoit le meilleur petit et grand bon hommet que oncques ceigneït espée.'* This is still an outline view, but what follows is a combination of Stoic ideas and commonsense expounded without a hint of parody or irony.

At the end of the book (chapter 49 onwards) we return to the framework: the giant's size is magnified again, the authorial *I* form is used with great force, and the whole picture is again one of heroi–comic and burlesque delineation. For instance, in comparing the herb to the giant we have the famous line, 'car, comme Pantagruel a esté l'idée et exemplaire de toute joyeuse perfection ...'† (chapter 51) which has in parenthesis '(je croy que personne de vous aultres, beuveurs, n'en doubte)'‡ and takes us back to the first chapter of the *Tiers Livre*. There is a constant turning to the envisaged reader with a highly rhetorical flavour in the authorial *I*'s speech: 'Croyez la ou non, ce m'est tout un. Me suffist vous avoir dict vérité'§ (chapter 52). It is as if the Olympian author has arranged for every point of view to be presented and then asks us, the envisaged readers, to make our own choice of focus.

Within this burlesque framework, the narrative technique has matured: the omniscient technique is now in full voice. It takes over the narrative almost completely and there is much greater control of dialogue – for instance the dialogues between Panurge and Pantagruel take up half the book. We shall see how the shape of the book conditions the narrative technique in later chapters but it must be noted here that dramatization, characterization, timing and tempo have undergone a sea-change and the subtle metamorphosis in ideas is reinforced by the change in narrative from

---

* For I once told you, and again tell it you, that he was the best, little, great Good-man that ever girded a Sword to his Side.

† for as Pantagruel hath been the Idea, Pattern, Prototype and Exemplary of all Jovial Perfection and Accomplishment ...

‡ (in the truth whereof, I believe there is none of you, Gentlemen Drinkers, that putteth any question) ...

§ Believe it if you will, or otherwise believe it not, I care not which of them you do, they are both alike to me, it shall be sufficient for my Purpose to have told you the Truth ...

the story of giants to something which is looking forward in novelistic directions.

With the *Quart Livre* the authorial *I* plays again the 'disruptive' rôle that the envisaged reader quickly recognizes. With a sea voyage, which takes uncommon and marvellous events as part of the narrative, the appeal to wonder is one of the main qualities of the book. Given this new subject, very different from the other three books previously published, the created author was to vary his narrative method. Like Lucian with his marvellous tales in the *True History*, the created author wants to keep his fantasy at as great a distance as possible from the envisaged reader: he does not want to discourage the suspension of disbelief without which the readers will fail to enjoy the fantastic episodes and will become disoriented. And yet, the created author does not want to shatter the established conspiracy between himself and the envisaged readers which was in evidence in the other three books. How does he manage to keep firm control over both reactions?

The *nous* technique, by which Alcofribas speaks for himself and for the whole company, now comes into full play: and it is one way of keeping the cable of suspension taut. Alongside this technique all the others keep intertwining themselves, sometimes rather incoherently, sometimes with fine magnificence. For in the *Quart Livre* we come as close as we can to direct presentation of events by Alcofribas and yet, we always preserve the distance of the Olympian author. The reader follows, even participates in, the story through the remarks of Alcofribas and is able to find an intimate narrative framework in the ship's voyages in and out among little islands. There is no logic about the way events are described in this *nous* technique: sometimes Alcofribas sees details that no one else in the company has seen, sometimes *nous* is not used in a group of episodes, so that we as readers are under its direction for only parts of the book. In other parts we are totally under the *I* technique of the Olympian author. To see how this works one must look at the two versions published: the first version of the *Quart Livre* which came out in 1548 with ten complete chapters and an unfinished eleventh one; and the final version which came out in 1552.[14] Thus we can examine the final version's twenty-five chapters, i.e. to the end of the partial edition. For if we observe the created author at this point, where he has the opportunity of consciously adding, altering or omitting phrases or episodes, we may discover clues as to how important this *nous* technique was for him in the art of fiction-making.

In the first chapter we have the *I* technique explicit in both versions: *Et suis en ceste opinion* (p. 74) and in 1552 the phrase repeated with the addition *sauf meilleur jugement** (p. 35). This *I* device creates a distance between the readers and the furniture of the fictional world, a distance which is closely related to the detachment that comes from the created author's prevailing note of intellect in all four books. The envisaged readers expect the *I* to intervene, jesting, parodying *merveilleux* stories, giving an anecdote a contemporary allusion and elaborating in an encyclopaedic way as he does with the Pantagruelion in the *Tiers Livre*. Furthermore he provides continuity between the third and the fourth books; he reminds us that all the ships are loaded with Pantagruelion and reminds us also of their number – 'le nombre des navires fut tel, que vous ay exposé au tiers livre'.† It is only the 1552 version which goes further and tells us the types of vessel involved.

The beginning of chapter 2 (in both versions) leads us to expect that there will be nothing new in the narrative technique for the whole voyage: the *leur* mentioned is the whole company and the story so far is presented by an omniscient narrator. But the second sentence in the 1548 version begins immediately with a *nous* device, 'ja commençans tournoyer le pol peu à peu, nous esloignans de l'Equinoctial, descouvrismes une navire marchande faisant voile à horche vers nous'.‡ This will in the later version form the introduction to the same episode – the debate between Panurge and Dindenault – in chapter 5. But what is interesting is that the created author did use this device in 1548. It enters unostentatiously,

* And it is my Opinion, with Submission to better Judgements.
† the number of Ships was such as I described in the Third Book.
‡ [On the fifth Day] we began already to wind by little and little about the Pole, going still farther from the Equinoctial Line, we discovered a Merchant-man to the windward of us.

but is artistically rather crude: we pass straight from one sentence with *leur* to a second sentence with *nous* and have to register that *nos fortunes* are henceforth going to be the same as those on board ship.

In the 1552 version chapters 2, 3 and 4 are added – the episode at Medamothi, and the exchange of letters between Gargantua and Pantagruel. The *I* device disrupting the story is heard, outside and above it, making satirical remarks on the painting each member bought on the quayside, perhaps having a dig at the Neo-Platonists' theories about fine arts and altogether revelling in the rôle that has been so firmly established for him. It gives encyclopaedic information on the Tarand, and then suddenly the narration changes to a *nous:* 'Ce que sus tout trouvasmes en cestuy tarande admirable est que . . .'* The *nous* device is a witness to all the things happening on board ship; it is able to observe details which any of the company can see and also to comment on them from a superior perspective. In other words this is another trick of the Olympian author: elevating us to the right hand of the god who is controlling the scene, so that we may look down at the puppets and their behaviour with delight. Let us see how the narration between Dindenault and Panurge works out (chapter 3 in the 1548 version; chapters 5–8 in the 1552 version). First there is the introduction to the debate, assigned to the omniscient narrator: *L'occasion du débat feut telle*† (the same in both versions). From that moment on, the spotlight falls on Panurge who takes charge of the narrative. The only point which we need to notice here is that Pantagruel in 1548 was in the game, 'Panurge dist secretement à Pantagruel et à frere Jean',‡ while he is pushed into the background completely in the 1552 version, when the exchange is between Panurge, Epistemon and frere Jan. This is quite important for the shaping of the rôle that Pantagruel is to play – as leader of the company and the one who conducts the assembly at every juncture. At the end of the debate comes the startling climactic sentence, 'Soubdain je ne sçay comment, le cas fut subit,

---

* But what we found most surprizing in this Tarand is, that . . .
† The occasion of the Fray was thus.
‡ Panurge tipp'd the wink upon [Pantagruel] and Friar Jhon. [Motteux is following the 1552 version throughout, and thus has Epistemon in the place of Pantagruel here.]

je n'heu loysir le considerer, Panurge (sans autre chose dire), jecte en pleine mer son mouton criant et bellant'* (1548 version). It does not shed much light to say that the created author here followed the story in Folengo word for word; for why should he have invented so much (even in 1548 and far more in the later version) in order to enrich the episode, only to copy Folengo at the climax and to revert to the *I* technique to carry on the narrative. If we look back to the beginning of the episode, we find that Alcofribas has been so busy with the Lanternois – asking after their habits – that he has not heard Panurge quarrelling with Dindenault, and has to have the story recounted to him. This is done in a straightforward way in *L'occasion du débat feut telle*. The real interest in the debate is in the dialogue, which is highly rhetorical and vastly amusing. (For more detailed comments, see chapter 7 below.) But with the opening of chapter 3 (chapter 6 in the 1552 version) there is a change of sides, for with the expectation that Panurge has something up his sleeve in order to get his revenge on the merchant, who in 1548 (but not in 1552) is called *glorieux*, we as envisaged readers are ready for the fun which Panurge has at the expense of the whole shipload of sheep and their master, Dindenault. Panurge takes all the mockery thrown at him by the merchant, all the high-flown sales-talk and his only request is to buy one of the sheep. An intervention from the pilot helps speed on the climax, the merchant agrees on a price, Panurge chooses a wether and the climax itself is introduced by the *I* technique. We are thus placed once more outside the story, laughing at Panurge's joke, at the doltishness of Dindenault and the stupidity of sheep. The present tense is effectively used and the whole episode can be seen from the distance of the Olympian author.

In the next chapter (chapter 4 and 9) the *nous* device is narrowed down to include only Alcofribas himself, who has noticed certain things that he wants to tell us. At various moments Alcofribas then enters and the episode is much enriched in the 1552 version. The punning, the enjoyment of splitting a metaphoric title or

---

* On a sudden, you would wonder how the thing was so soon done; for my part I can't tell you, for I had not leisure to mind it; our Friend Panurge without any further tittle tattle, throws you his Ram over-board into the middle of the Sea bleating and making a sad Noise.

image into two halves, the general playing with language which is the main interest in the island of Ennasin involves not only frere Jan, Panurge, Carpalim but also Alcofribas – who therefore gives us quite a close viewpoint and actually joins in the fun himself. There is no suggestion that he is any different from the other members of the company, and this is a great advantage in keeping the readers involved in the fantasy of the episode. Indeed if this were the only way in which we as envisaged readers were accompanying the group on their sea voyage, we should have a straight piece of prose fiction seen through the eyes of an explicit witness – the eye-witness to all that happens. But this is not so!

In the 'storm at sea' episode which takes up seven chapters in the final version (three chapters in the 1548 version), this device is interesting, for a short time and then once more the light is focused on Panurge and frere Jan. We start off with the usual *nous* framework (in both versions), Panurge encounters the ship-load of monks going to the *Concile de Chesil* and we have the pilot seeing the tempest brewing on the horizon. He immediately 'commenda tous estre à l'herte, tant Nauchiers, Fadriers et Mousses que nous autres Voyageurs'* (the same in both versions). So *nous* are in the middle of this crisis and it is through *nous* that we the readers are able to feel the effects of the storm. In the graphic, nautical description of the storm that follows, it is *our* vessels and *our* sails that are being battered; *nous* can see nothing in the darkened sky but lightning; *nous* are surrounded by *psoloentes, arges, elicies* and *nos aspects tous estre dissipez et perturbez*. The last sentence in this part of the description is a fusion of the created author's *I* technique and the effects that *nous* feel, 'Croyez que ce nous sembloit estre l'antique Cahos, on quel estoient feu, air, mer, terre, tous les elemens en refraictaire confusion.'† This is all that the *nous* and the author's *I* are allowed to do; for immediately after, we are back in the grotesque framework with attention concentrated on Panurge.

* call Hands upon Deck, Officers, Sailors, Foremast Men, Swabbers, and Cabbin-boys, and even the Passengers. [Note that the narration in Motteux's version takes no notice of the *nous* technique here.]
† Believe me, it seem'd to us a lively Image of the Chaos, where Fire, Air, Sea, Land, and all the Elements, were in a refractory Confusion.

If we, the readers, seem to be participating in the voyage our-selves through the *nous* technique, the whole pattern of events in the book gains a greater air of verisimilitude; it is easier for the reader to suspend disbelief. But the intertwining of this *nous* device with all the other narrative techniques makes it impossible to suspend disbelief for any length of time. In certain episodes, however, it works splendidly and in order to see all the techniques *tutti forti* let us look at the famous chapters 55 and 56 – the 'frozen words'. The episode starts with the *nous* device, 'En pleine mer nous banquetans, gringnotans, divisans et faisans beaulx et cours discours . . .'* Then in this fantastic tale which is about to be recounted by the omniscient narrator, it is Pantagruel who first hears eerie disembodied sounds coming from the air around them:

Pantagruel se leva et tint en pieds pour discouvrir à l'environ. Puys nous dist: 'Compaignons, oyez vous rien? Me semble que je oy quelques gens parlans en l'air, je n'y voy toutesfoys personne. Escoutez'. A son commandement nous feusmes attentifz, et à pleines aureilles humions l'air, comme belles huytres en escalle, pour entendre si voix ou son aulcun y seroit espart . . .†

The envisaged readers, *nous* – Alcofribas and the whole company and Pantagruel – are standing there trying to hear what could not be heard and there is a hint of the comic in the simile of the oyster shells. There is a great eerie sensation of disembodied sounds – *ce que nous effraya grandement* – until finally we can hear the sounds.

There is a rich counterpoint between Panurge who is imme-diately terrified and Pantagruel who remains calm and sane. Pantagruel attempts a rational interpretation of the phenomenon, giving four possible ways in which they could understand the legend of the Arimaspiens and the Nephelibates. But in the next chapter the captain gives us the real explanation, and from here on rationality takes a backward place, as in great imaginative detail the created author makes us look at, feel and hear these disem-

---

* When we were at Sea, Junketing, Tipling, Discoursing and telling Stories . . .
† Pantagruel rose and stood up to look out; then ask'd us, Do you hear nothing, Gentle-men? Methinks I hear some People talking in the Air; yet I can see no body; Hark! According to his Command we listen'd, and with full Ears suck'd in the Air, as some of you suck Oysters, to find if we could hear some Sound scatter'd through the Sky.

bodied words. The words remain unintelligible to the whole company, Pantagruel included, and they spend little time trying to decipher what they could mean.

The created author goes on to embroider upon the fantastic stories and also the various aspects of human language suggested by the stories. Thus at the level of narrative writing one gets the delight in handling words, 'et sembloient dragée perlée de diverses couleurs',* they are azure, gold, sand coloured; one that frere Jan has bursts like roasting chestnuts, 'feist un son tel que font les chastaignes jectées en la braze sans estre entonmées, lors que s'esclattent ...'† Here is a poet fascinated by the whole pheno-menon of language and the relationship between words and objects; the real life that words seem to have, an animated move-ment which is on the confines of articulation. The created author takes great joy in elaborating on one of the mysteries of language – how words have colours, shapes and sounds which are 'tangible': we talk of *paroles douces, ameres, glacées* and are thinking about them as objects. Alcofribas sees all this on board ship, 'Et y veids des parolles bien picquantes, des parolles sanglantes',‡ and we feel the strange, almost magic power that words have of striking fear, of charming and stimulating people and evoking visually a battle of long ago. In fact it is their power of perpetuating transitory, perishable events so that even if unintelligible to clear reason they have this element of survival, of bursting forth in the imagination of men. The extreme jubilance of the whole company is expressed when they are playing with these pretty coloured words, the jumbled jigsaw of thawing words, sometimes caught at the level of mere sound as in – *hin, hin, ticque, torche, bou, bou, bou, trr trr.* Some make a noise like trumpets and drums, some the clash of weapons and horses in battle and some like bugles and pipes. All in all, 'Croyez que nous y eusmez du passetemps beaucoup'.§ The main success of this episode is the interaction between all on

---

* which seem'd to us like your rough Sugar-Plumbs, of many Colours ...
† having been warm'd between Fryar Jhon's Hands, gave a sound much like that of Chestnuts when they are thrown into the Fire without being first cut ...
‡ I perceiv'd some very sharp Words, and some bloody Words ... we also saw some terrible Words, and some others not very pleasant to the Eye.
§ Believe me, we had very good Sport with them.

board ship sailing in the frozen, eerie Arctic sea and the fantasy they create out of 'frozen words'.

The whole company enjoys the exploration of sound, and Alcofribas comes into close contact with Pantagruel. 'Je vouloys quelques motz de gueule mettre en reserve dedans de l'huille ... Mais Pantagruel ne le voulut ....'* He gets the answer that swearwords are always to be had *entre tous bons et joyeulx Panta-gruelistes*. This conversation almost gives us the feeling that Alcofribas and Pantagruel have broken away from the created author and that Rabelais is watching his characters behave and act without his having predetermined the issues.

Alcofribas gives an insider's point of view to parts of the *Quart Livre:* and his use of *nous* has the effect that we, the envisaged readers, are there when the company calls upon islands; we have him as an eye-witness to the description of the inhabitants, with him we can also joke as a member of the company led by Panta-gruel. We are not allowed to become involved in the story or attached to any religious or philosophical senses any island could have – from the fictional point of view. For both Alcofribas and the created author can extend their vision and Alcofribas can narrow it down to give an eye-witness account of visits. There is no selection of detail in this eye-witness account: these are merely the things that catch our eye, given through an elliptic form, in the present tense and in brief graphic descriptions. We almost feel that we are really in the midst of events.

This is one of the exciting devices that the Olympian author has experimented with: he develops it most surely in the *Quart Livre*, though, as we have seen, it occurs in several places in the other three books. In one way it is like the picaresque novel in Spain where as in *Lazarillo de Tormes* the autobiographical thread is there from the beginning: the reader has a very narrow eye-piece through which he views the story. But the interesting point that one must make at once is that this eye-witness device in the *Quart Livre* is only one of the techniques through which the story is told. All the techniques found in the other three books are here

---

* I wou'd fain have sav'd some merry Odd Words, and have preserv'd them in Oil ...
  But Pantagruel would not let me ...

as well, particularly the Olympian author. The distance at which we are placed is totally contrasted with the single view that one is given in the picaresque novel, which takes as its main thread of narrative society versus the *picaro*. Rabelais by using this Olympian author technique has extended his view to take in all the possible ranges of distance, and yet it is quite an organizing and unifying device. We started off with no steady view, no basic focus from which to view the story and we end on what Professor Friedman called, 'the free verse of fiction'.[15]

In asking the question, 'Who talks to the reader?', we have a clear answer: the created author's *I*. From the beginning of the prologue to *Pantagruel* we are drawn into the mesmerizing, word-spinning account presented by the author and we never leave it. Thus on matters like the fact that he has some highly critical things to say about religion, fictionally he does not commit himself: he is content to let some things suggest themselves to the readers, but he never speaks out in defence of his own opinions and the reader's reaction must be 'Whether you believe him or not, this is how things are'. The mask or *persona* of the author is very definitely still the satiric personage: the free-verse form in which he chose to write is still vital for irony, parody and satire. The reader has, as it were, escalated to the seat that the Olympian author sits on: he is far away from the story and close to the creator of it. And the creator can be seen above all the events; he is creating the fictional world from a god-like vantage point. The choice of this point of view is as positive as the next choice Rabelais will have to make: that is, what kind of fictional form will be suitable to contain his irony, parody, satire, philosophical range and finally, and probably the most important, his linguistic inventiveness.

THE CHOICE OF FORM

The panoramic Olympian author has to choose a fictional form which will condition the way the work develops. The structure of the four books reinforces on one level the basic aim of a comic work: for each one ends on a burlesque note. *Pantagruel* promises more books of a similar type with grotesque and horrific adventures; *Gargantua* ends with an *enigme en prophetie* which is interpreted by Gargantua and frere Jan in different ways; the *Tiers Livre* finishes on the Olympian author's praise of the herb Pantagruelion and the *Quart Livre* ends on the scatology of Panurge's fear. Even the fifth book, which we are not discussing in this work, ends with the figure poem of the bottle and the word *Trinch*. Within this burlesque framework the Olympian author has taken the general outlines of *Pantagruel* and *Gargantua* from romances and epic stories, the *Tiers Livre* from a topic which was argued about by rhetoricians of the time – marriage – and the *Quart Livre* from the traditional topic of a sea voyage. If we look at it on another level, the work seems an encyclopaedia of Renaissance topics and problems where Rabelais dons a satiric mask to get a message across safely. Is Professor Keller right to regard Rabelais as a story-teller[1] or are Professor Screech and his predecessors right in just calling him a novelist? Are the 'loose unconnected adventures ... of which you may transverse the order as you please'[2] as true of Rabelais as of Cervantes?

Let us start our investigation with a review of the structure of the four books in turn.

'Pantagruel'

I Grotesque parody of an epic birth, plus a long genealogical list. The Olympian author conducts this first chapter.

II to V Birth, childhood and adolescence of Pantagruel. The gigantic *merveilleux* and realism juxtaposed. Parody of epic heroes from antiquity and from *chansons de geste*. Satire of historiography, of religion, of rhetoric and of universities.

Some verses on the death of Badebec.

It is clear that there is a thin narrative line modelled on epic stories. But equally clear is the fact that it is loose. One notices that the narration is mixed quite thickly with topical satire – for instance the lawsuit of Baisecul and Humesvene – with verse interludes; and with lists of places, people and books which hold up the story for a whole chapter. Furthermore, we are transported into a make-believe world full of grotesque wonders, with giants having as their henchmen persons who symbolize speed, industry, cunning and bravery. We do not identify ourselves with any character or with any event in this story. The characterization of Panurge could start a line of comedy but, in this first book, he is created in order to give rather coarse comic effects such as the way to build walls in Paris and how to play tricks on women. We conclude that we are more interested in the casual or rhetorical interpolations from the Olympian author than in a transparent narrative line.

'Gargantua'

I	Olympian author parodies genealogies.
II	Verse interlude of the *fanfreluches antidotées*.
III to IV	The origin and pre-birth of Gargantua.
V	Another interlude – the drinkers' discourse.
VI	The birth of Gargantua, with the satirical criticism of the Sorbonne (omitted from later editions).
VII to XII	Childhood of Gargantua, with a great deal of the comic and the satire coming from the Olympian author.
XIII	The finding of the best arse-wiper.
	Verse interludes intervening in the story.
XIV to XVII	Satire of education and of universities as Gargantua makes his grand tour of them.
XVIII to XX	Grotesque satire on Janotus de Bragmardo.
XXI	Gargantua's education.
XXII	Intervention of list of games which he used to play.
XXIII and XXIV	Continuation of Gargantua's education.
XXV and XXVI	The beginning of the war.
	The gigantic *merveilleux* of *Pantagruel* is dropped and we are introduced to a comic fool – Picrochole.
XXVII	Siege at Seuillé; introduction to frere Jan, a comic and satirical character who is much better developed than the Panurge of *Pantagruel*.
XXVIII	Main action is clumsily switched to Grandgousier at his home.
XXIX	Grandgousier's letter to Gargantua, which is serious in intent.
XXX to XXXIII	Picrochole in focus.
XXXIX	Frere Jan meets the whole company of *Gargantuistes* and harangues them. The beginning of a social comic scene.
XL to XLIV	Gargantua and frere Jan act as foils to each other in this parody of an epic war.
XLV and XLVI	Grandgousier deals with the vanquished and the prisoners of war in a serious and realistic manner.
XLVII to XLIX	Other episodes in this war.
L	Serious speech of Gargantua to the defeated.
LI to the end	The victors are rewarded and frere Jan is given the Abbey of Thélème. Description of that abbey.

There is a far greater sophistication in the Olympian author of *Gargantua* than in *Pantagruel*. The narration is also easily diverted to comic dramatization in the case of Picrochole, to a burlesque satirical portrait in the case of Janotus de Bragmardo and to a lively characterization of frere Jan. The parody of epic wars gives way to a heroi–comical treatment, with a far larger circle of characters. But around these clusters of episodes we find satire of religion, of rhetoric, of topical things like *imprese*, not to mention things like law and the church as symbolized by the Sorbonne. Furthermore, one has the same formlessness as in *Pantagruel*: much more so in fact. For in the first ten chapters we notice many more verse interludes, much more seriousness juxtaposed with buffoonery, and in the last chapters there is a constant ambiguity in the description of the Abbey of Thélème. If we agree with Sterne, who said 'digressions, incontestably, are the sunshine; – they are the life, the soul of reading! – take them out of this book, for instance, – you might as well take the book along with them ...'[3] we should not want to omit anything from *Gargantua*, but we should puzzle over the interventions from the Olympian author, which make us lose the narrative thread altogether. Finally, there are apparently serious episodes – like the speeches of both giants – which do not come into focus properly in this gigantic framework.

The 'Tiers Livre'

I and II, and
XLIX to the end   An absurd burlesque framework is established and is exceptionally well articulated.
In this framework there is in chapter 2 a clear formulation of
a norm of social and philosophical ideas around Pantagruel.
Furthermore, it is clear that Panurge stands alone in the
company of *Pantagruelistes*. In this second chapter, however,
he is given both some satire and a comic–rhetorical inventiveness.

If we follow through the structure of this third book, however, it will appear as neither the social comedy that this second chapter promises, nor as a Christian comedy as Professor Screech calls it.[4]

III and IV Panurge makes his speech on the praise of debts.

V Pantagruel replies sanely and moderately whilst Panurge is the same anti-hero that he was in *Pantagruel:* for instance, he says things like 'the lasses of Salmiguondy shall fart and my body shall be their cure'.

VI and VII The marriage-theme is announced.

VIII Instead of continuing this theme, Pantagruel offers the readers the sound of Panurge talking on a nonsensical topic. Verse interludes intervene towards the end of the chapter.

IX The question of Panurge – should he get married, and if so, will he be a cuckold? – answered by Pantagruel by echo.

X Vergilian and Homeric lots are tried; an accumulation of examples and quotations.

XI and XII Pantagruel and Panurge take the opposite interpretation from each other and this establishes a pattern.

XIII and XIV Consultation by dreams.

XV This chapter has nothing to do with the marriage theme. It is simply an excuse for more fun on the part of frere Jan and Panurge.

XVI and XVII Grotesque parody of a consultation with a sibyl.

XVIII Pantagruel solemnly gives one interpretation of this consultation whilst Panurge gives another totally diverse one.

XIX Pantagruel suggests a consultation with a deaf mute.

XX Nazdecabre, the deaf mute, is again interpreted solemnly by Pantagruel. One suspects that the Olympian author is having fun, making everyone play the game of interpreting signs. This episode is reminiscent of the Thaumaste scenes in *Pantagruel*; but while the Thaumaste episode was crude, artistically, this episode with Nazdecabre can skilfully bring in the Pythagorean symbolism of numbers, all the classical allusions and all the anecdotes from ancient writers to prove a nonsensical case. This seems a satirical dig against the current fashion of over-allusiveness, in the same way as the colours of the livery of the boy Gargantua were solemnly symbolized according to the *Blason des couleurs*.

XXI to XXIII The consultation with Raminagrobis.

Frere Jan and Epistemon are the only guides to Panurge.

The only focus in the *Tiers Livre* is the one given by the framework: once one has caught the tone there, one can enjoy the irony, the comedy, the satire, the rhetorical *ivresse verbale* and even the grotesque encyclopaedic ramifications. Within the framework provided by the beginning and end of the book, there is a piling-up of episodes: the story moves around Panurge, Pantagruel or frere Jan. For instance, attention may focus on the sheer linguistic gratuitousness around Panurge; or it may be on the opposition between himself rhetorically proving a non-sensical case and Pantagruel holding forth at great length on a normal point. Grotesque parodies mingle with serious episodes;

other episodes could well have come earlier or later in the book; it is written with the same formlessness as we have noticed in *Gargantua*. To call it a novel does not really get one very far in fictional terms, for the verisimilitude which is essential to that form is irrelevant to the *Tiers Livre*.

Quart Livre

The sea voyage can be seen as providing a narrative, with longer episodes separated by shorter, almost accessory episodes. The former touch real life more closely and are more satirical; whilst the latter may start from satire, but before they end they have transported us as readers to the world of pure fantasy. This alternation between the fantastic and the real, with all the shades of the phantasmagorical and the gratuitous intervening, is a framework which fits the structure of the voyage supremely well.

But even in this *Quart Livre* there is a thick mixture of satire, of long lists, of erudition and accumulation: for instance, the description of Quaresmeprenant by Xenomanes (chapters 30–2) is a list of his external anatomical features and behaviour; the list of cooks by frere Jan in chapter 40 could well have been in *Gargantua*; the banquets and sacrifices of the Gastrolatres (chapters 59 and 60) could have been in any of the previous books; and finally the long zoological list spewed forth by Eusthenes in chapter 64 takes us back to the lists of *Pantagruel*.

There is certainly a thin narrative line in all four books, but the texture round this narrative framework – or even outside it – is dense and rich. The Olympian author is not just writing a parody, he is not interested in systematically parodying epic heroes or epic values. Even where he is adapting a framework of fabulous events which brings in the supernatural, such as God's voice before one of the battles (*Pantagruel*, chapter 29), there is a constant tendency to self-parody or else a superior assurance that the readers and the author are on the same side. The Olympian author's voice is never very far from his fictional world.

In fact Rabelais has chosen a loose-shifting Menippean satire for his fictional form. Professor Northrop Frye in his *Anatomy of*

Criticism[5] writes that the 'novel-centred view of prose-fiction is a Ptolemaic perspective which is now too complicated to be any longer workable' and proceeds to put Rabelais in the same category as Lucian, Swift and Voltaire – all Menippean satirists.

My own use of the term Menippean satire must be defined at this point. Menippean satire was a free mixture of prose and verse invented by a Greek Cynic called Menippus. It passed over to Latin literature, through Varro: to quote Macrobius, 'There were also quite a number of other slaves who later became famous philosophers, among them Menippus on whose works Marcus Varro modelled his *Satires* which others call *Cynic* but he himself called *Menippean*.'[6] But in Latin literature the term is slightly unclear. First because the term *satura*, a 'medley', came to be thought of as satire in the Horace/Juvenal manner – a poem in which vices or follies are held up to ridicule – and was thus regarded by Quintilian: *satura quidem tota nostra est*. Secondly because the writers associated with Menippean satire are so diverse; for example, Varro himself, Seneca in the *Apocolocyntosis*, and Petronius in the *Satyricon*. I am using the term in a rather free sense to mean a mixture of verse interludes, of prose in different styles, parodies of epic, encyclopaedic erudition, serious episodes, humour, and satirical criticism of topical events. This use of Menippean satire as a generic description of the works of Rabelais is confirmed by another sixteenth-century French work that actually took as its title *Satyre Ménippée*. This anonymous collection of Menippean satires first came out in 1593, after the Religious Wars, and one of its authors (subsequently identified) was Passerat, who had written a *Commentaire sur Rabelais* which is no longer extant. In this first edition there are no verses and the title is *Abbregé et l'Ame des Estatz convoquez en l'an 1593*. In the second edition, published in 1594, the title has changed to *Satyre Ménippée*, there are verses composed by Passerat and there is a discourse to the reader apparently written by the printer Jamet Mettayer but possibly by Passerat. In the dialogue between the printer and a fictitious cousin of the author, the printer writes of the author of the book thus:

il a affecté ce tiltre nouveau de *Satyre Ménippée*, que tout le monde n'entend pas, veu qu'aux copies à la main y avoit l'*Abregé* et l'*Ame des Estats* ... Ceste question ... ne peut tomber qu'aux esprits ignorants: car tous ceux qui sont nourris aux lettres sçavent bien que le mot de *satyre* ne signifie pas seulement un poëme de mesdisance pour reprendre les vices publics ou particuliers de quelqu'un, comme celles de Lucilius, Horace, Juvenal et Perse, mais aussi toute sorte d'escrits remplis de diverses choses et de divers arguments, meslez de proses et de vers *entrelardez, comme entremets de langues de boeuf salés* ...[7]

(The italics are mine.)

Passerat, if it was he, continues by justifying the use of the word *satyre* for such a work,

encore qu'elle soit escrite en prose, mais farcie et remplie d'ironies gaillardes, picquantes toutesfois et mordantes le fond de la conscience de ceux qui s'y sentent attaquez, auxquels on dit leur veritez; mais, au contraire, faisants esclater de rire ceux qui ont l'ame innocente et asseurée de n'avoir point desvoyé du bon chemin.

The discourse then proceeds to tackle the adjective Menippean:

Quant à l'adjectif de Ménippée, il n'est pas nouveau: car il y a plus de seize cents ans que Varron ... a faict des *Satyres* aussy de ce nom, que Macrobe dict avoir esté appelées *Cyniques* et *Ménippées*, auxquelles il donna ce nom à cause de Ménippus, philosophe cynique, qui en avoit faict de pareilles auparavant luy, toutes plaines de brocards salez et de gausseries saulpoudrez de bons motz, pour rire et pour mettre aux champs les hommes vitieux de son temps. Et Varron, à son imitation, en fist de mesme en prose, comme depuis fit Petronius Arbiter, et Lucien en la langue grecque et après luy Apulée; et, *de nostre temps, le bon Rabelais, qui a passé tous les autres en rencontres et belles robineries si on veut en retrancher les quolibets de taverne et les saletez de cabarets.* (The italics are mine.)

It is interesting that the writer of the discourse chooses Rabelais as the first modern Western European to have taken this title of Menippean satirist and places him in the long tradition of Varro, Lucian, Apuleius and Petronius. Almost a century later, when we read le Père Rapin's *Réflexions sur la poétique d'Aristote et sur les ouvrages des poëtes anciens et modernes,* we can establish the general lines of this kind of satire and at which point Rapin places Rabelais. On ancient Menippean satire he writes:

La Satyre qu'a fait Seneque sur l'apotheose de l'Empereur Claudius ... est une des pieces des plus delicates de l'Antiquité, et l'Auteur ... paroist d'autant plus plaisant en cet ouvrage, qu'il est plus grave et plus serieux dans tous les autres. La pluspart des Dialogues de Lucien sont des Satyres de ce genre-là: l'Auteur est un bouffon agreable ...

When he turns to modern Menippean satire he states: 'Nous avons deux satires modernes, lesquelles surpassent tout ce qu'on a écrit en ce genre dans les derniers siècles. La premiere est espagnole, composée par Cervantes ... L'autre satire est françoise, faite du temps de la Ligue ...' He follows this reference to Cervantes and the *Satyre Ménippée* almost immediately with, 'La Satyre de Rabelais, toute spirituelle qu'elle est: est neanmoins écrite d'une maniere si bouffonne, et si peu conforme à l'honnesteté du siecle où nous vivons, que je ne la croy pas digne des honnestes gens.'[8] *Le bon Rabelais* is damned with faint praise.

Let us take the fictional form of Rabelais's books as being Menippean satire – and see what that entails.

In the first two decades of the century the Greek and Latin writers who were known as Menippean satirists were edited, translated and 'imitated'. Erasmus had collaborated with Thomas More and Josse Bade to produce in 1506 a Latin translation of a number of Lucian's dialogues; the *editio princeps* of Petronius' *Satyricon* was published in Milan in 1482 (though the most exciting part of it, the *Cena Trimalchionis*, was not discovered until the seventeenth century); there was an edition of Seneca's *Apocolocyntosis* in Rome in 1513; there was a 1520 edition of Petronius, published in Paris, which Rabelais could have read at about the same time he was enjoying the complete works of Folengo; Erasmus had written his *Praise of Folly*, Thomas More his *Utopia*. All these facts suggest that there was a vogue for this kind of satire in the humanist circles of the time.

Satire is the most rhetorical of all kinds of literature, but Menippean satire is rather different from Juvenalesque satire so that we must briefly say on which points it differs from the satire with which we are familiar. The Olympian author controls everything: in Rabelais's case this means the framework of the books, the comic, the fantastic, the satirical, the erudition, the linguistic inventiveness, the serious, the high style and the low style – and this was the most essential feature of the Latin Menippean satirists. Thus Seneca, for example, in the *Deification of Claudius the Clod*[9] establishes an authorial *I* in the first few lines of his funny account of Claudius' death, 'I wish to place on record the proceedings in heaven on October 13 last, of the new year which begins this auspicious age. It shall be done without malice or favour. This is the truth. Ask if you like how I know it? To begin with, I am not bound to please you with my answer ...'[10] The narrative line is more consistent than in Rabelais; it is a parody of how Claudius reaches heaven, listens to the brisk debate between the other gods as to whether he shall be deified or not, how he is then rejected from heaven and passes to the Underworld where he is sentenced to play for ever at dice with a dice-box which is bottomless. Nevertheless since parody and burlesque are at the root of this genre, there is also parodic verse imitating epic ways of telling the time; for example, before the story has really begun one has, 'Now had the sun with shorter course drawn in his risen light, And by equivalent degrees grew the dark hours of night ...' followed by, 'I shall make myself better understood, if I say the month was October, the day was the thirteenth. What hour it was I cannot certainly tell; philosophers will agree more often than clocks ...' Vulgar events are described in epic diction and the poeticization of language is rampant throughout Seneca's piece. Similarly the gods and goddesses of mythology are introduced in lofty language and then made to perform sordid or trivial actions. This exaggeratedly low style is part of the conspiracy between the author and his readers: the contemporary reader would recognize the jesting and the play on words, and would enjoy too the author's rambling style. The problem of tone was much easier for contemporary readers than it is for us, since Seneca's literary allusions, his imitations and his parodies would have an immediate response and the amount of pleasure would be greater because of the instant recognition of incongruity between the language and the things he was describing. His oscillation between parodied epic style and a down-to-earth matter-of-factness would bring a smile to those knowing readers.

Now Rabelais had the two things that were important for Menippean satire: an audience and the technique. The audience was humanist: people like Erasmus and Erasmians, Tiraqueau, Bouchard, Marguerite de Navarre and Vivès. The technique was imitation: in an age like the sixteenth century, imitation of the best writers of the past was rhetorically, and that meant poetically and fictionally, crucial. Imitation of writers like Petronius and Apuleius was considered by Erasmus in his *De duplici copia verborum ac rerum* as the appropriate means of deriving irony, satire and humour. Rabelais opted for the 'Asianic' style, with its rich copiousness of vocabulary, and he created a work which was devoid of the stridently moralizing note which is so often the characteristic of the Roman prose tradition.

Rabelais started off with raw materials like the gigantic framework, the parody implicit in the different situations in which his giants find themselves, and the topical satire of an anti-clerical nature; he too makes digs at contemporary rhetoric and philosophy, uses the humour of incongruity – low events described in lofty language – and comedy. Into this mixture he can inject his own language as a verbal tempest, which hurls the reader into the circle of the game, and turns the commonsense notion that all experience is true and reliable into ridicule. His encyclopaedic ramifications are not just satires of topical events; they create a world which is phantasmagorical. The disadvantages of the form are evident: the temptation to be artistically formless, the problems of tone, the self-indulgence which allows one to go on and on inexhaustibly, and the deliberate rambling digressions. The one thing which must be well-managed is the authorial control. Rabelais adapts Menippean satire for his own use – as did Varro, as did Seneca, and as did Petronius. We shall look at three major features of Menippean satire in turn.

Parody

It is important for a parody to be recognizable, and this usually means assuming that your reader has the same social and literary culture as you have yourself. For example, one might write divorce announcements in the manner of *The Times*' announcements of marriage and one would expect the readers of the newspaper to detect it, to savour the humour of it and to linger on the turns of speech one had used. Ancient authors had all the gods and goddesses of mythology whom they could deform, to make their love affairs ridiculous. But in both cases, an author would be aiming at a fairly well-read public, intelligent, with a certain amount of literary and aesthetic taste and a liking for – or at any rate a knowledge of – what was in fashion at the time of writing. To enjoy Rabelais's parodies, one could not be part of an illiterate crowd, but ideally a member of the highest literary class in the first half of the sixteenth century – the humanists.

The first thing Rabelais had to parody was the *Cronicques*, which came out a few months before he wrote *Pantagruel*. The passage describing the engendering of Gargantua by his mother and father runs thus:

Grant gosier qui fut le premier au bas de la montaigne regardoit venir Galemelle: et prenoit plaisir a regarder lentredeux de ses chausses (car ilz estoyent tous nuds). Adonc que Galemelle fut descendue: il luy demanda quelle chausse elle auoit la. Adonc luy respond en eslargissant ses cuysses quelle auoit celle playe de nature. Grant gosier regardant la playe large et rouge comme le feu sainct Anthoine: le membre luy dressa: lequel il auoit gros comme le ventre d'une cacque de haren: et long a l'aduenant: il dist a Galemelle que il estoit barbier et que de son membre feroit esprouuette pour scauoir si la playe estoit parfonde: a laquelle playe il ne trouua nul fons: toutesfoys si bien leur agrea le ieu que ilz engendrerent Gargantua.[11]

This is a realistic sexual act described on a pretty low and coarse level. When Rabelais has the same marriage and childbirth to describe in *Gargantua* he starts this way, 'En son eage virile, espousa Gargamelle . . . belle gouge et de bonne troigne, et faisoient eux deux souvent ensemble la beste à deux doz, joyeusement se frotans leur lard, tant qu'elle engroissa d'un beau filz'* (chapter 3). He has made comic all the sexual bits that he has kept in: for instance Gargamelle is simply *'une belle gouge et de bonne troigne'*; instead of *'si bien leur agrea le ieu'* one has *'joyeusement'*; but then Rabelais, instead of stopping at the conception, shoots away with the authority of all the *anciens Pantagruelistes* to prove that children can be carried in the womb for eleven months before they are

---

* In the vigor of his age he married Gargamelle . . . a jolly pug, and well mouthed wench. These two did often times do the two backed beast together, joyfully rubbing and frotting their Bacon 'gainst one another, insofarre, that at last she became great with childe of a fair sonne.

born. The disruptive technique of the authorial *I* is used so that the readers do not take the words too seriously – for is not this *I* always the buffoon and jester? Parody is normal to Rabelais; he can allow himself to treat anything humorously; he can always laugh at his own exaggeration; and can always find place for additional buffoonery.

Of course Folengo had been parodying heroi–comic epics in a fine way before Rabelais started writing. And it was perhaps in Folengo's *Baldus* that Rabelais learned how superlatives, hyperbolical expressions, and high-falutin rhetoric could be made incongruous if the content was ridiculously low. Listen to this invocation to the muses in Folengo, 'O muses oignez-moy un petit les levres de beurre frais, apportez-moy quelques lesches d'un jambon de Mageance rosties sur la braise ardente, puis tirez-moy un bon hanap de ce brouet de la cave, pour rendre mon discours digne d'iceluy'.[12] Folengo's use of the muses who feed him with macaroni and *polenta* takes off excellently all the invocations to the gods and goddesses in the ancient epic stories; and Rabelais, about to start his battle in chapter 28 of *Pantagruel*, can do the same thing:

O, qui pourra maintenant racompter comment se porta Pantagruel contre les troys cens geans! O ma muse, ma Calliope, ma Thalie, inspire moy à ceste heure, restaure moy mes esperitz, car voicy le pont aux asnes de logicque, voicy le trebuchet, voicy la difficulté de pouvoir exprimer l'horrible bataille que fut faicte.

A la mienne volunté, que je eusse maintenant un boucal du meilleur vin que beurent oncques ceux qui liront ceste histoire tant veridicque.*

The mockery of narrative convention is so blatant here in this *histoire tant veridicque* that one can expect the battle to be described in a burlesque way.

The genealogies at the beginning of *Pantagruel* and *Gargantua* are of course parodies. Lefranc, who held sway over the rationalist

---

* O who were able now condignely to relate, how Pantagruel did demean himself against the three hundred Giants; O my Muse, my Calliope, my Thalia, inspire me at this time, restore unto me my spirits; for this is the Logical bridge of asses! here is the pitfall, here is the difficultie, to have ability enough to expresse the horrible battel that was fought; Ah, would to God that I had now a bottle of the best wine, that ever those drank, who shall read this so veridical history.

archiepiscopacy of Rabelaisian studies for over half a century, could not have read Rabelais in the right way, for the argument is manifest in the very tone of the story. Furthermore, the juxtaposition of reality with parody was an explicit technique in literary precedents: thus burlesque medieval plays parodied or even destroyed the solemnity of many ceremonies and mysteries of the church. In the genealogy of Pantagruel we can recognize the Old Testament model which Rabelais is mocking: for instance, in Genesis, chapter v or chapter x we have the lists of families: the sons of Japheth, Gomer and Magog, Madai and Javan, Tubal and Meshech and Tiras. Pieces of the history of the human race are brought in, 'And Cush begat Nimrod; he began to be a mighty man in the earth ... and unto Eber were born two sons; the name of one was Peleg; for in his days was the earth divided.' The same features and the same style are parodied by Rabelais, 'Qui engendra Sarabroth, Qui engendra Faribroth, Qui engendra Hurtaly, qui fut beau mangeur de souppes, et regna au temps du deluge ...' Rabelais mocks gently at the Hebraic names by coining new ones with the same characteristics of sound as the real ones in the Old Testament. The genealogy of Pantagruel follows clearly the Old Testament rather than the crisp list of names which the New Testament provides (Matthew, chapter i and Luke, chapter iii). Rabelais could have given the reader both of the Biblical genealogies and abdicated responsibility for hidden blasphemy and satire. But the fact that he concentrated on the Old Testament account is something that we shall develop when discussing the giants later on in the study (chapter 8). From the fictional point of view, one sees the parody as uncontrolled; the idea is good but it is rather inartistically worked out.

In the gigantic framework all the marvellous deeds are parodies of epic stories. For instance, the birth of Gargantua (chapter 6): the conventional marvellous story, like *robert le diable* has 'a la peine de l'enfantement demoura par l'espasse dun mois en travail', accompanied by 'des terribles signes qui furent ouyes et veues au naissement'. We saw in the passage analysed in chapter i how Rabelais introduces a comic vision into his account of Gargamelle's pregnancy and how the medical terminology was so full of grotesque fantasy that we could laugh. In the life of Robert, this was the start of the marvellous; in Rabelais we suspect that we are to believe neither mythology nor parallels produced from classical or contemporary authorities.

In the miraculous cure of Epistemon in *Pantagruel* (chapter 30) there is a parody of Richard in the *Quatre fils Aymon*: he was resurrected by Maugis with an ointment and a good dose of wine. In Rabelais the miracle is overladen with fantasy and buffoonery, 'Adoncq noctoya tres bien de beau vin blanc le col, et puis la teste ... synapisa ... oignit ... et les afusta justement veine contre veine, nerf contre nerf, spondyle contre spondyle ...'* Panurge sews some stitches and then applies a final ointment *qu'il appeloit resuscitatif*. Here there is the same mixture of fabulous medical erudition and gigantic prowess, and the whole resurrection is done by Panurge.

Let us take the parody of one episode in *Pantagruel* – the epic battle between LoupGarou and Pantagruel, chapter 29 – to see how it is worked out. It is neatly enclosed between two statements which are themselves ironic: the first is, 'Les geans, voyans que tout leur camp estoit noyé, emporterent leur roy Anarche à leur col, le mieulx qu'ilz peurent, hors du fort, comme fist Enéas son perc Anchises de la conflagration de Troye.'† This recalls to the readers the whole destruction of Troy as recounted by Vergil, and the sign that convinced Anchises that Troy's fortune was still in the hands of his son as he left the burning city on Aeneas' shoulders. A double miracle had been the cause of Anchises' surrender: a flame playing around Ascanius' head and a comet blazing through the night to land on Mount Ida where the exiles were later to gather. Thus the significance of this very vivid tableau of the father, carrying the household gods and himself on his son's back, is very great:

'No more, no more lingering! I follow, I'm there, where you guide me!

---

* Then cleansed he his neck very well with pure white wine, and after that, took his head and into it synapised some powder of diamerdis ... he anointed it ... and set it on very just, veine against veine, sinew against sinew, and spondyle against spondyle ...

† The Giants seeing all their Camp drowned, carried away their King Anarchus upon their backs, as well as they could, out of the Fort, as Aeneas did to his father Anchises, in the time of the conflagration of Troy.

Gods of our fathers, guard this family, guard my grandson!
This sign is yours, and Troy is still in your heavenly keeping.
Yea, I consent. I refuse no longer, my son, to go with you.'
He had spoken; and now more clearly over the town the fire's roar
Was heard, and nearer rolled the tide of its conflagration.
'Quick, then, dear father', I said, 'Climb onto my back, and I will
Carry you on my shoulders – that's a burden will not be burdensome.'[13]

Rabelais's use of the simile is grotesque: the opposing army are giants too, their whole camp has been deluged by Pantagruel's pissing, they hoist up their king, Anarchus, and so are like Aeneas carrying forth Anchises. The dimensions are vast and gigantic, but not serious, and into the picture comes a simile which deliberately, instead of heightening the emotion, destroys any identification with the army or with the giants as a race.

The other sentence is the first one of chapter 30: 'Ceste desconfite gigantale parachevée, Pantagruel se retira au lieu des flaccons, et appela Panurge ...'* The absolute participial construction, modelled on the Latin ablative absolute, and the use of the adjective *gigantale* imply that this has been a marvellous epic fight which Pantagruel as usual has won.

Panurge's rôle in the battle is to increase the anti-heroic thread around Pantagruel. For instance, the courage of Eusthenes is enveloped by an epic simile comparing him to David killing Goliath, but rendered grotesque by the words *ce gros paillard Eusthenes* who is as strong as four oxen. Pantagruel's doubt about his own physical prowess in this battle is answered by Panurge in a burlesque epic comparison, 'That is well cack'd, well scummered, (said Panurge) do you compare your self with Hercules?' The reasonable answer would be in the negative, but Panurge says, 'You have by G— more strength in your teeth, and more sent in your bum than ever Hercules had in all his body and soule: so much is a man worth as he esteems himself.' There is no comment on these words; the arrival of LoupGarou starts the fight between him and Pantagruel. They are both *gigantesque* in the weapons they use; LoupGarou's mace is even enchanted, for 'tout

---

* This Gigantal victory being ended, Pantagruel withdrew himself to the place of the flaggons, and called for Panurge ...

ce qu'il en touchoit rompoit incontinent'.* When he is advancing on Pantagruel in tremendous ferocity, Pantagruel addresses himself in prayer to God. Here we have a serious speech within the *merveilleux* context: the tone of his address to God is serious, and the content is serious. As soon as he has finished, 'Alors fut ouye une voix du ciel, disant: "Hoc fac et vinces"; c'est à dire: "Fais ainsi, et tu auras victoire" '.† This is a voice from heaven, not in the manner of Vergil or Homer – where at least it would not create surprise, in that it would be dramatically conceived, placed in a better position and better worked out in the character of the hero. Here there is nothing to save it from being bathetic: Pantagruel's next words are in a completely different tone – '*A mort, ribault! a mort!*' where the word '*ribault*' from *ribauder/paillarder* is in context with the rest of his character, whereas his serious speech is rather wooden and staid. Furthermore there is the added touch that the Good Lord is at the side of his hero, for Pantagruel would have died but for God's help: 'De faict, en donna si vertement que, si Dieu n'eust secouru le bon Pantagruel, il l'eust fendu depuis le sommet de la teste jusques au fond de la ratelle.'‡ The description of the rest of the fight is hilarious: the tableau moves into action, LoupGarou says that he will mince Pantagruel's flesh, the latter kicks him in the belly till he falls backwards, and then picks him up and uses him to tack down all the other giants. Medical and *fantaisiste* comedy win the day and the whole chapter ends on a burlesque comparison when LoupGarou's corpse is hurled into the town square 'et tomba comme une grenoille sus ventre en la place mage de ladicte ville, et en tombant du coup tua un chat bruslé, une chatte mouillée, une canne petiere, et un oyson bridé'.§

We are on the perimeter, or at the end of the long perspective consciously used by the Olympian author, which prevents our feeling any identification with either side in the battle: it is like

---

* but contrarily all that it did touch, did break immediately.
† There was heard a voice from heaven, saying *Hoc fac, et vinces:* that is to say, Do this, and thou shalt overcome.
‡ He so sprightfully carried himself, that if God had not succoured the good Pantagruel, he had been cloven from the top of his head to the bottom of his milt.
§ where falling like a frog upon his belly, in the great piazza thereof, he with the said fall killed a singed he-cat, a wet she-cat, a farting duck, and a brideled goose.

watching a Hollywood western where one knows who are the goodies and who are the baddies and expects to enjoy seeing how it all turns out. Parody ages quicker than any other form of literature, and clearly this quality of Rabelais, where he concentrates on both the style and thought of the original in admiration not in contempt, would have been more immediately recognizable in the sixteenth century than it is today. But, and this is quite crucial, both the classicist and the non-classicist today can appreciate the burlesque comedy which Rabelais's exaggeration, fantasy and grotesqueness turn an episode, such as the one we have looked at now, into a masterpiece. Rabelais outdistances the kind of bookish parody that the humanists adored and achieves that high degree of self-consciousness which makes him see himself humorously.

Erudition and word-games

When Rabelais played with the corrective conundrums (*Gargantua*, chapter 2) it was as enigmatic for his contemporary audience in 1534 as it is now in 1970. This whole poem on *bagatelles* is a nonsensical *coq-à-l'âne* of the sort favoured by Mellin de Saint-Gelais and Marot. Reading Rabelais, one does not necessarily find a linear narrative with a story carrying one on: one can open him at any page and there is this linguistic inventiveness, this conception of language as the one thing that distinguishes humans from animals. This is one of the meanings that strikes one on reading the prologues to each book. And it is one aspect of the delightful counterpoint of Pantagruel and Panurge in the *Tiers Livre*. (We shall look at this in detail in our next chapter.) Every trick or linguistic game has to be very ingenious; it may be dated, in that it relies so much on our own knowledge of sixteenth-century language; some things such as puns or spoonerisms came more spontaneously to the tongue of ancient Rome or of sixteenth-century France than they do today – perhaps because the audience were so formed by rhetorical and linguistic elements in their basic educational theories and practice. (The difference in attitude in Great Britain and France towards punning today is partly due to the educational systems in both countries.) Perhaps it was because they were not used to 'silent reading'. An oral tradition meant that authors could expect their words to be heard, and this stimulated playing with homophones in things such as rebuses, *imprese* or puns, much as it does for a schoolboy today or a foreigner living in another country. The technique was facile and fun-making.

Rabelais could also play with printing: the typographical process was sufficiently new for contemporary readers to see *la coupe testée* (*la teste coupée*) as comic, to be amused by word-listing from top to bottom or from side to side; an example of this is the books in sainct Victor's library (*Pantagruel*, chapter 7). Rabelais's linguistic exuberance is the condition for his Menippean erudition. Just as Burton, in *The Anatomy of Melancholy*, can start with a neat statement such as 'We are apish in the world' and then proceed to play on the *apish* conception, bringing in all his literary experience and knowledge of languages, '*asini bipedes*, and every place is full of *inversorum Apuleiorum*, of metamorphosed and two-legged asses, *inversorum Silenorum* ...' so Rabelais can start with Gargantua finding the best arse-wiper in the world and elaborate it into a chapter. He can set off on divination, on codpieces, on Pantagruelion or on messere Gaster's habitation and end up on a note that is very far removed from the starting point. For example, in the arse-wiping episode in *Gargantua* (chapter 13) Grandgousier comes back from a fabulous victory to ask Gargantua's governesses if they have kept him nice and clean. Gargantua replies, 'J'ay ... par longue et curieuse experience inventé un moyen de me torcher le cul, le plus seigneurial, le plus excellent, le plus expedient que jamais feut veu.'* The superlatives tell us immediately how we are to look at the episode. Then, through an enumeration of words, Gargantua conveys the delight of soft, delicious sensations: through velvet, satin, silk, a feather; through perfumes, like marjoram, roses, fennel; through country-smelling parsley, lettuce and spinach leaves; and through linens, carpets and

---

* I have ... by a long and curious experience, found out a means to wipe my bum, the most lordly, the most excellent, and the most convenient that ever was seen.

cushions. After a question by Grandgousier 'Where did you find the best arse-wiper?', Gargantua starts versifying,

> Shittard
> Squirtard
> Crackard
>   Turdous:
>
> Thy bung
> Hath flung
> Some dung
>   On us ...

and then switches to a *rondeau* with *En chiant* as the repetitive rhyme. Grandgousier brings him back to arse-wiping with '*Retournons à nostre propos*', and Gargantua promises he will gravel his father by syllogizing, 'Il n'est ... poinct besoing torcher cul, sinon qu'il y ayt ordure; ordure n'y peut estre si on n'a chié; chier doncques nous fault davant que le cul torcher.'* This is a good example of the contrast between the way a thing is argued and what is being argued. There is some gentle satire here on the whole way of arguing that human beings have employed over the centuries. But there is also a delightful unconcern with the moral potentialities of this theme; rather our attention dwells on the way he is getting the obscene comic going. The question of obscenity nowadays causes no difficulty: since anything human can be brought into literature provided that it is relevant; so that urination or sexual coupling can be introduced in *Ulysses* or *Finnegans Wake* as part of the normal activities of the day. In the sixteenth century obscenity was a characteristic of certain genres as practised by the humanists; it was also rife in fifteenth- and sixteenth-century sermonists, particularly Franciscans. Obscenity in Rabelais is traditional; more important for him, it is inherent in the Latin Menippean satirists. For the most part it is scatological and may at first excite, but it soon palls unless it is given larger comic implications such as this episode of the arse-wiping. Gargantua pursues his *propos torcheculatif* – echoing all the *ifs* that philosophy has created, still with a scholastic turn of phrase,

---

* There is no need of wiping ones taile ... but when it is foule; foule it cannot be unlesse one have been a skiting; skite then we must before we wipe our tailes.

'Mais, concluent, je dys et mantiens qu'il n'y a tel torchecul que d'un oyzon bien dumeté . . .'* '*Je dys et mantiens*' leads into the comparison between the nectar and ambrosia which the gods and goddesses are supposed to be enjoying in the Elysian fields and the sweet sensation of wiping your bum with a goose – which is what they are really enjoying. And that is the opinion of Duns Scotus! The theme is milked for its humour and through the improvisation of '*torcheculs*' there is a wealth of medicine, botany, zoology, contemporary satire and costume lore; and the style ranges from the obscene, the farcical, and the scholastic to the last paragraph's somewhat lofty style. This use of lyrical rhetorical language for an indecent subject is common enough in literature, as is the use of elegant prose for erotic frivolities, but it was particularly used by the Latin Menippean satirists. This frank and glorious acceptance of the physical side of life is often called a Renaissance characteristic, but it is more important to see it as a modern link with the ancient world in Seneca and Petronius – who were not trying to do 'dirt on life', but who were aiming at a fairly sophisticated public in the empire.

Some of the scenes which interrupt the straight narration are masterpieces, like the discourse of drinkers in *Gargantua* (chapter 5) which we commented on in our first chapter. But the encyclopaedic erudition only succeeds when the linguistic facility of Rabelais is used for comic effects. Thus all the chapters in the *Tiers Livre* on divination or on dreaming, or the episodes describing the livery of Gargantua and the herb Pantagruelion are uncontrolled, inartistic (from the point of view of a twentieth-century reader) and flat. To the specialist, the following out of culinary terminology, of theories that are medical, botanical and philosophical, or of fashions such as colour-symbolism bring back laughter to these out-dated chapters. But a note of warning here. The encyclopaedic mania that bursts forth at every corner has to be seen as being controlled by the Olympian author. Take Pantagruelion, that famous crux that has been chewed over for cen-

---

* But, to conclude, I say and maintain, that of all torcheculs [arsewisps, bumfodders, tail-napkins, bunghole cleansers and wipe-breeches] there is none in the world comparable to the neck of a goose, that is well douned . . .

turies in attempts to derive a meaning from it. Professor Saulnier in one of his articles reviews all the theories that have been put forward hitherto and then adds his own theory.[14] Pantagruelion equals hemp, and according to Professor Saulnier there are 'indications qu'il y a une vérité à démêler dans ces chapitres'. He sees this hemp as the secret talisman of Pantagruel; this may mean, tacitly or allegorically, Pantagruel's Christian attitude; the sea journey which he is prepared to undertake is allegorically the myth of the search for truth; and Professor Saulnier then proceeds to disentangle the profound symbolism behind all the books of Rabelais. This is an elaborate and ingenious theory, but listen to the tone in which the whole episode is written. The *enfleure du ton* in the protestations that what the reader is going to read is true, 'Par ces manieres (exceptez la fabuleuse, car de fable jà Dieu ne plaise que usions en ceste tant veritable histoire)'* (chapter 51), is the usual tone of the Olympian author, as we saw in the last chapter. The rhetoric of the whole episode is similar to Panurge's praise of debts: Rabelais takes it almost wholly from Pliny the Elder, he interlards it with topical notions like classical allusions, etymologies, and scholastic terminology. We know that it is Rabelais's Olympian author who is in control here, and so we can accept a *jeu de mots* like, 'Je vous jure icy, par les bons motz qui sont dedans ceste bouteille là qui refraichist dedans ce bac, que le noble Pantagruel ne print oncques à la guorge, sinon ceulx qui sont negligens de obvier à la soif imminente ...'† knowing that this is the *I* technique of the Olympian author.

Satire

We approach satire – as we define it today, that is to say, 'a poem, now occasionally a prose composition, in which prevailing vices or follies are held up to ridicule' (*OED*) – with a word of warning.

---

* By such like means ... (the fabulous ways being only from thence excepted; for the Lord forbid that we should make use of any Fables in this a so venerable History).

† I swear to you here, by the good and frolick Words which are to issue out of that Wine-bottle which is a cooling below in the Copper Vessel full of Fountain Water, that the noble Pantagruel never snatch'd any Man by the Throat, unless it was such a one as was altogether careless and neglective of those obviating Remedies, which were preventive of the Thirst to come.

The background of Rabelais's ideas, the variety of interests he showed in aspects of contemporary life and his intellectual temper have been discussed by other critics and we shall not be concerned with them. To examine in detail every satiric device used by Rabelais is not the intention of this study. In looking at satire fictionally I want to take a few examples and suggest some ways of understanding it.[15]

Satire inheres in the unmasking of the ridiculous and the laughable in institutions, events, human gullibility, superstition, pride, vanity and *amour-propre*. An author can modify, without basically challenging, the accepted code of his century. Unless we are able to identify ourselves with the criticism, to be on the same line as the author, the shaft of his criticism is either lost or misinterpreted. In satire the author–reader conspiracy is a delicate balance: the author, to keep this sympathy intact, must not lose his temper, not get too indignant with an institution, or else the reader will turn away from the author's attack. Satire is an art-form which tends to be related to morality: the author is either implicitly asserting a certain ethical viewpoint or is generally concerned with aesthetic and intellectual principles. It is vital that the satire in Rabelais should be seen alongside the comic fantasy, the grotesque and the burlesque: they combine ultimately to make up a way of looking at the universe.

Rabelais is not like Swift nor Voltaire: in the country of the Houyhnhnms, for instance, man in civilization and on the earth that supports him strikes Swift in this way: 'when I behold a lump of deformity, and diseases both in body and mind, smitten with *pride*, it immediately breaks all the measures of my patience ...' It is true that it is Gulliver, the narrator, who says this, but there is a very narrow margin between Swift's fictional world and his real world at this stage. Would not the breaking 'of my patience' be very similar to the chapter in the *Tiers Livre* on clandestine marriages? The tone of this chapter, 48, is entirely different from others in the book: Gargantua breaks into an outburst of indignation which is expressed in violent and bold language. He questions the church's claim to exclusive inspiration in matters of morality and citizenship; he clearly stands for civil law and against ecclesiastical law. He lashes out against the church, and particularly against monks who were prepared to perform marriages without the consent of parents. (We must remember that the sixteenth century and Erasmus condemned marriages without the consent of parents, and in 1556 Henri II passed an edict forbidding such marriages.) Gargantua even goes so far as to admit the justice of killing the suitor–husband in vengeance and in treating such a marriage as a rape. The contemporary institution has aroused anger and indignation and invective replaces satire. Satire demands some detachment from too intense a personal involvement, and here Rabelais has criticized an abuse without any recourse to humour, comedy or wit. Even where there is enumeration, 'n'est ruffien, forfant, scelerat, pendart, puant, punais, ladre, briguant, voleur, meschant . . .'* each word is intended to be seen as an accurate and realistic description – none of these types of men would stop at anything to marry a rich and noble woman. In the same way the appeal to the senses in Swift gives a tinge of emotional, even of horrible colouring to his view of man. Rabelais does not go so far in this particular example, and it is itself an exception, but one can here see him trying to portray the 'man of reason' fuming against certain man-made institutions of the sixteenth century.

Now compare this example with the inscription on the door of the Abbey of Thélème, which is an invective written in verse. It is a kind of battering ram or spell-binding curse. The instruments it uses are enumeration, epithets, simile, metaphors, epigrams and word-coinages – all intended to bring out the ridiculous aspects of the thing it anathematizes. The message is that entry to the abbey is forbidden to all the people whom the Olympian author hates. Listen to the first strophe:

> Cy n'entrez pas, hypocrites, bigotz,
> Vieulz matagotz, marmiteux, borsouflez,
> Torcoulx, badaux, plus que n'estoient les Gotz,
> Ny Ostrogotz, precurseurs des magotz
> Haires, cagotz, caffars empantouflez
> Gueux mitouflez, frapars escorniflez,

---

* there is no scurvy, mezely, leprous or pocky Ruffian, Pander, Knave, Rogue, Skelm Robber or Thief . . .

Befflez, enflez, fagoteurs de tabus;
Tirez ailleurs pour vendre vos abus.*

There is a fifteenth-century curse against doctors which uses the same ingredients: the sound of the language, the rhymes and the tone,

> Les Maux terminés en ique
> Font aux medecins la nique:
> Hydropique, étique, phtisique,
> Paralitique, apopletique, lethargique.

But the differences between this medical curse and the strophe of Rabelais is immense: first of all the movement and the ebullience from '*Cy n'entrez pas*' to '*Tirez ailleurs*' are striking; secondly, the effectiveness of past participles like '*borsouflez*' used as rhymes; thirdly, the alliteration and assonance within each line – like '*Haires, cagotz, caffars empantouflez*'. Furthermore, the content of the verse is essentially simple: anyone who is obsessed with hypocrisy, unnaturalness and with fostering divisions is not to knock at the door. But this splendid curse is sustained by fantastic word-making; starting from bigoted hypocrites, words are added on an analogy of sound and sense so that, although one can analyse each new formation and trace it back to linguistic reality, the words themselves seem to take on life and become a monstrous mass of swarming, seething, puffed-up, black-coated creatures. The word-coinages always have a foot in both worlds: their roots are in the heritage of the language – they must follow the phonetic, morphological and syntactic scheme of that language – yet they can project themselves into the no-man's land of non-existence and chaos.

The framework is a verse interlude and is thus comic: comic

---

* Here enter not vile bigots, hypocrites,
  Externally devoted Apes, base snites,
  Puft up, wry-necked beasts, worse then the Huns
  Or Ostrogots, forerunners of baboons:
  Curst snakes, dissembled varlots, seeming Sancts,
  Slipshod caffards, beggers pretending wants,
  Fat chuffcats, smell-feast knockers, doltish gulls,
  Out-strouting, cluster-fists, contentious bulls,
  Fomenters of divisions and debates,
  Elsewhere, not here, make sale of your deceits.

and fantastic devices leave the invective far behind. For instance, the rhyme scheme makes words like '*bigotz/magotz*' stand out, and one begins to link them with '*matagotz/Gotz/Ostrogotz/cagotz*' realizing that the suffix -*got* has developed the sense of hypocrisy. Or again, the suffix -*flez* – repeated in '*borsouflez/empantouflez/ mitouflez/escorniflez/befflez/enflez/fagoteurs* – comes to mean something which is against nature. But unlike the invective against clandestine marriage, this inscription has overshadowed the content of the criticism by its own word-play. The technique draws the reader's attention precisely to itself – and not to the point of criticism. The detachment of the author is supreme in this example; there is no note of anger or indignation. The technique of exaggeration and exuberance has one effect on the reader: it arouses his laughter – not against anything in particular, just pure laughter.

The device of using a detached observer to mock by ridicule is frequent in Rabelais. Thus in the prologues he constantly makes mock of contemporary writers who pretend their works are deep when they are only dark, and in writing something obscure, expect their readers to look for deeper meanings and abstruse truths where there are none. For example in the prologue to *Gargantua*, he ridicules symbolical allegorization by turning the books that his *bons disciples* read into tomes with such fanciful names as *Fessepinte*, and then goes on to draw a comparison between the outer covering and the inner nourishment, 'Lors congnoistrez que la drogue dedans contenue est bien d'aultre valeur que ne promettoit la boite, c'est-à-dire que les matieres icy traictées ne sont tant folastres comme le titre au-dessus pretendoit.'* This seemingly innocuous sentence could be linked to the phrase *sugcer la sustantificque mouelle*, which occurs later, and it could be interpreted on one level only. But we realize that there is a possibility of two or three meanings inherent in the whole prologue. The best minds of the age may indeed be the humanists, yet Rabelais can mention Poliziano in the same paragraph as

---

* Then shall you finde that it containeth things of farre higher value then the boxe did promise; that is to say, that the subject thereof is not so foolish, as by the Title at the first sight it would appear to be.

Thomas Walleys (a professor at Oxford in the fourteenth century) on whom he can confer as a nickname the title of *Frere Lubin* – a title which meant the stupidest of all monks. Rabelais can detach himself from the humanists and satirize the allegorical interpretations, the commentaries of Ovid and the true meaning of the Bible on a note that suggests his own non-involvement. There seems to be a serious note of literary criticism, or literary method in this prologue – and he aligns his own book with Homer and Ennius which must also be read without such allegorical interpretations. Yet there is also a certain amount of Olympian irony here: in the author's recognition that the world as we see it and know it is essentially paradoxical, and the detachment which the mode of narrative creates is essential for ambivalence. Take, for example, the image of the dog from this same prologue: Rabelais compares a dog getting to the marrow of his bone to a person reading a book. But the simile is of a disparaging kind. And although the dog is dramatized, is created accurately, the observation is sound, the details are complete, and the dog's movements are nimble, one does not interpret it on one level only. Perhaps the dig against allegorical interpretation was worth making, perhaps Rabelais was stating implicitly that there was something serious in his book, perhaps he was telling readers to read closely and not go through the book superficially and simply laugh, perhaps he was engaging in a little self-parody here, perhaps he was mocking his readers who wanted abstruse truth in everything they read – perhaps all of these meanings were and are in the prologue. Whenever a reader is not sure what the author's attitude is or what reaction is expected from him, we have irony with little satire. Rabelais, through this form of Menippean satire, amuses himself detachedly at the senseless illogicality of human professions, of rhetoric, philosophy and religion. His attitude is undogmatic: he sees constantly more than two sides of every question and the very manner of expression is gay detachment.

Furthermore, once satire is concerned with the concrete elements in a language rather than externally concerned with lashing out against the observances of the church or against monasticism in the sixteenth century, one is less interested in the overt criticism

Rabelais may be meaning to convey than in the means he uses to make us see the ridiculous. The distinguishing line between the grotesque satire and the comic is not a clear but a blurred one. For example, the Janotus de Bragmardo episode (*Gargantua*, chapters 18–20) as a whole is an obvious and direct satire on pedantry and obscurantism in the Sorbonne, but it is precisely the kind of satire one might expect from a critical and intelligent student satirizing universities today. It is not logic or Latin that are satirized but bad logic and bad Latin. Janotus himself is the pedantic fossil that all systems throw up sooner or later. What is interesting is the variety of resources that Rabelais uses in this grotesquely comic and rich episode.

When Janotus enters on the stage it is in this way:

Maistre Janotus, tondu à la cesarine, vestu de son lyripipion à l'antique, et bien antidoté l'estomac de coudignac de four et eau beniste de cave, se transporta au logis de Gargantua, touchant davant soy troys vedeaulx à rouge muzeau, et trainant après cinq ou six maistres inertes, bien crottez à profit de mesnaige.*

One has first of all the physical portrait: '*tondu à la cesarine*' which is a lofty and poetic way of saying that he was bald like Caesar; '*vestu de son lyripipion à l'antique*' – meaning a long appendage of a graduate's hood, that hung down when the hood was thrown back but could be used to secure it when one drew the hood over the head; in other words Janotus was formally dressed, with his doctor of theology's hood which had a lappet attached to it. Janotus's behaviour is then described; he has eaten a '*coudignac de four*' – the *coudignac*, without the addition of *de four* would be a delicate cake, with the addition it means simply bread; and has drunk '*eau beniste de cave*' – wine. The whole procession is evoked with the professor in the middle, moving slowly, dirty, drunkenly and unwillingly to the *logis* of Gargantua. We have a *jeu de mots* between '*vedeau*' (a calf) and '*bedeau*' (a beadle) coming after Janotus who was '*touchant*' his flock with their drunken red faces;

* Master Janotus, with his haire cut round like a dish *à la cæsarine*, in his most antick accoustrement Liripipionated with a graduates hood, and, having sufficiently antidoted his stomach with Oven-marmalades, that is, bread and holy water of the Cellar, transported himself to the lodging of Gargantua, driving before him three red muzled beadles, and dragging after him five or six artlesse masters, all throughly bedaggled with the mire of the streets.

they are 'trainant, inertes et crottez' and are moving like unsteady wooden horses towards the lodging. The robot inhumanity and automatic nature of this procession are even further stressed by Ponocrates's reaction, when he 'eut frayeur en soy, les voyant ainsi desguisez, et pensoit que feussent quelques masques hors du sens'.* We know from the previous chapter that Janotus is the oldest and the most *suffisant* of the whole faculty; and we know too that the reason for his speech – to ask that Gargantua should give back the bells – is invalid because Gargantua has already decided to give back the bells. The harangue by Janotus is a richly woven rhetorical parody, using physically grotesque coughings and drunken burpings, which makes a *reductio ad absurdum* of all formal occasions of address. As the parody progresses, striking concrete details are harnessed to the theme: the sausages and stock-ings promised to Janotus are singled out satirically to characterize woolly churchmen. The alternation between French and Latin combined with drunkenness is heightened by grotesque and fan-tastic word-coinage:

Si vous nous les rendez à ma requeste, je y guaigneray six pans de saulcices et une bonne paire de chausses que me feront grant bien à mes jambes, ou ilz ne me tiendront pas promesse. Ho! par Dieu, *Domine*, une pair de chausses est bon, *et vir sapiens non abhorrebit eam*. Ha! ha! il n'a pas pair de chausses qui veult, je le sçay bien quant est de moy! Advisez, *Domine*; il y a dix huyt jours que je suis à matagraboliser ceste belle harangue: *Reddite que sunt Cesaris Cesari, et que sunt Dei Deo. Ibi jacet lepus.*†

Nearly every line in this paragraph is grotesque satire: from the illogical state of mind, through the meaningless sonority of the talk, to the heaping up of ill-fitting proverbs and maxims in the same way as Cervantes makes Sancho Panza use them. Further-more, Rabelais uses dramatically the barbaric language – the mix-ture of bad Latin, of Latin used wrongly, and a matter-of-fact kind

---

* who was afraid, seeing them so disguised, and thought they had been some maskers out of their wits ...
† If you restore them unto us at my request, I shall gaine by it six basketfuls of sauciges, and a fine paire of breeches, which will do my legs a great deal of good, or else they will not keep their promise to me. Ho by gob, *domine*, a paire of breeches is good, *et vir sapiens non abhorrebit eam*. Ha, ha, a paire of breeches is not so easily got, I have experience of it myself. Consider, *Domine*, I have been these eighteen dayes in matagrabolising this brave speech...

of French. This language, and the drunken state of Janotus are exploited to evoke the blurred emotional, even sentimental phrases which the chaos of habits, training and linguistic convention can produce. Rabelais's humanist friends would enjoy the way Janotus juxtaposes completely opposite terms: like the academic formality of *Domine*, and the use of Biblical texts like 'Render unto Caesar therefore the things which be Caesar's, and unto God the things which be God's' (Luke xx. 25). The chaotic sequence of disintegrated formal elements, like Janotus's coughing – *hen, hasch, hasch, grenhenhasch* – the invention of imaginary word-families like *omnis clocha clochabilis*, the grotesque elements of good-living mingled with drunkenness – all of these techniques, speeding up as the speech goes on, mean that Rabelais is less interested in the social satire, and much more in evoking for his readers a grotesquely comic portrait of a silly old man.

In considering the Juvenalesque satire in Rabelais one comes to feel that there was much less moral concern than in Swift, for example. This appeared and will continue to appear rather offensive to people who approach literature with a strong moral sense. The qualities that morality and religion usually call ribald, obscene, subversive, lewd and blasphemous were not rejected by Rabelais and in an age that became less and less stable his type of humour was taken to be dangerously subversive. Rabelais, unlike Erasmus, indulged in light-hearted satire with no didactic purpose or educational theories, and he destroyed earnestness effectively. He is far from being a moralist or even a *moraliste* of the Renaissance.

Our investigation of the fictional form in which Rabelais couched his work produces three exciting results. First, we see the extreme flexibility of Menippean satire; the disjointed narrative, alternating between gigantic adventures and parodies of situations, serious episodes, realistic descriptions and fantasy. To talk of his work as a novel is meaningless and we can now dismiss that term. Secondly, the theory of imitation dovetails neatly with Menippean satire: for it is precisely in Roman literature that one can find germs of all that Rabelais is trying to do. And finally, this form was a form peculiarly apt to Rabelais's linguistic inventiveness. Our next stage is an examination of one book as a whole in order to use it as a test case for our hypothesis. The *Tiers Livre* throws sharp light on Menippean satire, and it is the book most debated by scholars. And so we shall analyse it in the next chapter to see what shape the book takes if it is considered as a Menippean satire.

THE 'TIERS LIVRE'

When we open the *Tiers Livre* – published in 1546, twelve years after *Gargantua* – the whole fictional world has changed. The Olympian author has left behind the parody of marvellous stories; he has abandoned gigantic size as a recipe for comedy; he has a far larger circle of characters; Pantagruel has grown from an adolescent warrior to a young prince; and Panurge and frere Jan are now together in the same book for the first time. Scholarly criticism over the last sixty years has surmounted many barriers and erected a gate for the twentieth-century reader. It has explained the *Tiers Livre* in the context of sixteenth-century ideas, values and attitudes. But once the reader has stepped through that gate, he is confronted with a labyrinth of conflicting pathways where there are no signposts and he must take one or other critic's personal interpretation of what Rabelais meant to say. To examine the difficulties that are thus posed I am first going to take two critics, Lefranc and Professor Screech, who have taken opposite directions.

Firstly, can one see the *Tiers Livre* as Lefranc saw it, as Rabelais's contribution to the *Querelle des Femmes*?[1] There was certainly a rhetorical argument in mid-sixteenth-century France, with books from the feminists carrying on a running controversy with books from the anti-feminists; with speeches from the anti-feminists on the ancient theme that woman was a botched male: the result of a blunder by nature at the moment of conception, which produced a woman instead of a man. Any and every argument was used by the rhetorical books like Tiraqueau's *Laws of Marriage* to demonstrate that woman was a second-class citizen; all the way from the fact that God created woman last and used Adam's rib to fashion her, right to the nature of woman – deceitful, insatiable, extravagant, stupid, unfaithful and lustful. Conversely, the feminists argued that God, starting with the lowliest animals, worked up the scale of perfection till he reached man, and finally woman, as the summit of his creation. Man was made from earth whereas woman was made of human matter and was superior in elegance, *finesse*, honour, prudery and modesty. The interpretation of the *Tiers Livre* as simply another anti-feminist addition to this controversy may very well satisfy a historian of feminism in the sixteenth century but it fails to take account of the other elements in the book.

Secondly, has Rabelais stated the problem of marriage in flesh and blood terms in order to explore much wider issues like the relationship between the individual and his destiny or fate?[2] Was he primarily a Christian writer who saw the possibility of creating an 'excitingly original Christian comedy'? This hypothesis of a Christian comedy is unconvincing; it gives Rabelais a single and limited intention and imposes on all the chapters a philosophical framework; it makes Panurge into a grotesque fool who capers through the book experiencing, when he is lectured at by Pantagruel, an anguish little short of that of a Lutheran monk. That the *Tiers Livre* is complex and syncretic is undeniable, but a term like 'Christian comedy' needs to be treated with caution if we are to see all the themes that Rabelais is exploiting in the work. If the *Tiers Livre* leads two scholars to give partial interpretations of the work, it may be because neither of them is concerned primarily with the finished product of the artist's mind. I think that both their views relate to the content of the work but not to the fictional form it adopts. Paradoxically, that fictional form enables the reader to focus on the ideas in a linguistic context which changes them from what Lefranc or Professor Screech saw.

The form of the *Tiers Livre* provides the pattern into which fall the comic, the serious, the farcical, the grotesque threads which run through it. Once again, the standpoint of the Olympian author determines the viewpoint and we must look in greater detail at the way this technique is used. The very first words of chapter 1 show us the Menippean satirist, 'Pantagruel, avoir entierement conquesté le pays de Dipsodie, en icelluy transporta une colonie de Utopiens en nombre de 9876543210 hommes, sans les femmes et petitz enfans ...'* The Olympian author is in great

* Pantagruel having wholly subdued the Land of Dypsodie, transported thereunto a Colony of Utopians, to the number of 9876543210 Men, besides the Women and little Children ...

glee playing with the reversed sequence of cardinal numbers and in making little jokes like '*sans les femmes et petitz enfans*' (which are also found in a sermonist such as Maillard). The device can be compared with the historiography of the giants in the first chapters of *Gargantua* and *Pantagruel*. Moreover, the prince Pantagruel is still *le bon Pantagruel* and his way of colonization is full of humanity: his policy is to subdue the conquered people in the most humane way, and the reader approves intellectually but without any emotional involvement at all. The editorial essay on colonization is elaborated encyclopaedically, taking us first through the wrong way of ruling a vanquished country and then through the right way. Authorities are quoted as they might be in an adage of Erasmus, and we reach the conclusion that Pantagruel is approached with the same emotional detachment that we would feel towards the hero of a superhuman world where everything is conceived in Utopian terms – idealized and static. But the Olympian author prevents us from resting in a static approach for, as in his previous books, we as readers are expected to join him in participation: we are still the *Goutteux fieffez* of all the prologues.

When we move forward to the second chapter we notice that Pantagruel gives Panurge the lairdship of Salmygondin – which was hitherto in the hands of Alcofribas (*Pantagruel*, chapter 32). This is to be borne in mind for the characterization of Panurge: he has changed and matured into a comic character. In *Pantagruel* he had already captivated the company surrounding his master Pantagruel, and also us as readers, by his linguistic facility and his constant devouring of food and swilling of wine; he was fascinated by reetoric and could use it both well and badly; he was introduced as a man of about thirty-five years of age but, throughout the first book he had not grown up beyond his schoolboy jokes and lavatory graffiti. Now he will delight readers by revealing himself as both a fool and a clever knave: a fool, with all the more apparent sense and brain but with plans which are based on wrong principles and which come to nothing; but a clever knave in his development in purely linguistic terms of a universe which suits his egocentricity and *philautia* or self-love. In the presentation of Panurge in *Pantagruel* there are certain suggestive threads of character which fit in to this new rôle: the knave–fool is witty, cunning and clever; he is amoral and is always insisting on his pleasures with women and with the world; he is fond of money and can diddle everyone to get it; he is an exhibitionist. Let us look at the counterpoint of Panurge and Pantagruel in this second chapter to see how the Olympian author 'places' his characters at opposing ends of a scale of values and dramatically offers the reader the comedy of a fool set against the norm.

First of all he gives a delightful comic and poetic sketch of Panurge, 'Et se gouverna si bien et prudentement Monsieur le nouveau chastellain qu'en moins de quatorze jours il dilapida le revenu certain et incertain de sa chastellenie pour troys ans'.* The irony here is immediate: *'si bien et prudentement'* – meaning the opposite; *'Monsieur le nouveau'* – the appellation calling attention to the newness of the Lairdship; *'revenu certain et incertain'* – the second epithet cancelling the first; and the whole sentence leading up to *'troys ans'* which is juxtaposed with *'quatorze jours'*. We feel that this Panurge is going to make us laugh in a subtler way than we did before at his antics in church or the affair with the Parisian lady. The next sentence starts with a repetition of the same verb *dilapider*:

Non proprement dilapida, comme vous pourriez dire en fondations de monasteres, erections de temples, bastiments de collieges et hospitaulx, ou jectant son lard aux chiens, mais despendit en mille petitz bancquets et festins joyeulx ouvers à tous venens, mesmement tous bons compaignons, jeunes fillettes et mignonnes gualoises, abastant boys, bruslant les grosses souches pour la vente des cendres, prenent argent d'avance, achaptant cher, vendent à bon marché, et mangeant son bled en herbe.†

We are still in the realm of reality at first, with the Latin root *lapis* leading on to a list of monasteries, colleges and temples, but by the

---

* Now his Worship, the new Laird, husbanded this his Estate so providently well and prudently, that in less than fourteen days he wasted and dilapidated all the certain and uncertain Revenue of his Lairdship for three whole Years.
† Yet did not he properly dilapidate it, as you might say, in founding of Monasteries, building of Churches, erecting of Colleges, and setting up of Hospitals, or casting his Bacon-Flitches to the Dogs; but spent it in a thousand little Banquets and jolly Collations, keeping open House for all Comers and Goers; yea, to all good Fellows, young Girls, and pretty Wenches; felling Timber, burning the great Logs for the sale of the Ashes, borrowing Money before-hand, buying dear, selling cheap, and eating his Corn (as it were) whilst it was but Grass.

time the sentence closes we are sailing away on the wings of fantasy. The first half sets out what he could do to spend his income in fourteen days, but did not do, and the second half shows by contrast what he *did* do: he starts with '*prenent argent d'avance*', and ends with '*mangeant son bled en herbe*'. Panurge is creating a little cosmos where everything is turned upside down and he is the master of it. He is still the court jester of the company, as one would expect after *Pantagruel*, and is still *sympathique*. This hail-fellow Panurge is still the hearty eater and drinker, still the lascivious lover of beautiful wenches and still the liker of rhetoric. With '*mangeant son bled en herbe*'[3] a current proverbial metaphor is brought back to the literal sense it had lost. The comedy of language makes him highly *sympathique* to the reader and his delight in words is set against the seriousness and moderation of Pantagruel.

The latter is presented in outline view first of all, 'Pantagruel, adverty de l'affaire, n'en feut en soy aulcunement indigné, fasché ne marry.'* The Olympian author has already told us about the tolerance of the giant in *Pantagruel* and again reassures us on the point: 'Je vous ay ja dict et encores rediz que c'estoit le meilleur petit et grand bon hommet que oncques ceigneït espée ...'† But after this, we feel that the Olympian author is getting into his stride as he offers us this judgement on the character:

Toutes choses prenoit en bonne partie, tout acte interpretoit à bien. Jamais ne se tourmentoit, jamais ne se scandalizoit. Aussi eust il esté bien forissu du deificque manoir de raison, si aultrement se feust contristé ou altéré. Car tous les biens que le ciel couvre et que la terre contient en toutes ses dimensions: haulteur, profondité, longitude, et latitude, ne sont dignes d'esmouvoir nos affections et troubler nos sens et espritz.‡

---

* Pantagruel being advertised of this his Lavishness, was in good sooth no way offended at the matter, angry nor sorry ...

† For I once told you, and again tell it you, that he was the best, little, great Good-man that ever girded a Sword to his Side ...

‡ He took all things in good part, and interpreted every Action to the best Sense: He never vexed nor disquieted himself with the least pretence of Dislike to any thing; because he knew that he must have most grosly abandoned the Divine Mansion of Reason, if he had permitted his Mind to be never so little grieved, afflicted or altered at any occasion whatsoever. For all the Goods that the Heaven covereth, and that the Earth containeth in all their Dimensions and Heighth, Depth, Breadth, and Length, are not of so much worth, as that we should for them disturb or disorder our Affections, trouble or perplex our Senses or Spirits.

Pantagruel's emotions are not aroused by terrestrial matters; nothing is worth serious involvement or unreasonable anxiety; hence a detachment from external things, things outside man's control, so that they are evaluated in terms of what is reasonable; since they are indifferent in themselves it is the attitude of mind that endows them with value. The tranquillity and independence shown by Pantagruel here also appear later when he performs altruistic acts for Panurge. This is a purely Stoic attitude: the wise man does not *concern* himself with other men, but he serves them; he engages in action without positive desire.

In these two paragraphs the counterpoint is clear between Panurge and Pantagruel: Panurge is the knave–fool, creating comedy by his linguistic ingenuity, delighting at the way in which words, while often not meaning anything, can be exploited merely for their sound and alliteration; but in so doing he is the egocentric figure whose lavishness with money corresponds to a completely unrealistic attitude to everything in this world. Pantagruel, on the other hand, is sane, serious, moderate but tolerant. The beginning of the next paragraph emphasizes this, 'Seulement tira Panurge à part, et *doulcettement* luy remonstra ...'* (my italics). He says that Panurge will never be rich unless he shows some sense of thrift; immediately Panurge leaps in on the word *riche*, 'Riche? ... Aviez-vous là fermé vostre pensée? Aviez-vous en soing pris me faire riche en ce monde? Pensez vivre joyeulx, *de par li bon Dieu et li bons homs*!'† (My italicizing of the archaic expression.) Panurge brings in Rabelais's *joie de vivre* and in addition, is given an archaic expression, of the same type as that spoken by the Olympian author in the prologue to *Pantagruel*, so that we infer here a further self-parody of the author and perhaps a sly dig at the seriousness and commonsense of Pantagruel. The statement that follows this one, 'Autre soing, autre soucy, ne soit receup on sacrosainct domicile de vostre celeste cerveau ...'‡ is

---

* He drew only Panurge aside, and then making to him a sweet Remonstrance and mild Admonition, very gently represented ...
† Rich! ... Have you fixed your Thoughts there? Have you undertaken the Task to enrich me in this World? Set your Mind to live merrily in the Name of God and good Folks ...
‡ Let no other Cark nor Care be harboured within the Sacro sanctified Domicile of your Celestial Brain ...

too close to the paragraph on Pantagruel's *deificque manoir de raison* to be without some ironic meaning.

Panurge goes on to define himself unwittingly in comic terms, in this paragraph, 'Tout le monde crie: mesnaige, mesnaige! Mais tel parle de mesnaige, qui ne sçayt mie que c'est. *C'est de moy* que fault conseil prendre. *Et de moy* pour ceste heure prendrez advertissement . . .'* (The italics are mine.) In this world which Panurge is creating the *moi* is alone; one can see the fool isolated from the rest of mankind; his views on husbandry are against the commonsense of all people; and his rhetoric is engaged in proving right, through all reasonable arguments, a nonsensical case. Comedy does not reside in the virtue of one side winning in the end against the vice of the other side; in fact terms such as virtue and vice are irrelevant in comedy; it does not matter whether the man is as sincere as Alceste or as evil as Don Juan; what does matter is that the audience knows that everyone is against the fool; he is the only man marching out of step. Molière made sure that he 'placed' his norm, which is not moral but social, in the opening scene of *Le Misanthrope*: Alceste says,

> Je ne puis plus tenir, j'enrage, et mon dessein
> Est de rompre en visière à tout le genre humain,

whereas Philinte states firmly,

> Le monde par vos soins ne se changera pas.

Commonsense reason is played against the *atrabilaire amoureux*. Similarly the readers are 'in the know' about Panurge and Pantagruel: Panurge is to prove that terrestrial matters like money or love concern a man very much, whilst Pantagruel is to remain moderate, tolerant and full of commonsense – and this establishes him as the norm of the comedy.

But Rabelais has done more than that in this second chapter: Panurge is, as well as the fool, a clever knave. And so it is that in

---

* Every body cries up thrift, thrift, and good Husbandry; but many speak of Robin Hood that never shot in his Bow; and talk of that Vertue of Mesnagery, who know not what belong to it. It is by me that they must be advised. From me therefore take this Advertisement and Information . . .

speaking rhetorically well about anything, that is when proving
his nonsensical case, he delights the reader by his linguistic and
erudite ingenuity. Take for example what he does with the phrase
'*bled en herbe*': he embroiders his power of giving life and vitality
to a language by conjuring up very concrete pictures of all aspects
of the tender grass. The first simile, 'comme un hermite, vivent de
sallades et racines,'* establishes the angle of vision, and then
Panurge takes the reader literally through the work he saves all
mankind: the mowers who do not have to mow; the threshers
who do not have to thresh, and the millers who do not have to
grind it into flour. Verbs are enumerated to prove that the
properties of the grass are magical, 'It will make you have a current Belly to trot, fart, dung, piss, sneeze, cough, spit, belch, spew,
yawn, snuff, blow, breath, snort, sweat and set taunt your Robin
...' He ends with *et mille autres rares adventaiges*. Over and above
our amusement at the sheer inexhaustible fund of verbs, coupled
by their alliteration and assonance, we see here the suspension of
our customary habit of linking words with reality. With a serious
metaphor one has the literal and figurative meanings together in
the same word or phrase and we get a sublime insight which is
both emotional and intellectual when the resemblance between
the two things makes itself known. With a comic metaphor, it is
an intellectual reaction from the reader: the pleasure in making a
green salad and a green sauce out of the *bled en herbe* is irrelevant,
comic and aesthetic. Panurge piles one thing on top of the other
in his delight with the play of language; words have to him but a
tenuous connection with reality. The world created by Panurge
is an upside-down world and the reader laughs at the juxtaposition of normal and abnormal outlooks.

In fact Panurge is playing with language here in exactly the
same way as the Olympian author had done in chapter 11 of
Gargantua, and he interrupts in the same way as the Olympian
author does in the prologues: for instance, Panurge says, 'donnant
à repaistre aux bons (notez bons) ... aux bonnes (notez bonnes) et
jeunes gualoises (notez jeunes: car scelon la sentence de Hippo-

---

* like an Hermit feeding upon Sallets and Roots ...

crates . . .'* This is what makes many critics say that Rabelais and Panurge are one: but this is so simple and so naive that, fictionally, it does not take us very far. The brilliance with which Rabelais has 'placed' his comedy astounds one: every time Panurge appears in the book, stylistically there is a whiff of parody about his rhetoric; but readers laugh at him because the content of his linguistic worlds is nothing but egocentricity. Further, in the second chapter, there are hints of encyclopaedic knowledge associated with Panurge: this will be developed extensively in the next chapter, but already he has the recognizable features of a fool, an erudite fool, a fool who can use all his learning, all his erudition and scholarship to support any argument he likes.

The first two chapters of the *Tiers Livre* are crucial: they present the two leitmotifs of the Olympian author and social comedy, clearly established. Rabelais has taken over the dominant thread of thought of his time – Stoic Christianity, and in particular, the theory of indifference – and used it as the framework for comedy. This is going to be concentrated in Pantagruel's rôle, but it can be seen in the other characters such as frere Jan or Epistemon. Panurge is a living fool: where Petronius in the *Satyricon* had a problematic narrator Encolpius who, in some senses, becomes alive, Rabelais has a fool–knave. So we are beginning to see Menippean satire recede into the background and its place being taken by social comedy. But it is carried out in unexpected ways, and the oscillations between the two modes are striking.

Panurge continues his famous speech on the praise of debts. Now the satirical eulogy was very popular amongst humanists in the first two decades of the century: Lucian had been translated into Latin; Erasmus had used the convention in the *Praise of Folly*, and a number of his *Colloquies* also used the same technique for satirizing scholastic philosophy.[4] But in letting Panurge deliver the speech the Olympian author can do two things at once: by dissociating his own rôle from that of the actor who is Panurge he is not necessarily sympathizing or disagreeing with any satiric criticism or with any values that Panurge expresses; and secondly,

---

* and likewise to the good (remark the good) and young Wenches: For according to the Sentence of Hippocrates . . .

he transforms the satirical eulogy by having it delivered by Panurge. This is really brilliant: we knew already what a spinner of rhetoric old Panurge is, and we knew too how he could parody the Olympian author. Rabelais was not interested in borrowing as a moral problem at all but only in the additional dimension it gave the character of Panurge as a comic fool. He can use specious arguments to defend an obviously nonsensical case: they are ridiculous and funny only because Panurge is misusing them. Professor Mayer[5] makes an important point when he says, 'lyricism in the description of a vice or an unpleasant animal or disease is precisely one of the common features of the satirical eulogy'. This lyricism and this comico–poetic ingenuity are two traits that this episode needs and Panurge is comic precisely because he uses wrong principles for perfectly valid reasons. This comedy is what is going to take him through the *Tiers Livre* and the *Quart Livre* and is one of the traits which suggest that Rabelais is trying his hand at comic romance.[6]

Thus Panurge, in this speech, uses scholastic terminology, philosophical ideas, and classical allusions, and parodies them as in: 'Dea en ceste seule qualité je me reputois auguste, reverend, et redoubtable, que sus l'opinion de tous philosophes (qui disent rien de rien n'estre faict) rien ne tenent, ne matiere premiere, estoys facteur et createur'* (chapter 3). The initial step for normal people is to pay debts; it is a false perception to think that to be in debt is really a good thing; everyone would see here the upsetting of a normal outlook; but Panurge, having made the initial error of judgement then goes on perfectly logically to build a whole cosmos as if it were the normal one. For example, he has the thrill of creation – *'facteur et createur'* – the good gestures of men in his upside-down world – 'car les hommes sont nés pour l'aide et secours des hommes', good qualities like charity are praised, whilst faith, hope and charity would be exiled from this world were it not for debts. Every reason taken alone is perfectly valid, but put

---

* And yet did I, in this only respect and consideration of being a Debtor, esteem my self worshipful, reverend and formidable. For against the Opinion of most Philosophers, that of nothing ariseth nothing; yet, without having bottomed on so much as that which is called the First Matter, did I out of nothing become such Maker and Creator.

together under a huge umbrella of debts every reason is invalid. We are watching Panurge develop into a creatively comic character – one who causes laughter because of his inherent risibility and rhetoric as fool–knave. When he has raised the whole macrocosm and microcosm into a happy harmony of elements, Panurge exclaims in ecstatic bliss, 'Vertus guoy, je me naye, je me pers, je m'esguare, quand je entre on profond abisme de ce monde ainsi prestant, ainsi doibvant ...'* and the reader laughs at the extremely Panurgian way this is expressed.

At the end of the speech there is a fitting conclusion: the final link in the 'chain of being' comes from the fact that men and women are meant for each other: men have testicles and women have wombs, 'where Nature hath prepared for it very fit Vessels and Receptacles, through which descending to the Genitories by long Ambages, Circuits and Flexuosities, it receiveth a Competent Form, and Rooms apt enough both in the Man and Woman for the future Conservation and perpetuating of Human Kind'. This spermatological obsession is *une trouvaille*: in every future event Panurge will use the vocabulary derived from this obsession to elaborate his view of human nature. Thus, for example, in the sixth chapter, Panurge will say that after a year of marriage, 'ilz auroient tant taloché leurs amours de nouveau possedez ... et tant esgoutté leurs vases spermaticques, qu'ilz en restoient tous effilez, tous evirez, tous enervez et flatriz'.† Pantagruel will never share this highly erotic vocabulary with Panurge.

After Panurge has finished his harangue, Pantagruel offers on the one hand praise – 'me semblez bon topicqueur et affecté à vostre cause'‡ – and on the other hand a commonsense statement that even 'with all this fine speaking nothing will persuade me to contract debts'. The love which Pantagruel shows Panurge is important: never does he lose the basic tolerance towards this raga-

* Cops body, I sink, I drown, I perish, I wander astray, and quite fly out of my self, when I enter into the Consideration of the profound Abyss of this World, thus lending, thus owing.
† they so lustily bobb'd it with their Female Consorts ... that they had drained and evacuated their Spermatick Vessels; and were become thereby altogether feeble, weak, emasculated, drooping, and flaggingly pithless.
‡ I take you to be very good at Topicks, and throughly affectioned to your own Cause.

muffin that he showed in *Pantagruel*. But Panurge praises his master, saying the love he shows him 'transcende tout poix, tout nombre, toute mesure, il est infiny, sempiternel ...'* This exaggeration, the ridiculous excess and the nonsensical way that Panurge uses it, point to the comic juxtaposition between Panurge and Pantagruel.

Professor Screech has made clear[7] that there is also a physiological–philosophical juxtaposition between Panurge and Pantagruel. Panurge is a Galenist: that is to say, he thinks that semen is a product of the testicles themselves, whilst Pantagruel adheres to the more 'poetic' theory of Plato – that semen is produced chiefly in the brain. The opposition between Galenic and Platonic medicine is tricky: from a twentieth-century point of view it is raving idiocy to have the serious man holding forth on a theory which is so totally out of accord with physiological knowledge. But Panurge, as we know now, is the fool, who by his excessive adherence to physical, nay physiological matters, is at one end of the scale; he cannot see anything further than the present moment; but the norm has a Christian, Platonic, Stoic, metaphysical framework. Thus, for example, in chapter 6 Pantagruel discusses the law of Moses, and the way he argues for it means that the 'social norm' which hitherto has been clearly established now expands to include his seriously felt ideas about God. A year's abstention from war is justified for newly-married men: for they should try to provide heirs and should test whether their wives are sterile or fertile so that, 'pour mieulx après le decés des mariz premiers les colloquer en secondes nopces: les fecondes, à ceulx qui vouldroient multiplier en enfans; les brehaignes, à ceulx qui n'en appeteroient et les prendroient pour leurs vertus, sçavoir, bonnes graces, seulement en consolation domesticque et entretenement de mesnaige'.†

Pantagruel has already referred to Deuteronomy xxiv, 5, in stating

---

* goeth far beyond the reach of any price or value; it transcends all weight, all number, all measure; it is endless and everlasting ...

† they might pitch the more suitably, in case of their first Husband's decease, upon a second Match. The Fertile Women to be wedded to those who desire to multiply their Issue; and the Steril ones to such other Mates, as misregarding the storing of their own Lineage, chuse them only for their Virtues, Learning, Genteel Behaviour, Domestick Consolation, Management of the House, and Matrimonial Conveniences and Comforts, and such like.

that for a year after marriage the man may enjoy his rights – 'ut uno anno laetetur cum uxore sua'; and now he fuses the allusion with a reference to Deuteronomy xx, 5–7, which makes it all the richer. He links the Jewish attitude to marriage as a potential joy, the emphasis on the family through the procreation of children, the significance of fertility in marriage and the suggestion that sterile wives can be married for mutual solace and for 'the Management of the House'. Pantagruel gives a Christian view of marriage, interlarded with Pauline and Old Testament comments, but to go further and say that in this chapter Rabelais comes out strongly in favour of the individual and turns the sixteenth-century concept of marriage almost into a twentieth-century partnership seems to be misleading. It is inconceivable that Rabelais would, like Erasmus, write dialogues with two women speaking in order to illustrate his views on the laicization of culture! Basically, Rabelais follows the line of all sermonists of the time in stressing the family inheritance – both theological and philosophical – as being the most important thing. And the fact that Pantagruel is given this view of marriage as the norm among enlightened French people of the sixteenth century, whilst Panurge is almost reactionary in his replies to Pantagruel here, with his references to those like *les prescheurs de Varenes* and frere Enguainnant who condemn second marriages, is important for the comedy. The chapter ends with these words by Panurge, 'Je ne l'ay demandé sans cause bien causée, ne sans raison bien resonnante. Ne vous desplaise.'*
With their word-play, on '*raison*' and '*cause*', they remind the reader of the earlier linguistic fun.

In chapter 7, Panurge appears in fancy dress which he will also wear throughout the *Quart Livre*: he has a flea set in a gold earring which he wears on the right ear 'after the Jewish fashion', he forebears the wearing of his codpiece and has on instead of his normal clothes a 'long, plain-seamed and single-stitched Gown'. His appearance is very funny and the Olympian author adds, '(c'est belle chose, estre en tous cas bien informé)',† thus making sure that the

---

* Under favour, Sir, I have not asked this Question without Cause causing, and Reason truly very ratiocinant. Be not offended, I pray you.

† O what a brave thing it is, in every case and circumstance of a Matter to be throughly well informed!

readers too will see this as comic. Pantagruel, still called *le bon Pantagruel*, understands nothing of the disguise and when Panurge explains the meaning of his clothes, Pantagruel replies in terms of the Stoic theory of indifference: external matters like food or clothing are neutral as regards value, what does matter is the attitude of the individual towards them, 'Chascun abonde en son sens, mesmement en choses foraines, externes et indifferentes, lesquelles de soy ne sont bonnes ne maulvaises, pource qu'elles ne sortent de nos cœurs et pensées, qui est l'officine de tout bien et tout mal ...'* This serious speech of Pantagruel's may be compared with speeches from Erasmus's *The Godly Feast*. Rabelais uses a syncretic fusion of Saint Paul and classical sources to explain the indifference of external things like food, clothing and drinking and to assert that the mind is *mesmement* (chiefly) important in such things as those.8 Pantagruel is shown as 'apathetic' in the Stoic sense, and this aspect will develop as the comedy with Panurge gets broader. Panurge's comic muddle-headedness and his extreme lust, 'j'endesve, je deguene, je grezille d'estre marié et labourer en diable bur dessus ma femme'† make his sexual desire blatant, and his view of marriage is one long orgy legitimized by a certificate. His foolish self-conceit is stressed when he touches on what he had said in chapter 2 – 'O le grand mesnaiger que je seray'. This would seem to be the comedy as Molière would see it – with Pantagruel as the *raisonneur* and Panurge the fool. But this is not the case with Rabelais. For again, Menippean satire holds the stage for a chapter. Pantagruel eggs on Panurge's rhetoric because it will be fun, 'Voulez vous ... maintenir que la braguette est piece premiere de harnois militaire? C'est doctrine moult paradoxe et nouvelle. Car nous disons que par esprons on commence soy armer ... Je le maintiens, respondit Panurge: et non à tord je le maintiens'‡

* Every one overflowingly aboundeth in his own Sense and Fancy: Yea, in Things of a Foreign Consideration altogether extrinsecal and indifferent, which in and of themselves are neither commendable nor bad, because they proceed not from the Interior of the Thoughts and Heart, which is the Shop of all Good and Evil.

† I itch, I tingle, I wriggle, and long exceedingly to be married; that without the danger of Cudgel blows, I may labour my Female Copes-mate with the hard push of a Bull-horned Devil.

‡ Will you maintain ... that the Codpiece is the chief piece of a Military Harness? It is

(chapter 8). As a fictional character, Pantagruel preserves his tolerance and his love of Panurge intact during this chapter. He cannot resist trying to make Panurge exhibit his rhetoric. Panurge starts proving again a nonsensical case: the praise of codpieces. Again he uses valid arguments, useful knowledge and good reasons, but they are put together for a world that is upside down. He starts with praise of nature who has created plants, trees, shrubs, herbs with a protective covering for eternity. Readers agree so far; but then he turns to the human race where man has been created naked and helpless, and in order to bring all the vegetable and sensitive creatures into his subjection has to arm himself with a codpiece! At this point Pantagruel says, 'Par la dive Oye guenet ... depuys les dernieres pluyes tu es devenu grand lifre-lofre, voyre diz je philosophe.'* When nature formed a weapon for man, it was for the protection of the most important part of him – the testicles. And again, Panurge expounds the Galenic view that it would be better to be without a heart or head than to be without genitals. The fool has one thing in his view of life, and in Panurge's case it is his sexuality. One can see how he is out of step with Pantagruel and out of step with the whole human race when he proves such a nonsensical case. Moreover, Panurge again parodies subtly the Olympian author: for example, he uses the same jokes about the *couilles de Lorraine* as we read earlier in *Gargantua* chapter 1, and he ends his speech with a verse interlude.

When this is over Panurge asks Pantagruel *avecques un profond souspir* for some advice on this question of getting married, 'je vous supply, par l'amour que si long temps m'avez porté'.† Pantagruel states that it is important for the individual to make his own decision, and put it into action knowing that the issue is uncertain. Again, the norm is suggested in Stoic terms and Pantagruel is able to say, 'une foys en avez jecté le dez ... plus parler n'en fault...'‡

a new kind of Doctrine very Paradoxical: For we say at Spurs begins the arming of a Man. Sir, I maintain it, (answered Panurge) and not wrongfully do I maintain it.

* By the holy Saint Babingoose ... you are become, since the last Rain, a great Lifre lofre, Philosopher, I should say.

† I humbly beseech you for the Affection which of a long time you have born me ...

‡ then ... seeing you have so decreed ... what need is there of any further Talk thereof ...

In chapter 10 he reiterates the same view, 'N'estez vous asceuré de vostre vouloir? Le poinct principal y gist: tout le reste est fortuit, et dependent des fatales dispositions du ciel.'* Here one must not give too much weight to things totally outside one's control: one must submit to them provided that one has examined the situation and has found all the pieces of evidence one needs to make up one's mind. There is a certain paradox in the 'apathetic' attitude in that neither free-will nor free action can affect destiny, yet one must play the rôle of someone who does use free-will. But the paradox was there in the ancient Stoic view and, apart from Calvinism, is there in the Christian attitude. Pantagruel insists on active acquiescence to the will of God, 'Il se y convient mettre à l'adventure, les œilz bandez, baissant la teste, baisant la terre et se recommandant à Dieu au demourant, puys qu'une foys l'on se y veult mettre. Aultre asceurance ne vous en sçauroys je donner.'† This shows 'apathy' enriched with a positive Christian *prise de position*. The rest of the chapter is an exploitation of the linguistic comedy of Panurge's purely rhetorical dilemma – *An sit nubendum*. Panurge runs through all the arguments for and against marriage: on the one hand, the loneliness of being a bachelor, destitute of children, deprived of the comfort of an honest wife; and on the other the fear of cuckoldry, and the terror of his own physical inadequacy ('estant malade et impotent au debvoir de mariage'). Each time he reaches a conclusion in one of his arguments Pantagruel echoes it: that is, Pantagruel is no longer taking any argument seriously – you can marshal as good arguments for the one side as for the other and so it does not get you very far in actually making a decision. The episode is comic because the two sides are not funny if taken singly, but when you get the juxtaposition of normal attitudes with abnormal ones they are seen in all their

---

* Are not you assured within your self of what you have a mind to? the chief and main point of the whole matter lieth there; all the rest is merely casual, and totally dependeth upon the fatal Disposition of the Heavens.
† It is therefore expedient, seeing you are resolved for once to take a trial of the state of Marriage, that, with shut Eyes, bowing your Head, and kissing the Ground, you put the business to a Venture, and give it a fair hazard in recommending the success of the residue to the disposure of Almighty God. It lieth not in my Power to give you any other manner of Assurance, or otherways to certifie you of what shall ensue on this your Undertaking.

absurdity. Furthermore, Panurge's rhetoric is exposed in all its glory: and so is the emptiness of arguing to persuade when truth is the only valid thing. To argue that you would do better to get married is as simple as to rationalize on the step once you have taken it, but Panurge is not any the wiser for his purely rhetorical argumentation. One might compare Panurge with Hircan in Marguerite de Navarre's *Heptaméron*: they both make everything revolve round women in a sexual way and they both play with opinions in a purely *gaulois* way. Panurge takes the indifferent things of this life on earth as the very stuff of living: the fear that in marriage he will lose his sexual virility – which is a basic fear in males – is seen in a comic light. The reader has no indication that Pantagruel reacts in any emotional way whatsoever to this fear: he merely gives an intellectual reiteration of his Christian and Stoic views.

If it is true, as many critics have claimed, that the next cluster of chapters around divination demonstrates the wherefores of knowing the future in general rather than the specific question of Panurge's marriage, it nonetheless makes this part of the 'novel' rather outdated and boring to read. If, on the other hand, one regards the *Tiers Livre* not as a novel but as a prose fiction taking the form of a Menippean satire, one is in a much better position to see all the ideas, all the characters and the whole *bouffonnerie* as interlacing with each other in every chapter of the book. This does not automatically decrease the boring qualities which the twentieth-century reader finds in these chapters, but at least one can see much more clearly what the Olympian author was doing. Pantagruel is given all the classical erudition to play with whilst Panurge is given all the superstitions and falsely used learning to juggle with. Every time the grotesque comedy flags, Pantagruel restarts it for the sake of the love he bears Panurge. And so in the divination chapters he suggests Vergilian lots as perhaps one way of knowing the future, but goes on 'Je ne veulx toutesfoys inferer que ce sort universellement soit infaillible, affin que ne y soyez abusé'* (chapter 10). In this statement one can see Pantagruel

---

* Do not you nevertheless imagine, lest you should be deluded, that I would upon this kind of Fortune flinging Proof infer an uncontrolable, and not to be gainsaid Infallibility of Truth.

insisting on a commonsense norm; his qualified attitude towards the result of Vergilian lots is important. But nonetheless, there are little humorous digs against Pantagruel – which come from the Olympian author. For instance, Pantagruel opens the Vergilian books 'with his nail' (repeated in chapter 11, when he says to Panurge *Ouvrez seulement avec l'ongle*); his calling up of erudite allusions, and his one theme – that it is up to the individual to make a decision and put it into action – have to be put side by side with his calling Panurge *un fillol*. Furthermore, the humanists, and Rabelais among them, loved to play at divination by Homeric and Vergilian lots – and this whole chapter (chapter 10) could be seen as a game played by Pantagruel and Panurge.[9] The whole of the *Tiers Livre* in some sense is a game: Panurge is a knave–fool who exploits all the traditional subjects of farce: an ageing booby who wants to take a wife; yet he fears marriage and cuckoldry because women are never satisfied by their husbands. Pantagruel is the *raisonneur* when he is treated seriously; but at other times he is just playing the game.

The social satire against the fool is equally manifest: for instance, in chapter 13 where the first entry of frere Jan makes this clear, 'Your meaning is, and you would thereby infer ... that the Dreams of all horned Cuckolds (of which number Panurge, by the help of God, and his future Wife, is without controversie to be one) are always true and infallible.' Here the Olympian author is exploiting in a new way the traditional farcical theme of the man who is married and cuckolded: Panurge is the man who wants to get married for the wrong reasons, and if he does get married everyone of his company knows that he will be a cuckold, and the reader knows it too. Frere Jan's remark here brings sharply to the reader's mind that the normal course of events runs inevitably against the fool; that indeed, every reason, every piece of logic that Panurge may use, will paradoxically and illogically work against him. It is important then to see frere Jan here on the same side as Pantagruel, for very different reasons, but playing a variation to Pantagruel in the bass clef: if it were a moral norm to which we had to agree, there would be no cause for frere Jan to like this foolish rogue. But in the next chapter (chapter 14) when

the whole company is gathered together, 'At Seven a Clock of
the next following Morning, Panurge did not fail to present
himself before Pantagruel, in whose Chamber were at that time
Epistemon, Fryar John of the Funnels, Ponocrates, Eudemon,
Carpalin, and others, to whom, at the entry of Panurge, Pantagruel said, Lo, here cometh our Dreamer', they all poke fun at
the riotous behaviour of Panurge. Furthermore, frere Jan sees all
the adventures of Panurge in trying to find a sure way of guarding
against the future as a huge joke: 'tu sera coqu, homme de bien,
je t'en asceure: tu auras belles cornes'.* He plays with words like
nostre maistre de Cornibus as he had done in *Gargantua* and keeps his
monkish habits of speech 'et je feray la queste parmi la paroece'. In
the next chapter he is invoked by Panurge who is hungry again;
but the cause of his present hunger – the divination by dreams,
which required him to go to bed without any supper – is almost
forgotten as he and frere Jan dance round with their nonsensical
reasons, culinary terminology, illogical spoonerisms and play on
words. At the end Panurge calls frere Jan a 'couillon velouté,
couillon claustral et cabalicque ... allons mon baudrier...'† If
readers were supposed to disapprove ethically of Panurge, the
play of comedy, grotesque, burlesque and linguistic exuberance
which is built up between him and frere Jan would be irrelevant.
Epistemon, frere Jan and Pantagruel would rather present a stiff
upper lip and tell us again and again that Panurge was morally
wrong. But the dilemma is not a moral one; it is the traditional
social comedy of a man who is a potential cuckold but who
does not believe anything that anyone is telling him. Rabelais
has seized on the topicality of marriage problems as shown by
the spate of books for and against women; he has used these as
raw materials to create a burlesque comedy, rather in the way that
Molière took up the religious questions of his day and turned
them into *Tartuffe*. The clearest proof that the *Tiers Livre* is
not a moral comedy is given by the grotesque consultation with
a sibyl.

* thou wilt be a Cuckold, an honest one, I warrant thee; O the brave Horns that will be
  born by thee! Ha, ha, ha. [The laughter is not in the French at this point.]
† my Plush-cod Friar, my Caballine and Claustral Ballock.

The critics suggest that Pantagruel has to be listened to seriously on everything; but to do so in this episode would mean the reader's whole view of Pantagruel being turned topsy turvy. For he goes into a long *exposé* of how one cannot know for sure that one will learn anything in this consultation, 'Que nuist sçavoir tousjours et tousjours apprendre, feust ce d'un sot, d'un pot, d'une guedoufle, d'une moufle, d'une pantoufle?'* Panurge will say exactly the same things about *apprendre* in chapter 25 when he agrees to consult Her Trippa, and so one hardly reads this passage with the same earnest attention as one listens to Pantagruel on other occasions. Epistemon and not Pantagruel is to accompany Panurge in this wild-goose chase. It is a grotesque parody of Vergil's *Aeneid*, book 6, where Aeneas, before his descent to the Underworld, consults the Sibyl at Cumae. Vergil depicts both the Sibyl and Aeneas as austere and aloof figures – quite the opposite of Panurge and Epistemon. The Sibyl goes into a terrifying trance; she gives an answer when she is lucid, and it is a warning of another war, of how a second Achilles awaits Aeneas' coming to Italy and of how a woman will again be the source of his misfortunes. It is a most powerful scene, splendidly handled by Vergil.

It would be easy to parody gently such lines as

> her features, her colour were all at once
> Different, her hair flew wildly about; her breast was heaving,
> Her fey heart swelled in ecstasy; larger than life she seemed ...[10]

but Rabelais goes much further in his grotesqueness so that one can only catch hints of the original parodic intention. Aeneas sails until he comes to the north-west bay of Naples, in the neighbourhood of Cumae and finds the temple up against the side of a cliff,

> There's a huge cave hollowed out from the flank of Cumae's hill;
> A hundred wide approaches it has, a hundred mouths
> From which there issue a hundred voices, the Sibyl's answers.

Rabelais gives Panurge and Epistemon three days journeying from Pantagruel and the court before they reach, 'à la croppe de

---

* What hindrance, hurt or harm doth the laudable desire of Knowledge bring to any Man, were it from a Sot, a Pot, a Fool, a Stool, [a Winter Mittam, a Truckle for a Pully, the Lid of a Goldsmiths Crucible, an Oil-Bottle], or old Slipper?

une montaigne, soubs un grand et ample chastaignier, leurs feut monstrée la maison de la vaticinatrice'.* The picture of the crone is absurd, her culinary activities are ridiculous and there is no hint that prophecy is about to possess her; 'La vieille estoit mal en poinct, mal vestue, mal nourrie, edentée, chassieuse, courbassée, roupieuse, languoureuse, et faisoit un potaige de choux verds . . .'† After the prophecy, Vergil makes an allusion to the golden bough which Aeneas must find and pluck from its tree before being allowed to go to the Underworld. Rabelais makes Epistemon remember the golden bough before the hag gives her prophecy, 'Nous ne aurons d'elle responce aulcune, car nous n'avons le rameau d'or.'‡ This is humorous enough but Panurge's reply heightens the grotesque parody, 'Je y ay . . . pourveu. Je l'ay icy dedans ma gibbesierre en une verge d'or . . .'§ and then offers to her six smoked ox-tongues, a pot of fresh cheese, some drink and some money.

Both Panurge and the hag produce mysterious scribbles; she uses ritual invocations: for example, she turns her spindles round three times three, but all this is mingled with grotesque actions like putting her apron over her head, 'comme les presbtres mettent leur amict quand ils voulent messe chanter'.¶ When she is possessed she 's'escria espovantablement, sonnant entre les dens quelques mots barbares et d'estrange termination . . .'** We can remember the shudder of awe when Vergil says,

> her voice came booming out of the cavern,
> Wrapping truth in enigma: she was possessed; Apollo
> Controlled her, shaking the reins and twisting the goad in her bosom.

* the House of the Vaticinatress standing on the knap or top of a Hill, under a large and spacious Walnut-tree.
† The old Hag . . . was ill apparelled, worse nourished, toothless, blear-ey'd, crook-shoulder'd, snotty, her Nose still dropping, and her self still drooping, faint and pithless. Whilst in this wofully wretched case she was making ready for her Dinner, Porridge of wrinkled green Colworts . . .
‡ nor shall we get from her any Response at all, for we have not brought along with us the Branch of Gold.
§ I have . . . provided pretty well for that, for here I have it within my Bag, in the substance of a Gold Ring . . .
¶ as a Priest uses to do his Amice, when he is going to sing Mass . . .
** hereupon she gave a most hideous and horribly dreadful shout, muttering betwixt her Teeth some few barbarous Words, of a strange termination.

There is nothing to echo this in Rabelais. His hag writes her words on sycamore leaves, throws them to the wind and says, 'Allez les chercher, si voulez; trouvez les, si povez: le sort fatal de vostre mariage y est escript.'*

The Olympian author in his guise of writing Menippean satire makes an entry once in this episode, 'je veidz qu'elle deschaussa un de ses esclos, (nous les nommons sabotz) ...'† so the readers take this consultation with a sibyl as part of the game. The topicality of the marriage question has caught Rabelais's imagination and he puts it in his book as one of the themes that he is satirizing in a burlesque and grotesque way. Pantagruel is hardly the norm here; he expounds the message but can the reader take him as the super-human wise man when he seeks knowledge of the future from this parodied consultation with the sibyl?

Panurge takes over the interpretation from Pantagruel because 'You understand as much (answer'd Panurge) in the veritable Interpretation, and Expounding of recent Prophecies, as a Sow in the Matter of Spicery.' Once again, the pattern of the comedy is repeated: for in Panurge's interpretation one has exactly the opposite meaning from the one that Pantagruel had offered: Panurge would be cuckolded, would see his wife pregnant by another man and would suffer the loss of his worldly goods. When Epistemon, at the end of the chapter, brings in Propertius, Tibullus, Porphyrius and Eustachius to prove a point against Panurge, we hear a very familiar voice reiterating very familiar words, 'Vrayement, respondit Panurge, vous me alleguez de gentilz veaulx. Ilz feurent folz comme poëtes, et resveurs comme philosophes; autant pleins de fine follie, comme estoit leur philosophie.'‡

It is time that Pantagruel intervened again with some rational arguments and so at the beginning of chapter 19 Pantagruel once

---

* Search after them if you will; find them if you can; the fatal Destinies of your Marriage written in them.
† In sequel whereof, she pulled off one of her wooden Pattens. [The *nous* form is not used by Urquhart.]
‡ Verily, verily, (quoth Panurge) brave are the Allegations which you bring me, and Testimonies of two footed Calves. These Men were Fools, as they were Poets; and Dotards, as they were Philosophers; full of Folly, as they were of Philosophy.

again gives a serious reason against Panurge – *L'esprit maling vous seduyt* – and this recalls all the theological reasons why God must have abandoned him, and why he is not capable of cooperating with the Divine Will. He is totally incapable of conducting himself according to his own reason. This is a serious religious argument, stressed by Pantagruel's tone; but in the second half of the sentence – *mais escoutez* – his own love and toleration emerge again. He offers Panurge a consultation – *par signes, sans parler* – with a deaf mute, and we can hardly help remembering the Thaumaste episode in *Pantagruel*. There is no loss of sympathy towards Panurge here – and again we must conclude that Rabelais was not 'proving' that Panurge had the wrong conception of marriage. The series of consultations with Nazdecabre, with Raminagrobis and with Her Trippa is a pretext for satirizing everybody: satire of Panurge for his 'diabolology' and of the learned men in all the erudition each consultation brings out. They are all seen from the Olympian author's perspective, and can be laughed at as the grotesque and farcical fools that all human beings can be at some time in their life.

The extended duologue between Panurge and Pantagruel is now one grotesque comedy. For in chapter 24 when the fool consults Epistemon he is told 'comment la voix publicque estoit toute consommée en mocqueries de son desguisement ...'*
When the consultation is between frere Jan and Panurge we have, as we are beginning to expect, the question of marriage seen from one point of view – that of virile potency. The traditional language of obscenity is here turned into a *blason* match: it is a vigorous, coarse and jolly dialogue listing appellations on *couillon*. The atmosphere is very much that of men amongst men. The leitmotif of Panurge's oscillations *pro et con* marriage is stressed at a purely physical, nay physiological level. The comic situation is exploited through the list of names and echoed by the sound of bells. Panurge uses onomatopoeic sounds, rhythm and repetition to suggest the advice they give, 'Marie toy, marie toy: marie, marie. Si tu te marie, marie, marie, tresbien t'en trouveras,

---

* how the open voice and common Fame of the whole Country did run upon no other Discourse, but the derision and mockery of his new Disguise ...

veras, veras. Marie, marie' (chapter 27). But the second time he hears the bells they are saying, 'Marie poinct, marie poinct, poinct, poinct, poinct, poinct. Si tu te marie, (marie poinct, marie poinct, poinct, poinct, poinct, poinct), tu t'en repentiras, tiras, tiras; coqu seras' (chapter 28). Amongst his ribald remarks, frere Jan mentions the important thing about Panurge – his age: we know that he is of an age when sexual performance is rather beyond him; we know too that this is his basic fear throughout the *Tiers Livre*. And so, when frere Jan says in chapter 28, 'Desja voy je ton poil grisonner en teste. Ta barbe ... une mappemonde ... les neiges sont es montaignes ... il n'y a pas grand chaleur par les valées de la braguette ...'* what we have perceived becomes obvious to those who see Panurge.

When chapter 29 opens it is Pantagruel again who presses a more serious reason on Panurge: 'chascun doibt estre arbitre de ses propres pensées, et de soy mesmes conseil prendre ... et autant vous en diz la premiere foys que m'en parlastez; mais vous en mocquiez tacitement, il m'en soubvient, et congnois que philautie et amour de soy vous deçoit'.† Pantagruel's point is taken a step further with this comment: he shows that Panurge is bedevilled by *philautia* or self-love. Every fool is self-centred; his whole universe is dominated by self, as Panurge's was in chapter 2; but still Pantagruel likes him. He suggests a serious consultation with a theologian, a doctor, a lawyer and a philosopher. The comedy will arise from the juxtaposition of Panurge and his advisers: at the beginning of each session Panurge starts afresh – should he take a wife and if so, will he be cuckolded? Panurge is the fixed point around which all the episodes turn. Obviously, this again could be serious from the point of view of content, but the treatment is entirely comic.

---

* I see thee waxing a little hoar-headed already; thy Beard ... the resemblance of a Map of the Terrestrial Globe ... when Snow is on the Mountains ... there is not then any considerable Heat to be expected in the Valleys and Low-Countries of the Codpiece.

† every one in the Project and Enterprise of Marriage, ought to be his own Carver, sole Arbitrator of his proper Thoughts, and from himself alone take counsel ... Such always hath been my opinion to you; and when at first you spoke thereof to me, I truly told you this very same thing: but tacitly you scorned my Advice, and would not harbour it within your mind. I know for certain ... that Philauty, or Self-love, is that which blinds your judgment, and deceiveth you.

Let us look at Hippothadée's consultation, to see how laughter
is aroused in this potentially serious chapter. The theologian goes
straight to the point with a *modestie incroyable*: 'Mon amy, vous
nous demandez conseil, mais premier fault que vous mesmes vous
conseillez.'* The first questions in his catechism is, 'Sentez vous
importunement en vostre corps les aiguillons de la chair?'† This is
a serious theological question using the words of Saint Paul, if it is
taken in its proper context. But, as readers, we know that Panurge
will not take it in the right way: his answer is, 'Bien fort ... ne
vous desplaise, nostre pere'.‡ The theologian's second question is,
'avez vous de Dieu le don et grace speciale de continence?'§
Again the reader can say with Panurge – *'Ma foy non'*. The
question is only comic because we know the character involved,
we know the whole story up to now, and we know that Panurge's
lust gives a quick answer to such questions. The serious side of the
problem is clearly Pauline (cf. the answers to love and marriage
in Marguerite de Navarre's *Heptaméron*) as the next question
shows, 'Mariez vous donc, mon amy ... car trop meilleur est soy
marier que ardre on feu de concupiscence',¶ which is almost a
direct translation of Saint Paul (1 Cor. vii. 9), 'But if they cannot
contain, let them marry: for it is better to marry than to burn.'
This doctrine was an aspect which the church saw as a strong
principle in the Christian approval of legitimate marriage – it was
a divinely-appointed remedy for those whose lust demanded
an outlet. But Panurge's attitude is apparent: Hippothadée's mind
is working on one level whilst Panurge is totally on another level –
and the two never meet each other. For Panurge invites him to
the wedding feast, 'C'est parlé cela ... gualantement, sans circum-
bilivaginer autour du pot. Grand mercy, monsieur nostre pere!'**

* My Friend, you are pleased to ask Counsel of us; but first you must consult with your self.
† Do you find any trouble or disquiet in your Body, by the importunate stings and prick-
lings of the Flesh?
‡ That I do ... Be not offended, I beseech you, good Father, at the freedom of my
Expression.
§ have you obtained from God the Gift and special Grace of Continency?
¶ My Counsel to you in that Case (my Friend) is, that you marry ... for you should
rather chuse to marry once, than to burn still in Fires of Concupiscence.
** That is spoke gallantly, without circumbilivaginating about and about, and never hit it
in its centred Point. Grammercy, my good Father.

With delight he says, 'Je vous convie à mes nopces. Corpe de galline, nous ferons chere lie.'* But the second worry soon pops up – Will I be a cuckold? The answer from Hippothadée is again perfectly orthodox, 'Nenny dea, mon amy ... si Dieu plaist.'† Panurge reacts to this in his usual way – a long wail followed by ridicule: 'Oh you are sending me to the private bedchamber of the Lord. Tell me, my French compatriots, how does one proceed to reach there'. Trivial concerns take over in the discussion for a while, as Panurge tells him not to come to his wedding after all, 'Je vous envoiray du rillé en vostre chambre, de la livrée nuptiale aussy. Vous boirez à nous, s'il vous plaist.'‡ Hippothadée goes on, however, to shake off the ridicule cast at him by Panurge and to suggest that there was nothing scandalous in his words, for God is the giver of all and the conserver of all things; and he gives man this advantage that he has announced his will through the Holy Scriptures. The study of the Scriptures and the seeking of God's divine will in them is the best way of arriving at his *privé conseil*. The theologian then expounds morally on the duty of a wife and the duty of a husband and goes on exhaustively, while Panurge does not listen. He has closed his ears to any more scriptural comment and is ready for the next session, with the doctor.

We shall just briefly look at the consultation with Rondibilis to show that it is not merely the scriptural point of view that is used as a comic butt. Rondibilis prescribes five methods of quelling Panurge's lust – all of them based on the medical opinion that one must find ways of using up excess vigour which would otherwise be used by the body to produce semen. Firstly, intemperate drinking – and Rondibilis illustrates its effects with reference to Bacchus the god of drunkards, who was effeminate, beardless, and like a eunuch. Secondly, the taking of drugs to quell incontinence. Thirdly, hard labour – and Rondibilis proves this in a long passage which ranges from the chaste goddess Diana, who works so hard

---

* I invite you to my Wedding: By the Body of a Hen, we shall make good Cheer ...
† By no means ... if it please God.
‡ I will send you some good Things to your Chamber, together with the Bride's Favour, and there you may drink our Health, if it may stand with your good liking.

that she never has time to be lascivious, to athletic men who are as impotent as eunuchs. Fourthly, by fervent study – here Rondibilis gives a delightful picture of the scholar at work, with all his bodily activity suspended and all his energy diverted and concentrated in the brain so that one would think that he was in ecstasy, transported to a world of his own. When Rondibilis comes to the fifth remedy, which is *par l'acte Venerien*, Panurge jumps in and with great relief says, 'Je vous attendois là ... et le prens pour moy. Use des præcedens qui vouldra.'* Dramatically one can see Panurge waiting for the doctor to go exhaustively through all his medical knowledge before he comes to the most obvious course – the sexual act. Panurge again promises a great marriage banquet: he must feast his wife and her family and neighbours and everyone will be happy.

But in the next chapter Rondibilis has to explain in medical terms, how Panurge will be a potential cuckold, like every man getting married. This chapter 32 is the main evidence of Rabelais's anti-feminism, particularly Rondibilis' exposition of the behaviour of women: they are in the sway of a little animal who is hungry for copulation. He says, 'Quand je diz femme, je diz un sexe tant fragil, tant variable, tant muable, tant inconstant et imperfaict, que Nature me semble (parlant en tout honneur et reverence) s'estre esguarée de ce bon sens par lequel elle avait créé et formé toutes choses, quand elle a basty la femme.'† This is the ancient doctrine of women as botched males. Later Rondibilis moves to the notion commonly held in the ancient world, the middle ages and in the sixteenth century, that the womb is an autonomous animal which is capable of self-movement and can distinguish smells. He compares the woman to the moon: she takes her light from the sun, is fickle, unpredictable and shines best when the sun has set, 'elles prennent leur adventaige, se

---

* There did I wait for you ... and shall willingly apply it to my self, whilst any one that pleaseth may, for me, make use of any of the four preceding.
† When I say Womankind, I speak of a Sex so frail, so variable, so changeable, so fickle, inconstant, and imperfect, that, in my opinion, Nature, (under favour nevertheless of the prime Honour and Reverence which is due unto her) did in a manner mistake the Road which she had traced formerly, and stray exceedingly from that Excellence of Providential Judgment, by the which she had created and formed all other things, when she built, framed, and made up the Woman.

donnent du bon temps, vaguent, trotent, deposent leur hypocrisie et se declairent …'* As regards her individual nature, woman is defective because nature had more regard for 'la sociale delectation de l'home et à la perpetuité de l'espece humaine, beaucoup plus qu'à la perfection de l'individuale muliebrité'.†

This is told without parody or irony and in chapter 33 Rondibilis is given a delightfully fantastic fable, which is listened to by the whole company. What we have here is a social gathering enjoying jokes about women because they are and always have been topical: even Hippothadée makes a comment on forbidden fruit; Carpalim, Ponocrates and Epistemon tell their own witty anecdotes, and they all laugh heartily, men amongst men. The last part of Rondibilis' advice is treated as a farce: he will have to see the bride's urine, and feel her pulse, and Panurge promises that he will be paid for all he does – Cela s'entend.

From the Stoic point of view, the comedy is very much that of Pantagruel versus Panurge: Pantagruel's ethical solution lies in the disposition of his soul, the successful end being virtue or 'consistency in life' – knowing your own nature and living in accord with it. Panurge on the other hand is the opposite of consistency; his is the rôle of the foolish, unphilosophical man, always restless and always undecided – the man in the crowd with no answer to life's problems, simply a tremendous gift for talking his way into or out of crises. Pantagruel's supreme tolerance could be called Stoical too; he repeatedly asserts that Panurge's excessive lust and extremely sexual vocabulary and thoughts are not to be condemned in themselves but only in so far as they are seemly or unseemly for the individual. Pantagruel is happy in his own existence in the Tiers Livre: he is a wise man who bows to Fate or to the 'play of fortune' and who is prepared in his own mind to accept everything that Fate brings him because he enjoys a serene disposition – 'jamais ne se troubloit jamais ne se vexoit'. The

---

* forthwith they take their advantage, pass the time merrily, desist from all labour, frolick it, gad abroad, lay aside their counterfeit Garb, and openly declare and manifest the interiour of their Dispositions …
† by a great deal more respectful heed to the delightful Consortship, and sociable Delectation of the Man, than to the Perfection and Accomplishment of the individual Womanishness, or Muliebrity.

Stoic view of the universe is coloured by optimism and it is here that Pantagruel rejects implicitly the views of Saint Paul and the whole of the Christian fathers. For the question of sin does not really enter; one could contrast Saint Paul's views on sexual sin, for example in the Epistle to the Ephesians, chapter v, where he seems to stress the initial sex-relationship between Adam and Eve as the origin of human sin.[11] The element of Stoicism that was taken over by Christianity was very large, but in their ethical concerns there is a sharp contrast between the moral principles developed by Christianity and those preached and practised on the pagan side. Of course, Rabelais was writing a comic book. Therefore questions of evil and sin which reformers like Luther treated with emotional involvement are not so treated in Rabelais's books; we find an intellectual acceptance of indifference and not an emotional one.

The rest of the *Tiers Livre* moves away from comedy and into the grotesque: and this grotesque aspect is seen from the Olympian perspective. For example Panurge, at this climactic stage of the fiction, is isolated and experiences the same kind of reaction as he had in the presence of the sibyl, Raminagrobis or Her Trippa. The marriage quest is all but forgotten and the whole company laughs at the scene of fast dialogue between him and the ass Trouillogan – reminiscent of the *Chanson de Ricochet* in chapter 9. Satire of characters and topical attitudes to philosophy and to marriage are rampant and the reader laughs at everything in this Menippean satire. Where Pantagruel enters it is the Pantagruel we saw in chapter 8: for instance he and Panurge indulge in a *blason* match around the word *fol*. He even has a few jokes in his old manner, 'Si raison estoit pour quoy jadis en Rome les Quirinales on nommoit la *Feste des folz*, justement en France on pourroit instituer les Triboulletinales'* (chapter 38). Similarly, the trial of Bridoye is a piece of topical satire on the legal profession with Bridoye's rhetoric, as in the case of Panurge throughout the book, being used to prove nonsensical cases. Pantagruel and the rest of

---

* If there was any reason why at Rome the Quirinal Holiday, of old, was call'd, The Feast of Fools; I know not why we may not for the like cause institute in France the Tribouletick Festivals, to be celebrated and solemnized over all the Land.

the company excuse him on account of his *vieillesse* and *simplesse*, implying that he is a Pauline fool:

Et me semble qu'il y a je ne sçay quoy de Dieu qui a faict et dispensé qu'à ses jugemens ... toutes les præcedentes sentences ayent esté trouvées bonnes ... lequel ... veult souvent sa gloire apparoistre en l'hebetation des saiges, en la depression des puissans et en l'erection des simples et humbles.* (cf. St Paul, 1 Cor. i.27)

Pantagruel praises Bridoye for his humility and his recognition of the limits of his power in that he does not play dangerously with dice, but is in a genuine dilemma where knowledge and information are not enough to show the way clearly, so that he submits himself to God – 'se recommandoit humblement à Dieu le juste juge'. Thus the senile fool is regarded by the company as pathetic but excusable and by the readers as being very reminiscent of Humesvene and Baisecul's trial in *Pantagruel* where again the giant puts everything right.

The method of distancing everything in a mode of irony and satire becomes clear now, and in case we have not caught the tone of the work, the Olympian author enters at the end with Pantagruelion, and here the authorial *I* is used, 'je veids qu'il feist charger grande foison de son herbe Pantagruelion, tant verde et crude que conficte et præparée'.† Everything in the *Tiers Livre* has been 'placed'. The comic norm is established through Pantagruel and the fool-knave Panurge; but outside the narration one finds the Olympian author reminding readers that both Pantagruel and Panurge are fictional characters. Moreover, they are fictional characters devoid of verisimilitude: so that Pantagruel can and does change rapidly from one chapter to another in the same way as does Panurge, who sometimes dominates the scene with his

---

* Truly, it seemeth unto me ... there hath been ... extraordinary savouring of the un-speakable Benignity of God ... For it is usual (as you know well) with Him whose Ways are inscrutable, to manifest his own ineffable Glory, in blunting the Perspicacy of the Eyes of the Wise, in weakening the Strength of potent Oppressors, in depressing the Pride of rich Extortioners, and in erecting, [comforting, protecting, supporting, up-holding, and shoaring up] the [poor, feeble, humble, silly, and] foolish Ones of the Earth.

† it was observed, how he caused some of his Vessels to be fraught and loaded with a great quantity of an Herb of his called Pantagruelion, not only of the green and raw sort of it, but of the confected also ... (note that the English does not use the *I* technique here).

rhetorical ingenuity while at other times he is laughed at for being the sex-obsessed fool. This gives the readers a certain *insouciance* towards all the themes raised in the book. The long philosophizing and social reflection by Pantagruel needs to be set alongside his humorous tolerance of the fool. And similarly Panurge must be seen in his Janus-like rôle: both as fool and clever knave. This does change the emphasis of the whole book.

Firstly, it is clear that Rabelais's intentions were not philosophical nor religious but literary. The *Tiers Livre* was not meant to be a moral treatise: every episode is taken seriously only by critics who think Rabelais has a moral message to deliver. This is a critical tradition which takes moral strenuousness as equivalent to good art. Even the satire is not moralistic in tone and all the farcical, grotesque and subtle comedy are not there simply to sugar the pill of humanist Christianity: they are there for literary and fictional reasons. Secondly, the amused superiority of the Olympian author is not always in evidence when we look at Panurge. There is an artistic involvement, indeed a sympathy, which might be seen as the beginnings of a comic romance. We shall discuss this in the next chapter.

The Menippean satire circles around the traditional comic theme of a potential cuckold. If one looks back now at the views of Lefranc and Professor Screech one could say that they were both right, in that the *Querelle des Femmes* did spark off the *Tiers Livre* and in so doing provided an opportunity for discussing themes such as the individual and his destiny, *but* the real novelty of the book is the Menippean satire form which is so very flexible. It is here that one sees all the threads coming together.

7

CHARACTERS

Northrop Frye, classifying Rabelais as a Menippean satirist, goes on to assert that all satirical writers are concerned with mental attitudes and with stylized characters who must be the mouthpieces of the real author and not people who can be disengaged from the satiric narrative.[1] But in Rabelais's work we find comic characters, comic episodes and comic language being used in both a burlesque and a poetic manner. What we cannot be sure about is the uniformity of Rabelais's handling of comic language and creation of comic characters throughout the four books. Thus, for example, one needs to assess his linguistic skill 'by the extent to which he can develop freedom and variety of expression *within* the constraints imposed by the language' (my italics).[2] Yet the set of speech habits that the sixteenth-century writer in France had at his disposal was not narrowly restricted and is hard to delimit. Writers such as Rabelais or Calvin had different idiolects and registers, even different languages – French and Latin – to work with. One may compare the situation with Apuleius: his education was in Greek and his *Metamorphoses* was written in Latin; he translated philosophical works from Greek into Latin, yet wrote his own philosophical works in Latin; so in the second century of our era Apuleius was very aware of the bi-lingual nature of his culture and this was not untypical of the authors of Latin antiquity. It is well-known that the development of French as a language to express imaginative or philosophical concepts proceeds from the paratactic structure of the middle ages to a hypotactic structure in modern French.[3] Rabelais could draw on the humanist model of a highly hypotactic Latin or the native model of a highly paratactic French (for imaginative writing) in order to derive from them different levels of style, vocabulary and syntax; and the way he fuses them into a personal approach to language is one of the vital things that must be analysed in the next two chapters.

As for the creation of comic characters, is he not interested in characters at all except in so far as they can be used in order to propound mental attitudes and values which can then be thrown aside or re-affirmed as he wishes? His characters, on this theory, are merely extensions of the mask that the Olympian author donned in the prologues and throughout the four books. Indeed, most critics of Rabelais's fiction weave a romantic web around the biography of the real Rabelais when dealing with characters like Panurge or frère Jan. For instance, Professor Tétel says of Panurge 'c'est Rabelais lui-même tel qu'il était pendant ses années d'études. Nous pouvons l'imaginer . . .'⁴ making not the slightest distinction between the real Rabelais and the creator of Panurge. Obviously Rabelais's life must necessarily have been one of the main sources of the fiction that he was creating, but for the nature and significance of his characters one has to look in the works themselves and not at the biographical facts of the real Rabelais. The question is whether Rabelais's characters do transcend the stylized convention which the Menippean satirist erects. Take Voltaire's *Candide* as a point of comparison here: Candide is from his entry into the prose fiction a Lockian 'clean sheet' who goes through the *conte* occupying a middle position between the optimistic Pangloss and the pessimistic Martin; parodied picaresque adventures befall him as he tests each doctrine in the light of events. Voltaire manipulates the character to this specific end: never does he let Candide break free of the satiric outline that he has fashioned for him. Voltaire, with far more polish, far more subtlety in his ironical twists and with a far greater maliciousness than Rabelais, is not interested in the character of Candide at all; he expects his readers to look at this Bergsonian robot from the point of view of the author. Candide is a stylized character, a mouthpiece of the author's ideas, who learns eventually that work in society is the most useful activity of man.

Many of Rabelais's characters are Voltairian in shape, and his attitude towards them is the same: most of them are seen from the Olympian perspective and strike us as what E. M. Forster has called 'flat characters': 'Flat characters were called "humours" in the seventeenth century, and are sometimes called types, and sometimes caricatures. In their purest form, they are constructed round a single idea or quality ... they are easily recognised ... by the reader's emotional eye.'[5] Examples of flat characters in Rabelais readily come to mind: all the giants' henchmen, Janotus de Bragmardo, Homenaz, Du Douhet, Thaumaste, Rondibilis, Her Trippa, Nazdecabre, LoupGarou, Hippothadée and so on. If we spread out Rabelais's canvas of characters to its full extent, the comic framework in which he is working demands the sheer number of persons that he throws in as extras with lavish detail, like his schoolboy from Limoges with his pindaric jargon, half macaronic Latin, half French, who is sketched for us and then tossed away with extravagant pleasure. Such 'extras' or flat characters only come to life because of the author's own linguistic inventiveness, in much the same way as Balzac's characters live in *Les Illusions Perdues*. For Balzac conjures up a world of inexhaustible phenomena which has the savour of an unreal 'Arabian Nights' atmosphere: those who influence the hero's destiny are compared to sultans and pashas, the obstacles he comes across like the intrigues of booksellers, the chaos of *les Galeries de Bois*, the stink of human flesh and the traffickings among journalists are compared to dragons and evil spirits in fairy stories; exotic elements like the near-magic enchantments of the theatre or the firework dazzle of backstage life are visualized as if 'dans un palais du Cabinet des fées'; a comparison between Paris fashion and an 'espèce de princesse ... des Mille et un Jours pour qui chacun veut être le prince Calaf' is like a leitmotif, the temptations of the Evil Genii of the Lamp, the transformations of fortune, the bookseller who holds a levée every morning, the constant astonishment of the hero Lucien as he discovers enchanted countries in this Paris – all this mass of thick, swarming, pullulating life casts the story on a gigantic scale. Into this framework Balzac pours in hundreds of characters, some white, some black and some a murky or ash-coloured grey and it is his energy and his vitalizing force that galvanize his fictional world. Neither Rabelais nor Balzac 'créent des personnages, mais comme tout artiste, un monde cohérent et particulier' (Malraux). Hardly any of Rabelais's characters are entirely invented or created from scratch. Rather has he, like the bee in the recurrent sixteenth-

century simile, sucked here and there, among folk-literature and
medieval books, to make the honey specially perfumed and all
his own. To see how this world is peculiar to Rabelais we must
study first of all those 'extras' or flat characters that he invokes
through his necromantic arts.

We shall start with one example – that of the *saiges femmes*
present at the birth of Pantagruel (*Pantagruel*, chapter 2). Before
the giant himself is born, we have the grotesque sight of Badebec's
womb pouring forth dromedaries laden with masses of gammon,
followed by camels burdened with sausages and chitterlings
and finally twenty-five cart-loads of garlic, leeks and onions.
This whole procession is watched with stupefaction by the midwives. Some of them say, 'Voicy bonne provision. Aussy bien
ne bevyons nous que lachement, non en lancement; cecy n'est
que bon signe, ce sont aguillons de vin.'* The wit of the remarks
is dependent on two *jeux de mots*: the French pronunciation '*en
lancement*' is akin to *en landsman* (the German word being *Land-
mann*) as pronounced by the Swiss, meaning compatriot, peasant,
countryman; the joke is that '*boire en lancement*' carries over the
implication that all Germans drink like fish. The second joke is the
perennial one that '*de vin*' is akin to *divin* and is often used by
Rabelais elsewhere (e.g. *Gargantua*, chapter 27, frere Jan and
another monk dialoguing on *le service divin* and the *service de vin*).
The little scene is brought to life with the choice of *caquetoyent* and
menus propos and the popular level of joking the midwives are
given; for example, one of them with a true 'prophetic' spirit
says, 'Il est né à tout le poil, il fera choses merveilleuses; et, s'il
vit, il aura de l'eage.'† The next time we see the midwives
(chapter 3) is when they are mentioned by Gargantua: hints of
the created author creep up to the surface; for example, '(où sont
elles? bonnes gens, je ne vous peulx veoyr); allez à l'enterre-
ment . . .'‡ which immediately reminds one of the prologue to

---

* Lo, here is good provision, and indeed we need it; for we drink but lazily, as if our tongues
walked on crutches, and not lustily like Lansman dutches: truly this is a good signe, there
is nothing here but what is fit for us, these are the spurres of wine that set it a going.

† He is borne with all his haire, he is undoubtedly to do wonderful things, and, if he live,
he shall have age.

‡ (where be they, good folks? I cannot see them). Go you to my wife's interrement.

the *Quart Livre* where the *captatio benevolentiae* contains this phrase, 'Gens de bien, Dieu vous saulve et guard! Où estez vous? je ne vous peuz veoir . . .'* This example of playing dynamically with flat figures brings one up sharply against the created author's own stylistic characteristics: his use of leitmotifs, his short question and answer, his elliptical way of giving replies, his punning and joking and his command of language transferred into dialogue.

One may think of all the well-known features of Rabelais's style, such as the archaisms in the prologues, the bold and fantastic inversions of subject and verb, his use of parenthesis, the Villonesque vocabulary; yet, it is in creating dialogue for his characters that his dynamic relationship with patterned speech in the sixteenth century really comes to life. An example, which is particularly interesting is the introduction of Dindenault, a picaresque character, whose entry to the *Quart Livre* differs somewhat as between the 1548 and 1552 versions. By making a brief comparison between the two versions we can watch the artist very consciously pruning and enriching the development of character.

Into this episode, the created author has put his dramatic qualities – his skill as a story-teller, and his imaginative inventiveness (so transforming a story that is in Folengo's *Maccheronee*, chapter 11) and his mastery of dialogue. The bare bones of the episode were Folengo's – the story of the one sheep thrown overboard and all the others in the flock following it – but the richness of character and the liveliness of the dialogue between Panurge and Dindenault are Rabelais's.

The merchant of Taillebourg is given a simple character sketch. The 1548 version's *dedans la nauf quantité de moutons* has been omitted in the 1552 version; also the epithet *glorieux* used in 1548 to characterize Dindenault is cut out. This gives a better shape to the whole episode, as we are now free to read the story and participate in the dialogue, without having our attitude to this overconceited merchant pre-determined. Dindenault first chooses to tease Panurge about his fancy dress, and the reader, remembering

---

* Good people, God save and keep you; Where are you? I can't see you . . .

how everyone made mock of this in the *Tiers Livre*, joins in the laughter against Panurge: 'voyant Panurge sans braguette, avecques ses lunettes attachées au bonnet, dist de luy à ses compaignons, "Voyez là une belle medaille de Coqu".'* (The 1552 version is virtually the same.) Dindenault picks out the suggestive thread that Panurge, in his comic fancy dress, already *looks* for all the world like a cuckold. But Panurge is still the witty, erotic non-cuckold knave, who leaves off the wearing of breeches that he may be more ready for unchastity, and can reply to Dindenault, 'Comment diable seroys je coqu, qui ne suis encores marié, comme tu es, scelon que juger je peuz à ta troigne mal gracieuse?'† To make the difference more striking between the merchant, who is married, and Panurge, who is still given to bawdy talk about women and his own virile and free state, the 1552 version omits in the next reply of Dindenault the word *braguettes* and makes him say, 'non pour toutes les bezicles d'Afrique'. Moreover, Dindenault announces that he has a stupendous wife and a marvellous marriage, 'j'ay une des plus belles, plus advenentes, plus honestes, plus prudes [the last adjective was not in the 1548 version] femmes en mariage ...'‡ The conceit of the merchant of Taillebourg in capturing this splendid bride is heavily ironical, for all the superlatives are turned exactly into their opposite by Panurge's reply. In the 1548 version he simply says, 'J'avoye biscoté ta femme ...' which is but a coarse verb; in the 1552 version he picks up the superlatives and couples them with a verb for sexual play coined by Panurge himself, 'si ... j'avoys sacsacbezevezinemassé ta tant belle, tant advenente, tant honeste, tant preude femme ...'§ And again in the 1552 version Panurge, instead of calling Dindenault a *braguetier*, says, 'Responds, o belinier de Mahumet ...'¶ Thus

---

* seeing Panurge without a Codpiece, with his Spectacles fastened to his Cap, said to one of his Comrades, Prithee look, is not there here a fine Medal of a Cuckold?

† How the Devil should I be one of the hornify'd Fraternity, since I am not yet a Brother of the Marriage-noose, as thou art, as I guess by thy ill-favour'd Phyz?

‡ for I have got me the cleverest, prettiest, handsomest, properest, neatest, tightest, honestest, and soberest piece of Woman's-Flesh for my Wife ...

§ if ... I had Gingumbob'd, Codpiec'd, and Thumpthumpriggledtickledtwidl'd thy so clever, so pretty, so handsom, so proper, so neat, so tight, so honest and so Sober Female Importance ...

¶ Answer me, O thou Ram of Mahomet.

one can see the created author in 1552 cutting out the sexual vocabulary in Dindenault's speech but patterning it and keeping it strictly in Panurge's own speech. Dindenault also has the same stylistic characteristics as the Olympian author; for example, 'Qu'en as tu à faire? Dequoy te meslez tu? Qui est tu? Dont es tu? O lunetier de l'Antichrist, responds si tu es de Dieu.'* This time, however, the author characterizes for his readers the abrupt, imperious, inflammable and condescending manner that the man adopts towards Panurge, so that he stands out rather more clearly from the narrative than did the *saiges femmes*. Then Panurge asks the merchant to sell him one of his sheep, and from there on there is much sales-talk on Dindenault's side. The language used is at once mocking and insulting; the style is rhetorical, his speech stuffed with encyclopaedic information; Dindenault is playing with language and with erudite allusions in much the same way as Panurge had praised codpieces in the *Tiers Livre*. For instance, 'Ce sont moutons à la grande laine, Jason y print la toison d'or. L'ordre de la maison de Bourguoigne en feut extraict. Moutons de Levant, moutons de haulte fustaye, moutons de haulte gresse.'† The allusions to mythology, and to the House of Burgundy rise in a lyrical crescendo and the repetition of '*moutons*' forms a kind of descant, almost a verse interlude;

> Moutons de Levant
> moutons de haulte fustaye
> moutons de haulte gresse.

(Note the similar words in the prologue to *Gargantua: ces beaulx livres de haulte gresse*.) This reminds us of the lyrical praise of the Decretals (*Quart Livre*, chapter 51), where Homenaz almost plainchants their eulogy,

> O seraphicque *Sixiesme*!
> O cherubicques *Clementines*!
> O *Extravaguantes* angelicques.

---

* What hast thou to do with it? What's that to thee? Who art thou? Whence comest thou, O dark Lantern of Antichrist? Answer if thou art of God?
† They are long Wool Sheep, from these did Jason take his Golden Fleece. [The Order of the Golden Fleece of Burgundy was drawn from them. D.C.] Zwoons, Man, they are Oriental Sheep, Topping Sheep, Fatted Sheep, Sheep of Quality.

In both cases, the rhetorical style, the sequence in which the words are arranged and the ordering of phrases make the tone clash with the meaning; the sentences rise upwards when one reads them aloud whilst the meaning is crashing downwards. In Dindenault's case one has sales-talk furnished with fantasy and poetry.

The dialogue (added newly in 1552) is racy, with Panurge replying in short, sharp phrases like *Voire* or *Il vous plaist à dire* and the merchant building up to his joke – the comparison of Panurge and one of his sheep – and his onomatopoeic imitation of the bleating of a sheep. This type of dialogue is common in Rabelais: for example, in the *Tiers Livre*, chapter 9, where Pantagruel echoes the conclusions of the highly rhetorical Panurge as he tries to decide about marriage, one finds

> Poinct doncques ne vous mariez, respondit Pantagruel.
> Voire mais (dist Panurge) ...
> Mariez-vous doncq, de par Dieu, respondit Pantagruel.
> Mais si (dist Panurge) ...
> Poinct doncques ne vous mariez (respondit Pantagruel) ...*

and so on. The repetitions, the rhetorical expounding of his problem, with the other merely agreeing – give a type of dialogue that is amusing to read, and Rabelais is skilful in its use wherever there is an opportunity.

The virtuosity of the talking is heightened as Dindenault tells Panurge with detailed splendour what the sheep's fleeces are made into, what their skin is transformed into and what their entrails are useful for; 'Des boyaulx, on fera chordes de violons et harpes, lesquelles tant cherement on vendra comme si feussent chordes de Munican ou Aquileie.'† Now this is highly rhetorical, with parallelisms of construction, hyperboles and bold striving after effect; furthermore, it is symmetrical with the previous sentences and there is a studied use of alliteration and assonance which almost intoxicates the reader. The exuberant luxuriance of the

---

* Quoth Pantagruel, Then do not marry.
  Yea, but (quoth Panurge) ...
  Then marry, in the name of God, quoth Pantagruel
  But if (quoth Panurge) ...
  Then do not marry (quoth Pantagruel).
† Of the Guts shall be made Fiddle and Harp Strings, that will sell as dear as if they came from Munican or Aquileia.

speech is the means by which the created author 'places' this picaresque figure: the content is very low – all the parts of a sheep, from its horns to its urine – but the form is incongruously high. The excessive ornament, the grandiloquence and artificiality of style steadily degenerate into bombast throughout the merchant's speech. Rabelais's fund of erudition becomes almost a parody of erudition in Dindenault: classical allusions, classical authorities for every little detail, the lore of medicine, alchemy, magic, are all thrown into the mixing bowl. For example, at the most dramatic moment, when Panurge has thrown the one sheep into the sea, there is a delightful mingling of the different styles and levels: it is impossible to keep all the other sheep from following the one who has plunged into the sea and the created author cites Aristotle, '*lib. 9. de Histo. animal*', to support the commonplace observation 'comme vous sçavez estre du mouton le naturel ... estre le plus sot et inepte animant du monde'.*
While the merchant is trying to save his flock he is 'noyé en pareille forme que les moutons de Polyphemus, le borgne Cyclope, emporterent hors la caverne Ulyxes et ses compaignons'.†
The mixture of levels is extremely comic. There is a mock-epic allusion to the incident in Ulysses' travels when Ulysses and his companions, having avenged themselves on the Cyclops by blinding him, outwit him by clinging to the bellies of his precious sheep as they go out of his cave. Dindenault's drowning, brought about by his own much-praised sheep, is Panurge's comparable revenge. Panurge pushes away the drowning men as they try to climb back into the ship and treats them all to a piece of sermonizing on the miseries of life in this world exactly like Olivier Maillard or 'un second frere Jan Bourgeoys'. This episode shows how far Rabelais can go with dialogue and dramatic skill: he gives both a *reductio ad absurdum* of the kind of sales-talk that we hear in a fair-ground or market and a parody of style which 'places' the merchant of Taillebourg.

* for you know that it is in the Nature of Sheep ... marks them for the most silly and foolish Animals in the World.
† drowned, in the same manner, as one-eyed Polyphemus's Sheep carried out of the Den Ulysses and his Companions ...

In these examples Rabelais's linguistic inventiveness is finely used to animate flat characters who are, in E. M. Forster's words, 'little luminous disks of a prearranged size, pushed hither and thither like counters across the void or between the stars'. The dynamism is manifest in the way in which the Olympian author controls the episode, parodies his own style – in the prologues, in characters like Homenaz and Dindenault, in encyclopaedic ramifications – and exploits rhetoric for comic effects. But when we come to frere Jan and Panurge, would they qualify for Forster's adjective 'round'? That is, can they surprise us in a convincing way? Forster would say that the book ought to have, 'the incalculability of life about it – life within the pages of a book'.[6] Frere Jan and Panurge display rich linguistic inventiveness as they move very swiftly through a series of adventures. No moral judgement is asked from the reader. For in a work which is controlled by an Olympian author, where burlesque cancels out seriousness in the creation of comic characters, one is not called upon to assess those characters as moral, immoral or amoral people. In a nineteenth-century novel we take pleasure in approving or disapproving the hero; we sympathize with the hero when he is suffering or we smile at him when he comes face to face with the incongruities of life. But our criterion of verisimilitude – whether this or that is possible in life – is not valid for either frere Jan or Panurge.

The formlessness of the work, and indeed the very presence of an Olympian author in the rôle of a Menippean satirist make it impossible to have heroes. Frere Jan and Panurge are much like anti-heroes, in the same way as Scarron's La Rancune is: 'Le comédien la Rancune, un des principaux héros de notre roman, *car il n'y aura pas pour un dans ce livre-ci* ...' (*Le roman comique*, pt. 1, chapter 5; the italics are mine.) Both characters respond to events in ways that are appropriate to the particular episode and may indeed reveal contradictory traits in their characters. By contrast with Swift or Voltaire there is in the delineation of these two characters a lack of moral concern and an artistic detachment from them – neither will be in any way mouth-pieces of the Menippean satirist. With Panurge and frere Jan the form of the

Menippean satire begins to look like a comic romance. Fielding offers a detailed definition of comic romance in the preface to *Joseph Andrews:*

Now, a comic romance is a comic epic poem in prose; differing from comedy, as the serious epic from tragedy: its action being more extended and comprehensive; containing a much larger circle of incidents, and introducing a greater variety of characters ... *it differs in its characters by introducing persons of inferior rank* ... whereas the grave romance sets the highest before us: lastly, *in its sentiments and diction*; by preserving the ludicrous instead of the *sublime*. In the diction, I think, *burlesque itself may be sometimes admitted;* of which many instances will occur in this work, as in the description of the battles, and some other places, *not necessary to be pointed out to the classical reader, for whose entertainment those parodies or burlesque imitations are chiefly calculated.*[7] (The italics are mine.)

Without venturing into an argument about Epic, Tragedy and History as conceived by Fielding, and without considering his whole theory of the Comic which is irrelevant to a French work (and perhaps to most English works), we may nevertheless take up several points from this definition. Firstly, parody: parodied battle-scenes assume a 'classical reader', that is, a cultured literate class who can appreciate the allusion to a Homeric or Vergilian original. Secondly, the characters are of inferior 'manners'; this is contrasted with the grave romance where the 'highest' people are there for us to admire. Thirdly, the diction must preserve the ludicrous. And finally, as opposed to serious epic, the grotesque framework of the whole fiction excludes any deep feeling or serious tragedy. In all these points we may see the kind of fiction that Rabelais was writing in terms of such characters as frere Jan and Panurge. Use of the term comic romance will define more sharply the two characters; and it will show how Rabelais went beyond the satiric plot and beyond the gigantic parodied framework with which he started, when he saw in the counterpoint of frere Jan and Panurge an anti-heroic theme.

Let us look first at the way they are introduced. Panurge, in chapter 9 of *Pantagruel* is presented alone (this is important, as we shall see) in the street as he meets Pantagruel and his henchmen, 'rencontra un homme beau de stature et elegant en tous lineamens du corps, mais pitoyablement navré en divers lieux, et tant mal en ordre qu'il sembloit estre eschappé es chiens, ou mieulx resembloit un cueilleur de pommes du païs du Perche'.* Panurge is a picaresque hero here: he is coming from marvellous adventures in Turkey, with all the outward appearance of having suffered, but he is still *elegant* and *beau de stature*. Pantagruel is attracted to him precisely for this reason; 'Par ma foy, il n'est pauvre que par fortune, car je vous asseure que, à sa physionomie, Nature l'a produict de riche et noble lignée ...'† The picaresque novels of the seventeenth and eighteenth centuries have exactly the same characteristic: a *picaro* who is handsome and who has in his features a touch of distinction. One has only to read Mateo Aleman's *Guzmán* or the opening scenes of Sorel's *Histoire Comique de Francion* to see this. For instance, Francion meets a gentleman who falls for 'sa bonne mine ... où il esclattoit je ne sçay quoy de noble et de non vulgaire estoit un charme qui l'avoit invité a luy faire un nombre infini d'offres de son service' (Pléiade edition, *Romanciers du XVIIe siècle*, p. 93). And so the appearance of a noble *enfant terrible* with whom Pantagruel 'falls in love' need cause no surprise.

Nevertheless I am really taking this picaresqueness rather superficially. For the first Spanish picaresque novel *Lazarillo de Tormes* was not published until 1554 – after even the *Quart Livre* – though some scholars argue that it was probably written around 1525. It creates a new way of writing fiction: Lazarillo, existing permanently on the bread-line, has nothing to offer but himself – *aquí estoy yo*. The novel is an anti-heroic reaction to all the *gesta*, chivalric novels and pastoral romances, and the readers are made to participate in the story where they 'vean que vive un hombre con tantas fortunas, peligros y adversidades ...' Its form is autobiographical; and we are invited to see the events entirely from the viewpoint of Lazarillo himself. Nowhere is Panurge like

---

* he met with a young man of very comely stature, and surpassing handsome in all the lineaments of his body, but in several parts thereof most pitifully wounded; in such bad equipage in matter of his apparel, which was but tatters and rags, and every way so far out of order, that he seemed to have been a fighting with mastiffe-dogs, from whose fury he had made an escape, or, to say better, he looked in the condition wherein he then was, like an Apple-gatherer of the countrey of Perche.

† By my faith, he is only poor in fortune; for I may assure you, that by his Physiognomie it appeareth, that nature hath extracted him from some rich and noble race ...

Lazarillo. For one thing he is utterly non-realistic – which in a picaresque novel would be fatal, for it is precisely the conflict between the individual and society that marks it out as a novel. For another thing, Panurge does not pass from a poorer master to one a little more rich, revealing all the time that he is cleverer and more guileful than either of them. Yet one facet of Panurge's presentation is picaresque: this clever knave is both intelligent and witty; he can talk well, drink well, eat well, and in the first encounter with Pantagruel the two weave a pattern of comedy around each other.

Panurge immediately launches into various languages, some of them real, some non-existent, with no other practical purpose than to have fun at the expense of the company around the giant. In all the languages his discourse turns around two topics: he is starving and he is dying of thirst. Ravaging hunger and thirst is part of the lot of the picaresque hero in Spanish literature; for instance, in the first chapter of *Lazarillo de Tormes*, the first encounter between Lazarillo and the blind man, the *picaro* steals bread which in his hunger he promptly devours. And food becomes the common trait between Panurge and frere Jan. Panurge gratuitously plays with all the possibilities of language, the absurdities and the paradoxes, before finally turning to French. By speaking in Italian, Basque, Danish, Hebrew and so on, this *enfant terrible* produces a comic reductive parody of rhetoric and language which is very funny. Incidentally, the created author slyly puts into his mouth a dig at those people who think that Touraine is the home of good French, 'C'est ma langue naturelle et maternelle, car je suis né et ay esté nourry jeune au jardin de France, c'est Touraine.'*

Pantagruel also is brought to life, not as a fully rounded character in the manner of a nineteenth-century novel, but as a necessary genial companion to Panurge. For here he has a comic guise: he wants to help, and so asks a series of ordinary straightforward questions – but the answers are not answers to the questions at all and the giant is only there to act as a sparring partner for Panurge.

* It is my natural language and mother tongue, for I was borne and bred in my younger yeares in the garden of France, to wit, Touraine.

For instance, Pantagruel replies after Panurge has treated him to a speech in German, 'Mon amy, je n'entens poinct ce barragouin; pour tant, si voulez qu'on vous entende, parlez aultre langaige.'* And Panurge immediately starts speaking a non-existent language. The other members of the company chip in with their own views about which language Panurge is talking now, and the scene becomes a kind of dance around the *picaro*. Pantagruel, at the end of this encounter, remains as he was at the beginning, and the created author gives him a mock-epic allusion to the friendship between Aeneas and Achates to drive the point home, 'je vous ay ja prins en amour si grand que, si vous condescendez à mon vouloir, vous ne bougerez jamais de ma compaignie, et vous et moy ferons un nouveau pair d'amitié telle que feut entre Enée et Achates'.† Here you see the beginning of Pantagruel's feeling for Panurge, compounded of tolerance, gaity and delight in such a likeable rogue; Pantagruel will preserve it throughout the four books. On Panurge's side we see the rhetorical inventiveness and comic gratuitousness, which will develop wherever an episode calls for such qualities to appear. The language game that Panurge is playing changes the tone of the book: before, it had the shape of epic parody; now it has the beginnings of comedy. The guessing game that everyone indulges in sets the stage for similar episodes to come.

Let us turn now to the entry on stage of the second comic character – frere Jan in *Gargantua*. The scene is chapter 27, the siege of Seuillé, the abbey where we are about to meet frere Jan. The created author has already, before the opening of the chapter, indicated the activities of Picrochole's army by means of a vast enumeration of verbs, present participles, nouns and adjectives:

(the enemy) prindrent les champs les uns parmy les aultres, gastans et dissipans tout ... emmenoient beufz, vaches, thoreaux, veaulz, genisses, brebis, moutons, chevres et boucqs, poulles, chappons, poulletz, oysons, jards, oyes, porcs, truyes, guoretz; abastans les noix, vendeangeans les vignes, emportans les seps, croullans tous les fruictz des arbres. C'estoit un desordre incomparable ...‡

* My friend ... I have no skill in that gibberish of yours; therefore if you would have us to understand you, speak to us in some other language.
† I have already stamped in my minde such a deep impression of love towards you, that, if you will condescend unto my will, you shall not depart out of my company, and you and I shall make up another couple of friends, such as Aeneas and Achates were.
‡ they took the fields one amongst another, wasting, spoiling, destroying and making

The style here reminds one of Burton's *The Anatomy of Melancholy* where everything is thrown in together – nouns, participles, verbs and adjectives – to end in a rhetorical climax. There is a brisk rhythm here, an unlimited vocabulary and a drive towards the exhaustive catalogue. Verbs range indiscriminately over present participles, past historic and imperfect. The use of the past tenses was unsettled at this time, so one must not be over-subtle about these shifts between the imperfect and past historic. Yet one is aware of a tendency towards long sentences, made up of short phrases or words expressing the movement of thought. It is opposed to Latin style in that it tends to take one along a linear movement instead of seeing a sentence as a balanced structure, built up from clause to clause.

The beginning of chapter 27 is in the same style. Its exuberance derives from the accumulation of verbs, each item springing forward naturally, and from an ebullience of language which enacts the activity of the army. The Olympian author suddenly intervenes in the present tense, 'Dont vient cela, Messieurs? Pensez y, je vous pry.' A sentence which makes us see the satirical contrast between all the apothecaries, doctors and priests who caught the plague and the army which escaped unhurt. This prepares us for the robot-like action of all the monks in the monastery who, 'A toutes adventures feirent sonner *ad capitulum capitulantes*. Là feut decreté qu'ilz feroient une belle procession, renforcée de beaulx preschans, et letanies *contra hostium insidias*, et beaulx responds *pro pace*.'* In contrast to the flurry of activity that we have been led through by the army here one has the juxtaposition between the normal reaction to a siege and that of the monks: action is impossible to them, their training has fixed them in a rigid rut; their only reaction is to offer Latin phrases and this in itself removes any

havock ... drove away oxen and cowes, bulls, caves, heifers, wethers, ewes, lambs, goats, kids, hens, capons, chickens, geese, ganders, goslings, hogs, swine, pigs and such like. Beating down the walnuts, plucking the grapes, tearing the hedges, shaking the fruit-trees, and committing such incomparable abuses, that the like abomination was never heard of.

* At all adventures they rang the bells *ad capitulum capitulantes*: there it was decreed, that they should make a faire Procession, stuffed with good lectures, prayers and letanies, *contra hostium insidias*, and jollie responses *pro pace*.

possible sympathy one might have for them and leaves room for nothing but laughter.

Whereas Panurge was brought into the spotlight alone in a Parisian street, with no external preparation at all, frere Jan is introduced within this comic and satirical framework. He is presented thus: 'En l'abbaye estoit pour lors un moine claustrier, nommé Frere Jean des Entommeures, jeune, guallant, frisque, de hayt, bien à dextre, hardy, adventureux, deliberé, hault, maigre, bien fendu de gueule, bien advantaigé en nez, beau despescheur d'heures, beau desbrideur de messes, beau descroteur de vigiles...'* One feels the extreme vigour and joy in the adjectives which describe frere Jan, in the number of descriptive words and the absence of any conjunctions. The accumulation of adjectives and present participles moves us very rapidly from the purely physical and exuberant to the moral qualities of the monk. Paradoxical and unexpected combinations of words are directed at the habits of the clergy, for instance *'beau despescheur d'heures'* where the effect depends on the combination of disparate elements – the very robust and physical *'despescheur'* with the liturgical *'heures'*, which Urquhart has rendered into English as 'morning prayers'. The incongruity which is the basis of humour here refers back to the other monks who were not like this frere Jan. Later on he is described as, 'pour tout dire sommairement vray moyne si oncques en feut depuys que le monde moynant moyna de moynerie...'† This sentence is ridiculous; partly because the conditional clause cancels out the first part of the sentence and partly because it is fundamentally a play on words in which the created author uses *'moyne'* as a present participle, past historic and a noun.

From the lively character sketch one moves to the framework again – so that frere Jan stands out more strongly against the background of the other monks. The language he uses is racy, scattered inconsequentially with bad Latin (or rather with bits of

---

* There was then in the Abbey a claustral Monk, called Freer Jhon of the funnels and gobbets, in French *des entoumeures*, young, gallant, frisk, lustie, nimble, quick, active, bold, adventurous, resolute, tall, lean, wide-mouthed, long-nosed, a faire dispatcher of morning prayers, unbridler of masses, and runner over of vigils.

† to conclude summarily in a word, a right Monk, if ever there was any, since the Monking world monked a Monkerie ...

Latin mingled with French as for instance, *Seigneur Dieu, da mihi potum*), with swearings and oaths and abundant puns. To frere Jan there is one thing that is important in this invasion: saving the vineyard. His reaction is grotesque and contrasts with the other grotesque – the singing of chants and the muttering of masses. We suspect at once that the interesting thing about frere Jan will be how unlike a monk he is: this discrepancy between one's normal view of a monk and this original character is going to be one of the traits that make him burlesquely comic and also make us forget the satirical traits if the episode does not call for them to be displayed. The satirical traits are only the buttresses of a character who is created individually as a comic character. We accept all his gestures with detachment as a piece of fiction, responding appropriately to the medical humour, to the scatological turns of phrase and to the great love of eating and drinking that make him an ideal companion to Panurge. In both characters obscenity and vulgarity are always present: it is the simplest way of making readers laugh.

Just as Panurge in *Pantagruel* is treated in the war as a heroi-comic figure (e.g. in chapter 26 in the enemy's camp there were *150,000 putains, belles comme deesses* ... to which Panurge straightforwardly says *Voylà pour moy*) so also is frere Jan throughout the battles of *Gargantua*. For example, in chapter 44, we see frere Jan standing on the rock, brandishing a stout short-sword and laying low any one who comes near him. The burlesque level consists of the marvellous single-handed slaughter of hundreds from the other side; the discrepancy is between the normal attitude towards the killing of human beings and the abnormal, in this case the medical, in which human bodies become inanimate objects or animals. When frere Jan kills the guard one's normal reaction would be revulsion at such a cruel act, but the medical terminology forces the emotion out. Frere Jan has killed him with his sword, and immediately the created author provides us with a startling angle of vision: 'luy coupant entierement les venes jugulaires et arteres spagitides du col, avecques le guarguareon, jusques es deux adenes, et, retirant le coup, luy entreouvrit le mouelle spinale entre la seconde et tierce vertebre: là tomba

l'archier tout mort.'* We are made indifferent to the fact that
these are human beings because the massacre is related in this
technical vocabulary – and this is an essential part of the comedy
of both frere Jan and Panurge. Frere Jan's sentiments and diction
are both ludicrous: his love of punning and his schoolboyish
jokes turn this scene into a burlesque comedy. For instance, the
other guard, who has just witnessed the killing and desperately
calls out to frere Jan 'Ha, Monsieur le Priour, je me rendz!
Monsieur le Priour, mon bon amy, Monsieur le Priour!'† gets a
rapid answer: 'Monsieur le Posteriour, mon amy, Monsieur le
Posteriour, vous aurez sus voz posteres'.‡ Or later on in the same
repartee, frere Jan promises to make the man a cardinal; again the
technical terminology forms our response:

Lors d'un coup luy tranchit la teste, luy coupant le test sus les os petrux, et
enlevant les deux os bregmatis et la commissure sagittale avecques grande
partie de l'os coronal, ce que faisant luy tranchit les deux meninges et ouvrit
profondement les deux posterieurs ventricules du cerveau; et demoura le
craine pendent sus les espaules à la peau du pericrane par derriere, en forme d'un
bonnet doctoral, noir par dessus, rouge par dedans.§

The doctor's hood conceit is brilliant: the horror is increased by
the aptness but cancelled by the unexpectedness. One has the
clash of sublime and grotesque in the angle of vision and instead of
smirking at the 'grisly sick joke' one laughs at a complex and
subtle joke. In the first two books one is seeing both frere Jan and

* he cut clean thorough the jugularie veins, and the sphagitid or transparent arteries of the
  neck, with the fore-part of the throat called the gargareon, even unto the two Adenes,
  which are throat kernels; and redoubling the blow, he opened the spinal marrow betwixt
  the second and third verteber; there fell down that keeper stark dead to the ground.
† Ha, my Lord Prior, quarter, I yeeld, my Lord Prior, quarter, quarter, my good friend,
  my Lord Prior.
‡ My Lord Posterior, my friend, my Lord Posterior, you shall have it upon your pos-
  teriorums.
§ Then at one stroak he cut off his head, cutting his scalp upon the temple-bones, and
  lifting up in the upper part of the scul the two triangularie bones called sincipital, or the
  two bones bregmatis, together with the sagittal commissure or dart-like seame which
  distinguisheth the right side of the head from the left, as also a great part of the coronal or
  forehead-bone, by which terrible blow likewise he cut the two meninges or filmes
  which inwrap the braine, and made a deep wound in the braine's two posterior ven-
  tricles, and the cranium or skull abode hanging upon his shoulders by the skin of the
  pericranium behinde, in forme of a Doctors bonnet, black without and red within.

Panurge as heroi-comic figures and the rest of humanity as a kind of puppet-show: men enter and disappear, their rôle is mechanical and at no stage does one identify oneself emotionally with any of them. There is no room for pity.

Both of these characters have a syntactically dynamic language which creates amusement. To see this in detail, let us take one scene with frere Jan: chapter 39 of *Gargantua*, where there is a respite from warring and the whole company repair to Grandgousier's castle for a banquet. There is a hearty welcome from Grandgousier and later from Gargantua for this fine fighter. Frere Jan settles himself down to drink but will not discard his monkish garb. He starts talking; in this little monologue the structure is entirely paratactic. Sentences are fairly short like, 'Davantaige, je n'auray nul appetit'.* The link between them, though clear, is far from logical or even coherent – for example, *la cuisse d'une nonnain* seems to be the subject of a new sentence but it is followed by, 'N'est ce falotement mourir quand on meurt le caiche roidde.'† The next sentence is 'Nostre prieur ayme fort le blanc de chappon'.‡ Here one has an ellipsis of thought. Frere Jan is letting out all his physical and indeed sexual preoccupations within a spoken framework of religion. The juxtaposition of a nun's thighs with his religious superior and the white of a capon is startling and suggestive, and a quick dialogue with Gymnaste brings him back to his main subject. '... les cuisses d'une damoizelle sont tousjours fraisches ...'§ – this is the problem that he will be going into. All his linguistic training is to be applied to a subject which is incongruously low and vulgar. He parodies the scholastic way of arguing: *primo, secundo et tiercement* and we laugh not only at the incongruous mingling of the two languages but also at the clash between the form and its content. All three reasons are so absurd that frere Jan expects to have to pause while the whole company bursts into thunderous laughter; there follows the noise of drink being poured ... *Crac, crac, crac* ... and a

* And, which is worse, I shall lose my appetite ...
† the thigh of a Nunne. Doth not he die like a good fellow that dies with a stiffe catso?
‡ Our Prior loves exceedingly the white of a capon.
§ the thighs of a gentlewoman are alwayse fresh and coole ...

further pause while everyone drinks some wine. The three dots which the created author puts in occur throughout the chapter and indicate the pauses for drinking.

His next topic of conversation has no links at all with the previous one; his thinking is lively but the content is half-digested and his language is a mixture of habit, of monastic training and a traditional *gaulois* attitude: thus, his training prompts him automatically to make allusions to Scripture, and to use the Latin language, but his lively nature makes the juxtaposition of earthy and scriptural language extremely funny, 'Diavol! il n'y plus de moust: *germinavit radix Jesse*', the tree of Jesse (Isa. xi. 1) together with the half-fermented wine. All the remarks that are scattered in this monologue are either parodies of theologians or mixtures of clerical bad Latin and hardly better French, 'Par Dieu, Monsieur mon amy, *magis magnos clericos non sunt magis magnos sapientes*.'

This kind of monologue, interrupted by pauses for drinking, is inconsequential artistry on the created author's part. For here we have language used to express the process of half-thought in frere Jan; this is removed from the process of thought and far removed from the logical word-order of achieved thought. Rabelais is deliberately and skilfully evoking the atmosphere of a drinking party. The monologue hops about from subject to subject – from topical allusions, like the soldiers fleeing from the battle of Pavia, to Biblical anecdotes. Frere Jan brings in all these remarks as casually and inconsequentially as any man holding forth to a group of tippling companions. At the end of the episode one has the whole scene summed up by Eudemon, 'Foy de christian ... je entre en grande resverie, considerant l'honnesteté de ce moyne, car il nous esbaudist icy tous.'* This use of language is interesting: first, because it is a parody of the sermonists like Menot and Maillard, whose works were printed in a mixture of French and Latin as a kind of manual for less intelligent and witty sermonists than themselves, and secondly, it is consonant with the character that the created author has presented us with.

---

* By the faith of a Christian ... I do wonderfully dote, and enter in a great extasie, when I consider the honesty and good fellowship of this Monk; for he makes us here all merry.

Grandgousier and Gargantua are vastly impressed by this monk and it is with great delight that he sets forth as a marvellous anti-hero for the next few episodes. Rabelais revels in his account of frere Jan – whether it is the ironic way he uses the *couleurs de rethoricque Ciceroniane* or his way of proving to everyone what activity, industry, bravery and boldness he is capable of; there is never a moment in *Gargantua* when his tongue is not wagging. As part of this characterization Rabelais has given frere Jan certain features which will accompany him throughout the next two books: his love of wine, his courage and bravery, a certain robust coarseness as regards all the physical things in everyday life, an idiolect which is a mixture of Latin and racy French, an indulgence in vigorous action and a *joie de vivre*, as well as traditional monkishness.

Panurge, on the fictional level, is less well developed than frere Jan. He is fragmentary and disorganized in the first book: for example, he becomes a burlesque idealized hero when he is included in the marvellous lineage that makes him a heroi–epic figure in the battles. Yet there are signs of what he is to become in the *Tiers Livre*. He is presented alone, whilst frere Jan is set against the backcloth of other monks, their habits, their training, their gluttony and their indolence. And Panurge is close to the giant, so that when Pantagruel is in a tight spot during the war, his immediate thought is *Ha, Panurge, où es tu?*

We have already seen something of Panurge's comic rôle in the *Tiers Livre* and we need only stop briefly to look at some of his actions in the book. First of all, he carries on the 'diabolology' that was characteristic of him in *Pantagruel*, both in the oaths and swear words he uses and in the content of his talk: so that in chapter 17 of the *Tiers Livre* with its grotesque sibyl, the thought of the devils and the Underworld is enough to make him say, 'O les laydes bestes! Fuyons. Serpe Dieu, je meurs de paour. Je n'ayme poinct les diables. Ilz me faschent, et sont mal plaisans. Fuyons.'* The way that Panurge is obsessed by devils (cf. the consultation with Raminagrobis) is yet another mark of the fear he exhibits through-

---

* The Devils are breaking loose to be all here. O the foul, ugly and deformed Beasts! Let us run away! By the Hook of God, I am like to die for fear! I do not love the Devils; they vex me, and are unpleasant Fellows. Now let us fly, and betake us to our heels.

out the book – a fear which becomes sexual in the *Tiers Livre*, where he himself confesses that he fears impotence (chapter 9) – but which by the *Quart Livre* has broadened out to include almost every possible danger. Secondly, he shows the same fondness for quick witty sayings, and this love of talking becomes extended and the comic aspect is deepened. Rhetoric does not concern itself with the communication of truth but with persuasion, and Panurge's fondness for rhetorical technique dehumanizes him by reducing him to the level of a physically determined mechanism. But his linguistic inventiveness wins our sympathy and so makes him a living anti-hero in the book. When he says that in his book of life there appear only men, 'Je ne bastis que pierres vives, ce sont hommes'*, we think at first that this is nothing but a play on words, another instance of his linguistic talent and therefore not to be taken too seriously; yet we see that it is a part of his very life: men, the company of men, are essential to him, for without them his talk is nothing. Nevertheless, as a fool he is isolated from the rest of mankind. When he is providing the counterpoint with frere Jan in the *Tiers Livre* it is the physical aspect of life that is their main concern. Eating, drinking, making war were what interested frere Jan, so it is no surprise to find something like, 'Fiantoient aux fiantouoirs, pissoient aux pissouoirs, crachoient aux crachoirs, toussoient aux toussouoirs melodieusement, resvoient aux resvoirs, affin de rien immonde ne porter au service divin'† (chapter 15). He starts with the familiar and real, and ends up playing on words, with the fantastic '*resvoient*' and '*resvoirs*'. He amuses the company by syllogizing, for instance, 'Plus matin se levans, par la dicte caballe, plus tost estoit le beuf au feu; plus y estant, plus cuict restoit; plus cuict restant, plus tendre estoit, moins usoit les dens, plus delectoit le palat, moins grevoit le stomach, plus nourrissoit les bons religieux'‡ (chapter 15). He is

---

* It is all with Live Stones that I set up and erect the Fabricks of my Architecture, to wit, Men.

† They dunged in the Dungeries, pissed in the Pisseries, spit in the Spitteries, melodiously coughed in the Cougheries, and doted in their Doteries, that to the Divine Service they might not bring any thing that was unclean or foul.

‡ The more betimes they rose by the said Cabal, the sooner was the Beef Pot put on; the longer that the Beef was on the Fire, the better it was boiled; the more it boiled, it was the tenderer; the tenderer that it was, the less it troubled the Teeth, delighted more the

mon amy to Panurge, who calls him, at the end of this speech, *couillon velouté, couillon claustral et cabalicque*, and one can see that gastronomy is one of the links between frere Jan and Panurge and traditional obscenity. Leitmotifs like Panurge's fear of devils, his promises to the Lord Almighty, to whom he offers altars, chapels and religious ceremonies, his persistent light-hearted accusations of frere Jan and his exhibitionism weave in and out through the whole of the *Tiers Livre* and *Quart Livre*. Frere Jan likes him – *Car je t'aime du bon du foye* (*Tiers Livre*, chapter 21) – and enjoys his company because he is such fun. Both together involve the reader in laughter and in an appreciation of the physical sides of human nature. We enjoy the playing with words like *praedestiné*, the slanging match of obscene names, the quips about Panurge's age and physical adequacy, the parodied bits of the Bible that come from both frere Jan and Panurge and traditional tales like the story of the ring of Hans Carvel.

When we turn to the *Quart Livre*, the organization of the comic is increasingly taken over by these two characters. In the great social scenes of this book, such as the island of Ennasin, the island of the Papimanes and the adventures with the Andouilles, frere Jan and Panurge are characters about whom the reader already knows everything. Thus when frere Jan disappears into the kitchens of Panigon or of the Andouilles we already know that such behaviour is typical of him; when Panurge asks Pantagruel *Et quand boyrez vous?*, or is terrified at the storm over the sea, we know again that such acts are typical of him. We expect episodes like the heroi–comic battle of the Andouilles to show us the burlesque figure of frere Jan and in the same way we are not surprised at the joke that the company play on Panurge in the last two chapters. We expect Panurge to make excuses for frere Jan's absence from the company (e.g. chapter 10, *ne sçavoit comment l'excuser*) and we expect that frere Jan will enjoy the debate between Dindenault and Panurge – he already knows that Panurge has something up his sleeve, and sits back waiting for the joke. When frere Jan speaks, we expect his language to be the same as it

Palate, less charged the Stomach, and nourished our good Religious Men the more substantially.

163

was at our first meeting with him: so that, for instance, when he
ends a speech in chapter 10

Vertuz Dieu, *da jurandi*, pourquoy plus toust ne transportons nous nos humani-
tez en belle cuisine de Dieu? Et là ne consyderons le branslement des broches,
l'harmonie des contrehastiers, la position des lardons, la temperature des
potaiges, les preparatifz du dessert, l'ordre du service du vin? *Beati immaculati in
via.* C'est matiere de breviaire*

we recognize the same manner as in his speeches in *Gargantua*.

In the storm at sea episode (chapters 18–23) we can see frere Jan
and Panurge performing in all their glory. All the characteristic
elements in the counterpoint of the two comic characters are
there in intensified form. For example, frere Jan's leitmotif is still
the old cuckold–booby of a Panurge that he jested about in the
Tiers Livre: here he calls upon devils to come and punish this
wretch, 'Mille diables ... saultent on corps de ce coqu ...'† and
later on, 'si encores je te oy pioller, coqu au diable, je te gualleray
en loup marin ...'‡ On the other side the grotesque aspect of
Panurge is brought out sharply in the 1552 version by an addition
to the number of gifts he throws to the monks whom he sees at
the beginning (chapter 18): the *seze douzaines de jambons* of the
1548 version[8] become exaggeratedly, 'soixante et dix-huict douzaines de jambons, nombre de caviatz, dizaines de cervelatz,
centaines de boutargues ...'§ Throughout all the consultations in
the *Tiers Livre* he has always been ready to offer the consultant
grotesque gifts of material things (cf. the gifts to the sibyl, to
Nazdecabre and to Rondibilis). Later he is to call to mind this
encounter when the storm is raging, envying those *bons et béatz
Concilipetes*. Rabelais is metamorphosing his comic fool a further

---

* Ods-fish, *da jurandi*, why do not we rather remove our Humanities into some good
warm Kitchen of God, that noble Laboratory? and there admire the turning of the Spits,
the harmonious rattling of the Jacks and Fenders, criticize on the position of the Lard,
the Temperature of the Potages, the preparation for the dessert, and the order of the
Wine-service? *Beati Immaculati in via*, matter of Breviary, my Masters.
† A thousand Devils seize the Cuckoldy Cow-hearted Mungril ...
‡ if I hear thee again howling, thou Cuckoldly Cur, I'll maul thee worse than any Sea-
Wolf.
§ seventy eight dozen of Westphalia Hams, Unites of Pots of Caviar, Tens of Bolonia
Sawsages, Hundreds of Botargoes ...

stage beyond the *Tiers Livre* until he becomes the one who does
not act when the danger is upon him but is able, once the danger
has passed, to pick up the remnants of himself through his rhetoric
and language play and so sail through to the next incident as if
nothing had happened. His rhetoric in this episode can be illustrated by the fusion of classical and religious allusions: 'O que
troys et quatre foys heureulx sont ceulx qui plantent chous! O
Parces, que ne me fillastes vous pour planteur de chous! O que
petit est le nombre de ceulx à qui Juppiter a telle faveur porté
qu'il les a destinez à planter chous'* (chapter 18). The passage
starts with a parody of Vergil (which he had used before in the
Tiers Livre, chapter 4) *Aeneid* i. 94 – *O terque quaterque beati*,
coupled incongruously with a bathetic illustration – planting cabbages. This leads Panurge into a rhetorical display of the same
kind as his splendid praise of debts. He associates cabbage planters
with epic heroes, and then twists an *Apophthegma* of Plutarch to
suit his own purpose; the lofty style, full of exclamations and
lengthy sentences, and the incongruous application of mythology
to cattle and swine – both sufficient to delight his readers and at
the same time make them aware that this love of talking does not
lead anywhere. The end of the parodic speech, 'Ha! pour manoir
deificque et seigneurial, il n'est que le plancher des vaches',† is set
side by side with, *Ceste vague nous emportera, Dieu servateur*.‡
Intellectually we can enjoy this rhetoric and the grotesquely comical character of Panurge himself though we see that all he is
saying merely springs from the superstitious side of his nature. The
burlesque comedy between the two characters is excellently
managed: we know roughly what each is going to say, the general
level of the talk and the language that they will use. Thus for
example, the scatological vocabulary which is characteristic of
both, the jesting of Panurge – for example in 'nous sommes au
dessus de Ela, au dessus de toute la Game. Be be be bous bous.
Jarus. A ceste heure sommes nous au dessoubz de Gamma ut: Je

* O twice and thrice happy those that plant Cabbages! O Destinies, why did you not Spin
me for a Cabbage Planter? O how few are they to whom Jupiter hath been so favourable
as to predestinate them to plant Cabbage!
† Hah, for a Divine and Princely Habitation, commend me to the Cows Floor.
‡ Murthur! This Wave will sweep us away, blessed Saviour!

naye'* (1548 edition) and the joking about cuckoldry of frere Jan. Panurge's talk is characteristically full of references to frere Jan's guilt, constant allusions and vows to the good Lord who is going to save him, parody of Biblical phrases and swearwords.

After the two serious interventions from Pantagruel and Jamet Brahier, Panurge talks about making *quelque bon et beau veu* and we are off again on the familiar grotesque dialogue between frere Jan and Panurge. This is in fact another 1552 addition, and is in character with frere Jan, 'Acappaye, acappaye. Beuvons hau! Je diz du meilleur et plus stomachal. Entendez vous, hault, majour dome, produisez, exhibez. Aussi bien s'en va cecy à tous les millions de Diables. Apporte cy, hau, page, mon tirouoir (ainsi nommait il son breviaire).'† In other words, it reminds one of the great talking and drinking scene of *Gargantua*, chapter 39, where frere Jan keeps the whole company amused by his illogical rhetoric and his references to the *matiere de breviaire*. There is the same skipping from subject to subject and the same mixture of cooking, God, drinking, and everyday anecdotes, and the same elliptical leaps from one to the other. There is no danger of identifying frere Jan with the shipload of monks whom the company met at the beginning of the episode or of associating him with the satirical remarks that Rabelais makes against monkishness. The apparently inconsequential remarks of frere Jan are beautifully done: in the middle of shouts to the sailors to haul away, he can only think of wine and of All Saints' Day!

This development of frere Jan and Panurge as burlesque comic characters suggests that the Olympian author has in fact turned to comic romance. The sketchy realism that the Menippean satirist aims at is now subordinated to a fuller sympathy and to an eager interest in what is going to happen next to such creative characters. Thus the episode of the storm at sea cannot be regarded simply as an allegory, philosophical or otherwise, in which characters are

---

* we are above *Ela*. Above the pitch, out of Tune, and off the Hinges. Be, be, be, bou, bous. Alas! we are now above G *sol re ut*. I sink ...

† Let her drive, for the Lord's sake unhang the Rudder, hoh, let her drive, let her drive, and let us drink, I say of the best and most cheering, d'ye hear Steward, produce, exhibit, for d'ye see this, and all the rest will as well go to the Devil out of hand. A Pox on that Wind-broaker Aeolus with his Fluster-blusters, Sirrah, Page, bring me here my Drawer (for so he call'd his Breviary) ...

stripped down to their essential traits. The command of language which Rabelais always has is projected into dialogue between two characters of greater substance; and we can now link the appearance of frere Jan and Panurge in this *Quart Livre* to their previous entries in the other three books. There is no real development of them as characters at all, but there is a sense in which they have taken on flesh and blood, and now control the structure. The anecdotal and digressive expertise of the Olympian author is put into the hands of frere Jan and Panurge to a large extent: stylistically, they hardly ever use hypotactic structure (except to parody it); and they hardly ever run to periods. From the point of view of the reader, the gaiety, fun and rich texture of the narrative all spring from these two characters and the way they can create humorous incongruity by the unexpected exploitation of scenes or episodes in a nonsensical way. Admiration for the positive qualities of frere Jan permeates the whole of the *Quart Livre*. His courage and efficiency are at the opposite end of the scale to Panurge: since Panurge's maturation as a comic character in the *Tiers Livre* he is in a constant state of fear, but his linguistic exuberance makes him always *sympathique* to the reader.

Nevertheless the form is still that of Menippean satire: the narrative is disjointed and if the book were to be called a comic romance, one would have to forget all the parts that are not controlled by frere Jan and Panurge. What is more, the verse interludes, the wavering between different kinds of parody even in the *Quart Livre* (e.g. the battle of the Andouilles where the heroi-comical frere Jan plays exactly the same rôle as he did in *Gargantua*) and the satirical sorties against Neo-Platonism make us very hesitant to call the *Quart Livre* anything but a Menippean satire. Because of the appropriate looseness of the form, because of the comparative freedom it offered in terms of structure, theme and characters, and because Rabelais adapted it for his own use, what one can see, above all, is that the Olympian author is in complete control of all the books. In the last analysis both Panurge and frere Jan, despite a certain degree of near-independent life, are still seen as characters who are the unwitting butts of the Olympian author's gentle ridicule.

8

THE GIANTS

The creation of Grandgousier, Gargantua and Pantagruel is the axis, the imaginary straight line, about which Rabelais as a Menippean satirist revolves. It is here that one can bring together Rabelais the real man and Rabelais the creative author. For now the distinction between fiction and non-fiction fades away: the fictional world, which we have been discussing till now, fashioned by invention, becomes transmuted to the non-fictional world in the characters of the giants. These gigantic figures are permeated with the metaphysical, philosophical, moral and sociological assumptions that a writer like Rabelais would be making. For instance, the personal attitude to institutional religion, the satire on hypocrisy and superstition, the attacks on pedantic dogmatism, the abstract categorizing of human beings and the intellectual deductions are ultimately the real man Rabelais's attitudes. At the same time, the *joie de vivre* – that emphasis on exhilaration and merriment which is so marked a characteristic of Rabelais – permeates the giants and their world: the banquets they hold at every possible occasion, the drink which flows freely for their followers, the gay conversations in which ancient authorities are set side by side with everyday topics, the excitement and thirst for knowledge, the affirmation of violent activity and the sheer delight of the senses. What we shall analyse is the question of the convergence of two themes – the fictional and the non-fictional – which build up the main components of Rabelais's world.

The *credo* of the giants is well-known: Grandgousier, the first generation, is a simple Christian, devoted to prayer and faith in an omnipotent and creative God, with the leitmotif *fiat voluntas tua* always in his heart; he is also a good feudal lord. Gargantua, the second generation, has his father's views on Christian charity, benevolence and prayer, but has new views on education and the need for moderation in philosophy. He joins in the Erasmian anti-clericalism that was current at the time. The last generation is Pantagruel who changes from an adolescent warrior to a hero of

Stoic and scriptural spirit. These are roughly schematized in the giants and yet, from the beginning, these serious aspects produce a certain unease when set in a gigantic framework. Whereas Cervantes's Don Quixote gradually becomes a character whose preposterous deeds excite in the reader a loving reprobation, the question arises with the personalities of Rabelais's giants, do they merely become mouthpieces of the real man as Candide does? Do they make any impact on the reader as fictional characters or are they merely cardboard figures who are used rather abstractly and schematically by Rabelais in a Menippean satire?

We shall examine the giants in their generations and shall, by exploring the texture of this thick narrative, attempt to discover whether it is possible to reconcile the separate shapes assigned to them by the created author.

Grandfather Grandgousier is introduced in chapter 3 of *Gargantua* as a *bon raillard en son temps* who loves his victuals. The reader's interest is already quickened by the comic juxtaposition of the real and the gigantic: the giant has everything in excess, yet it is real and delicious, '*bonne munition* de ... *force* langues de beuf ... *abondance* de andouilles ... *renfort* de boutargues, *provision* de saulcisses ...'* (The italics are mine.) The reader shares with the Olympian author the intellectual pleasure of Grandgousier's marriage to Gargamelle, the pregnancy scene, the sudden bursts of realistic dialogue between the two parents, the almost gratuitous song-like discourse of the drinkers. Neither parent evokes much sympathy: the tone is of grotesque comedy, with a constant intrusion of the *I* technique (see chapters 3, 4, 5, 6, 7, 8, 9, 10, 11 and 12).

The first episode that presents us with father and son together in conversation is the famous arse-wiping scene in chapter 13. As we saw in the last chapter, Panurge and frere Jan come to life precisely because of their constant dialogue; the characteristic way in which they build up their phrases into sentences makes them

---

* he was ordinarily well furnished with gammons of Bacon ... with store of dried Neats tongues, plenty of Links, Chitterlings and Puddings in their season; together with salt Beef and mustard, a good deale of hard rows of powdered mullet called **Botargos**, great provision of **Sauciges** ...

stand out from their surroundings as flesh-and-blood comic characters. Here we have Grandgousier in the rôle of an inquirer and Gargantua as respondent: ' "Comment cela?" dist Grandgousier. "J'ay (respondit Gargantua) par longue et curieuse experience inventé un moyen de me torcher le cul, le plus seigneurial, le plus excellent, le plus expedient que jamais feut veu." '* From this moment on, Gargantua is almost given the rôle of the Olympian author in a Menippean satire: he varies his syntax by repetition, by inversion, by enumeration; he switches over from prose to verse; throws out exclamations and asks a host of rhetorical questions; where there is dialogue it is very often in the form of quick repartee with jokes at a crude level like, ' "Retournons (dist Grandgousier) à nostre propos." "Quel? (dist Gargantua) chier?" "Non (dist Grandgousier), mais torcher le cul." '† The whole passage of Menippean satire was examined in chapter 5 and so we can pass on to Grandgousier's speech expressing his delight in and admiration for his son's achievement:

O ... que tu as bon sens, petit guarsonnet! Ces premiers jours je te feray passer docteur en gaie science, par Dieu! car tu as de raison plus que d'aage. Or poursuiz ce propos torcheculatif, je t'en prie. Et, par ma barbe! pour un bussart tu auras soixante pippes, j'entends de ce bon vin Breton, lequel poinct ne croist en Bretaigne, mais en ce bon pays de Verron.‡

The humour is ironical and simple and so is the syntactic structure. Grandgousier indulges in exclamations and oaths, gently satirizes scholastic argumentation and brings in again his *joie de boire* with his promise of the good Breton wine. The grotesque but lovable and humorous traits of his character, which he showed in previous

---

*How is that, (said Grangousier?) I have, (answered Gargantua), by a long and curious experience, found out a means to wipe my bum, the most lordly, the most excellent, and the most convenient that ever was seen.

† Let us return to our purpose, (said Grangousier). What, (said Gargantua), to skite? No, (said Grangousier), but to wipe our taile.

‡ O my pretty little waggish boy ... what an excellent wit thou hast? I will make thee very shortly proceed Doctor in the jovial quirks of gay learning, and that, by G—, for thou hast more wit then age; now, I prethie go on in this torcheculatife, or wipe-bummatory discourse, and by my beard I swear, for one puncheon, thou shalt have threescore pipes, I mean of the good Breton wine, not that which grows in Britain, but in the good countrey of Verron. [Urquhart's translation of Bretaigne by Britain obscures the joke, which is that Breton wine comes not from the vineyards of Brittany, which were non-existent, but from the Loire valley.]

chapters, are heightened by the use of natural speech and satirical themes. He is grotesque when he looks into the education of his son; the model father is seen through a distorting mirror. For example, the father admires his marvellously quick-witted son, but the illustration of this wit is in his discovery of a 'means to wipe my bum'! His education must be the very best; for Grandgousier says that he 'participe de quelque divinité ... et parviendra à degré souverain de sapience, s'il est bien institué'* (chapter 14), but we can hardly conceive of Grandgousier as a human being when he is ready to kill maistre Jobelin for making his son so dim in comparison with the young Eudemon. And in chapter 16, when the gigantic mare to take Gargantua to Paris has come to Grandgousier as a gift from *Fayoles, quart roy de Numidie,* the framework is still grotesque and the jokes somewhat crude: 'Voicy ... bien le cas pour porter mon filz à Paris. Or ça, de par Dieu, tout yra bien. Il sera grand clerc on temps advenir. Si n'estoient messieurs les bestes, nous vivrions comme clercs.'† After all this we expect Grandgousier to remain a simple, but thoroughly grotesque character, humorous but lovable.

But we are proved wrong. When the story develops and a war is declared between Picrochole and Grandgousier there is a violent change in his character. At first, in chapter 28 he turns to God and says, 'Ho! ho! ho! ho! ho! mon Dieu, mon Saulveur, ayde moy, inspire moy, conseille moy à ce qu'est de faire!'‡ Here we have an appeal to God, who knows his strength and is aware that pursuing peace has been his first consideration throughout his life, for counsel and aid to bring Picrochole, who must surely be in the hands of the wicked spirit, back to the divine yoke once more. This self-abasement and entreaty for God's help is a piece of simple primitive piety matched by the same simplicity of syntax that we saw in chapter 13.

---

* doth participate of some divinity, and that if he be well taught ... he will attain to a supreme degree of wisdome.

† Here is, ... what is fit to carry my sonne to Paris. So now, in the name of God, all will be well, he will in times coming be a great Scholar, if it were not (my masters,) for the beasts, we should live like Clerks.

‡ Ho, ho, ho, ho, ho, my God, my Saviour, help me, inspire me and advise me what I shall do.

But the next chapter (chapter 29) is a letter written by Grand-gousier to his son, and the difference in syntactic structure is very striking. For the style is much more hypotactic,[1] with a web of subordinate clauses, a firmer use of word-order, using repetitions for stylistic effects, and with the words that link the phrases together – conjunctions, relative pronouns or adverbs – carefully organizing the whole structure. Let us look more closely at the beginning of the letter:

La ferveur de tes estudes requeroit *que* de long temps ne te revocasse de cestuy philosophicque repous, *sy* la confiance de noz amys et anciens confederez n'eust de present frustré la seureté de ma vieillesse. *Mais, puis que* telle est ceste fatale destinée *que* par iceulx soye inquieté *es quelz* plus je me repousoye, force me est te rappeler au subside des gens et biens *qui* te sont par droict naturel affiez.

Car, ainsi comme debiles sont les armes au dehors *si* le conseil n'est en la maison, *aussi* vaine est l'estude et le conseil inutile *qui* en temps oportun par vertus n'est executé et à son effect reduict.

Ma deliberation n'est de provocquer, *ains* de apaiser; d'assaillir, *mais* defendre; de conquester, *mais* de guarder mes feaulx subjectz et terres hereditaires, *es quelles* est hostillement entré Picrochole sans cause ny occasion, et de jour en jour poursuit sa furieuse entreprinse avecques excès non tolerables à personnes liberes.* (The italics are mine.)

The first paragraph has two quite long sentences, hinged on the antithetical '*mais*'; the second paragraph starts with a strongly emphasized '*car*' and the third paragraph contrasts one verb with another in a rhythmic balance. This already shows a marked contrast with the style of Grandgousier as we have seen it hitherto. Furthermore, this style, particularly in the third paragraph, through the rhythm created by the antitheses, is modelled on

* The fervency of thy studies did require, that I should not in a long time recall thee from that Philosophical rest thou now enjoyest; if the confidence reposed in our friends and ancient confederates had not at this present disappointed the assurance of my old age: But seeing such is my fatal destiny, that I should be now disquieted by those in whom I trusted most: I am forced to call thee back to help the people and goods, which by the right of nature belong unto thee; for even as armes are weak abroad if there be not counsel at home: so is that study vaine, and counsel unprofitable, which in a due and convenient time is not by vertue executed and put in effect. My deliberation is not to provoke, but to appease; not to assault, but to defend: not to conquer, but to preserve my faithful subjects and hereditary dominions: into which Picrochole is entred in a hostile manner without any ground or cause, and from day to day pursueth his furious enterprise with that height of insolence that is intolerable to free-born spirits.

Ciceronian Latin – the style beloved of humanists of the time. This is the formal style of Rabelais; his academic style, which we can contrast with the natural style – of the dialogues and mono- logues of his comic characters. Each sentence in the three para- graphs here is controlled: each word is strengthened by a syno- nym, like '*noz amys et anciens confederez*'; the use of logical link- words like '*ains*', '*car*' or '*mais*' gathers together the whole piece. This could simply be the difference between Grandgousier talking and writing. However, the differences in tone are striking and are underlaid by a change in the content and in the views that Grand- gousier is putting forward. The letter is not only serious; it is also rather stilted within the grotesque framework; moreover, it seems to be a pretext for the author to express certain ideas of his own. To take this last point first: Rabelais, the real man, was throughout his life as opposed to war as was Erasmus. As an author of a gigan- tic story, he exploits the opportunity to expound the view that the only justifiable war is one of self-defence. Erasmus in one of his adages – *Dulce bellum inexpertis*, first published in the 1515 edition – after stating that pacifism was the only true Christian attitude, that 'we are just like Turks fighting Turks', goes on to say,

I am not saying that I would absolutely condemn an expedition against the Turks, if they had attacked us first, and so long as we conducted the war ... in the name of Christ, with Christian minds and with Christ's own weapons ... Let us take to them a plain and truly Apostolic profession of faith ... If one examines the matter with close attention, one will find that almost all wars between Christians have arisen from either stupidity or wickedness ... Some young men ... go into war out of rashness rather than badness .... Some are urged into war by a secret hate, others by ambition, others by the fierceness of their character.[2]

War is seen in a deeply Christian context: letters and negotiations between ambassadors should be used to settle wars; the chief armour of a Christian is prayer and knowledge, and a confidence in God which serves to place that knowledge firmly in God's sphere. Erasmus regards those who start a war as wicked and foolish, and all humanity as smitten with this disease. Rabelais, through the mouth of Grandgousier, expresses opinions which are very close to Erasmus's. In the first paragraph, Grandgousier stresses his age, the violent shock he felt when he realized that the amicable friendship between old associates had been broken, and the necessity now for Gargantua to hasten home to defend his people. In the second paragraph, he says that study and knowledge need to be channelled into action, otherwise they are merely vain and abstract; in the third paragraph, he places the war firmly in Erasmian terms – with no thought of provocation but merely of defence – with his enemy from day to day waxing in strength in his *'furieuse entreprinse'*. The fourth paragraph sums up what Grandgousier has done to try to avoid war, and recognizes that Picrochole's conduct is that of a man who has free-will but cannot act rightly because he has been abandoned by God's grace, 'Dieu eternel l'a laissé au gouvernail de son franc arbitre et propre sens ...'* The last paragraph of the letter is an appeal from Grandgousier to Gargantua to come and help as soon as he can, for it is 'non tant moy (ce que toutesfoys par pitié naturellement tu doibs) que les tiens, lesquelz par raison tu peuz saulver et guarder'.† This is, as many critics have pointed out, a mixture of medieval and humanist comments: a feudal commander with ideas on war, ethics and Christianity of the kind that were topical in 1534. Nothing comic here: it is totally serious.

The stiltedness of the letter, placed as it is in such a grotesque framework deserves further consideration. The cause of the war is trivial; the commander Picrochole – an old friend of Grandgousier – is depicted as entirely comic; from the first news of the strife of the cake-makers, he is furious, 'Lequel incontinent entra en courroux furieux, et sans plus oultre se interroguer quoy ne comment, feist crier par son pays ...‡ (chapter 26). The battle that is waged around the abbey close is burlesque epic, especially with the introduction of frere Jan; it is a parody of all existing wars in epic stories. So, the letter with its serious arguments comes

---

* The eternal God hath left him to the disposure of his own free will and sensual appetite ...
† not me so much (which nevertheless by natural Piety thou oughtest to do,) as thine own People, which by reason thou mayest save and preserve.
‡ Picrochole incontent grew angry and furious; and without asking any further what, how, why or wherefore, commanded the ban and arriere ban to be sounded throughout all his countrey ...

as a surprise after the parodic setting. Furthermore, it sits awkwardly with the giant's character.

It seems as if we already have two different tones in the character of Grandgousier: the simple, boisterous, comic-loving giant and the seriousness of a Christian king. To the first tone we can assign his faith and confidence in God, which appear quite automatically – even when the company is enjoying frere Jan's talking (chapters 39 and 40) we find Grandgousier defending monks because they pray for mankind. To the second tone, that of his letters and speeches, belong such ideas as war, pacifism, anticlericalism and scriptural Christianity. In the last few chapters of the book we can still see the two tones at work in the same way: for example in chapter 45 Grandgousier treats his prisoners well, as a scriptural Christian should, and in chapter 46 his speech to Touquedillon is underlaid by ideas of acting out one's life in peace. Thus he can say,

Ainsi faut il faire entre voisins et anciens amys, veu que ceste nostre différence n'est poinct guerre proprement, comme Platon, *li.v.de Rep.*, vouloit estre non guerre nommée, ains sedition, quand les Grecz meuvoient armes les ungs contre les aultres, ce que, si par male fortune advenoit, il commande qu'on use de toute modestie.*

By means of the hypotactic syntax – with the conjunctions and the relatives once more firmly controlling the structure – the author follows Erasmus, who had summed up the Platonic argument in his *Institutio principis Christiani*. But we can hardly reconcile the dialogue that follows, in which Grandgousier plays the principal rôle, with his serious speech where he quotes authorities like Plato and ancient precedents such as Hannibal which are worked out rationally – Hannibal conquered countries and that was 'contraire à la profession de l'Evangile' – and also employs logically constructed arguments, all set out in a clear and systematic order.

The rôle that he takes up in dialogue is in the natural tone,

* So should good neighbours do, and ancient friends; seeing this our difference is not properly warre, as Plato, lib. 5. *de repub.* would not have it called warre but sedition, when the Greeks took up armes against one another, and that therefore when such combustions should arise amongst them, his advice was to behave themselves in the managing of them with all discretion and modesty.

whereas the part he plays in speeches and letters gives him a second tone which is overwhelmingly academic. In this second rôle, Rabelais provides no insulating property to enable us to be detached from Grandgousier – there is no irony, no satire or parody. But the commonsense, the reliance on reason and the appeals to God have as the underlying leitmotif the hatred of inhumanity and of cruelty. Grandgousier's innocence and simplicity, his perpetual good humour, his generosity of mind and the desire to extend to others the *joie de vivre* of his own court are all traits in a likeable character. There are times when Rabelais reduces his stature to a normal human being: for instance, at home in his castle (chapter 28), he tells stories as all good grandfathers do:

le vieux bon homme Grandgousier ... qui après souper se chauffe les couiles à un beau, clair et grand feu, et, attendent graisler des chastaines, escript au foyer avec un baston bruslé d'un bout dont on escharbotte le feu, faisant à sa femme et famille de beaulx contes du temps jadis.*

The picture we get of Grandgousier is rather uneven: the joy and perpetual spontaneity of his dialogues with Gargantua, the way he encourages the *cochonneries* of his son in chapter 13, the pride he shows in his son's natural invention, are fully delineated but the aspects of his character that are redolent of humanism are either bumpy or flat. The world he moves in is delightfully characterized as rather childlike: even sexual dialogues like the midwives discussing the sex of Gargantua (chapter 11) coexist with the healthy overflow of vitality which is one of the elements of a Rabelaisian world.

In the son we expect the delineation to be fuller, simply because he has a much larger rôle and takes up whole chapters himself in *Gargantua*. From the beginning he is set in the grotesque gigantic framework, and all we see of him as a baby and then as a child is comic. For example, at the sound of the flagons coming and going, full of overflowing wine (chapter 7), he falls into a

---

* the good old man Grangousier ... who after supper warmeth his ballocks by a good, clear, great fire, and, waiting upon the broyling of some chestnuts, is very serious in drawing scratches on the hearth, with a stick burnt at the one end, wherewith they did stirre up the firre, telling to his wife and the rest of the family pleasant old stories and tales of former times.

kind of ecstasy 'comme s'il goustoit les joyes de paradis'; the women looking after him thereupon play on the glasses with knives, while in his cradle he 's'esguayoit, il tressailloit, et luy mesmes se bressoit en dodelinant de la teste, monichordisant des doigtz et barytonant du cul'.* As a boy, he cracks one joke – very much a schoolboy's joke – in chapter 12. The seigneur de Painensac and his men come to visit his father and ask the gigantic boy to show them to the stables. Gargantua leads them up to the top of the house and shows them his own huge wooden horse! But all through these early chapters one is aware of the Olympian author firmly in control of the narrative. For example in chapter 11 when Gargantua is now adolescent, the narrative seems to stop, while a poetic and totally gratuitous extemporization is made on the phrases, 'à boyre, manger et dormir; à manger, dormir et boyre; à dormir, boyre et manger'. Here proverbs are turned upside down and expressions that centuries before had lost their literal meaning are suddenly given one again. While we are enjoying this playful twisting and turning of language by the Olympian author, our interest in Gargantua himself is diminished. With chapter 13 however, which we have looked at earlier from Grandgousier's point of view, there is an increased interest in the son as he talks with such scatological *finesse* about the sensation-producing qualities of the different kinds of 'bum-wipers'. In the next few chapters, on Gargantua's medieval schooling and on the new humanistic one, the author is satirizing the old system of education while at the same time aiming occasional shafts at the new. For example, in chapter 15, when Eudemon recites his Latin better than a Gracchus, the author's only conclusion is to describe Gargantua's reaction in a comic simile, 'toute la contenence de Gargantua fut qu'il se print à plorer comme une vache et se cachoit le visaige de son bonnet, et ne fut possible de tirer de luy une parolle non plus q'un pet d'un asne mort'.†

But in chapter 23 Gargantua is educated in a new way, and most

---

* he became gay, did leap for joy, would loll and rock himself in the cradle, then nod with his head, monocording with his fingers and barytonising with his taile.
† all the countenance that Gargantua kept was, that he fell to crying like a Cow, and cast down his face, hiding it with his cap, nor could they possibly draw one word from him, no more then a fart from a dead Asse.

critics seem to regard this as unequivocal praise of the new humanist education. Not only is the picture gigantic – as the critics recognize – but the author gives us, consciously and warmly, unmistakable cues for laughter. For example Ponocrates has to start afresh with his new student, and so 'le purgea canonicquement avec elebore de Anticyre et par ce medicament luy nettoya toute l'alteration et perverse habitude du cerveau'.*³ Then Gargantua is shown swimming along the Seine holding a book in the air with one hand, 'transpassoit toute la riviere de Seine sans icelluy mouiller . . .'† Furthermore the *I* technique intrudes once or twice: thus in order to exercise his voice-box Gargantua yells like all the devils in Hell, 'Je l'ouy une fois appellant Eudemon, depuis la porte Sainct Victor jusques à la fontaine de Narsay.'‡ In short we have here a huge slice of Menippean satire with fantastic and *merveilleux* exploits spread on thickly and gaily, and it is essential to see Rabelais's attitude first of all from an Olympian point of view. But what about Gargantua's religious views? And what about the development of his character fictionally?

To take the second question first, Gargantua remains in Paris for many chapters, still gigantic and still able to carry on playfully with all his physical and mental exercises. When he is called back (chapter 34) he rides on the huge mare, takes a huge tree as his lance, laughs when the pissing of the mare drowns a band of enemies, and treats all the bullets as grapestones or as flies buzzing around his head. Once home, he tucks in at his father's banquet and eats six pilgrims in a salad: the comedy is riotous and reveals to the reader that Gargantua is still the same as he was as a mere adolescent. There is no real development of his character at all, but he can fire jokes at us and make satirical sallies to arouse laughter amongst the readers. Is there any brilliant dialogue which might show us Gargantua a little more fully, as something more than just a gigantic sketch? In chapter 39 the meeting between him and frere Jan is conducted on a boisterous note, 'Hés, Frere Jean,

* the said physician purged him canonically with Anticyrian ellebore, by which medicine he cleansed all the alteration, and perverse habitude of his braine.
† crossing thus the bredth of the river of Seine, without wetting it.
‡ I heard him once call Eudemon from St Victor's gate to the fountain at Narsay. [D.C.]

mon amy, Frere Jean mon grand cousin, Frere Jean de par le
diable, l'accollée, mon amy!'* The repetitions, the thousand em-
braces and thousand hugs they exchange suggest that here are
friends for life. Frere Jan sits on a stool near Gargantua; the
grotesque framework begins to fade away and a burlesque one to
take its place. For in the next chapter, 40, Gargantua expounds in
very Erasmian terms how degenerate, ignorant and socially use-
less the monks are; they seem to be neither preaching nor giving
the world the true doctrine like a *bon docteur evangelique*. Here the
author has assigned to Gargantua ideas that have in themselves a
certain amount of verisimilitude; being of the second generation,
he has taken in all the opinions topical at the time, his interlocutor
is a monk, frere Jan, who is basically the reason for the speech; and
the vocabulary and syntax that he employs are by no means re-
mote from the sort of things we have heard from his lips before.
For instance, he uses phrases like *la merde du monde, conchier et
degaster, trinqueballer leurs cloches,* of the monks to lash out against
the inhabitants of abbeys. Furthermore, he earnestly maintains
that every true Christian prays for the monks and 'Maintenant tel
est nostre bon Frere Jean'. There follows a portrait of frere Jan:
'Il n'est point bigot; il n'est poinct dessiré; il est honeste, joyeux,
deliberé, bon compaignon; il travaille; il labeure; il defent les
opprimez; il conforte les affligez; il subvient es souffreteux; il
guarde les clous de l'abbaye.'† All these qualities that Gargantua
sees in frere Jan are important: bigotry and hypocrisy will be
condemned later by both Gargantua and Pantagruel (cf. the inscription at the door of the Abbey of Thélème); it is the joviality
of frere Jan and Panurge that will make them such good companions to the giants; resoluteness in action will be revealed, for
instance, in the storm at sea episode (*Quart Livre,* chapters 18–24);
and frere Jan has a willingness too to assist those like Panurge, who
are less fortunate than himself. These qualities are to be a leitmotif

---

* Ha, Friar Jhon, my friend, Friar Jhon, my brave cousin, Friar Jhon from the devil: let
me clip thee (my heart) about the neck, to me an armesful ...
† He is no bigot or hypocrite, he is not torne and divided betwixt reality and appearance,
no wretch of a rugged and peevish disposition, but honest, jovial, resolute, and a good
fellow: he travels, he labours, he defends the oppressed, comforts the afflicted, helps the
needie, and keeps the close of the Abbey.

of the company in the *Tiers Livre* and the *Quart Livre*; Gargantua says that they have nothing to do with being a monk but are the general human qualities in frere Jan that he admires. It is precisely Gargantua's charity and benevolence that make us see the realistic background to this burlesque and at times grotesque intrusion of frere Jan. In a comic book we are presented with life not apprehended as a form of experience but rather exhibited as a spectacle, and in this, what is necessary above all is humanity – otherwise it remains on a grotesque level. It is important that the benevolence of Gargantua should make an impression on us if we are to appreciate the linguistic dance that he and frere Jan perform in the Abbey of Thélème at the end of the book. Moreover, if we look back at the previous chapter (39), where frere Jan does all the illogical talking and keeps all the company merry, one sees that this scene is representative of all the joking, jesting and riotous living throughout the two books. Both the good humoured charity of the giant and the incalculable frere Jan provide comedy. (See, for instance, chapters 43 and 45.)

If we turn now to the question of Gargantua's religious attitude, the first thing that strikes us is that this is the most polemical and Erasmian of all the books, and it is not surprising to find Gargantua as Rabelais's spokesman. It is clear that there are features of religion assumed by Gargantua that would be anathema to traditional theologians, especially the Sorbonne, the theological faculty of the university. For instance, the stress on the Scriptures themselves, so by-passing the authority of the church or the intercession of the saints and the Virgin Mary: if we look back on his new system of education there is a distinct contrast between hearing twenty-six or thirty masses per day under *praecepteurs Sorbonagres* and reading the Scriptures and praising God. Anti-monasticism has taken over the essentially pre-reformist ideas of Grandgousier, but one can say that all the scriptural thinkers like Erasmus, Marguerite de Navarre and Marot were saying this sort of thing in the 1530s: 'Tous vrays christians, de tous estatz, en tous lieux, en tous temps, prient Dieu, et l'Esperit prie et interpelle pour iceulx et Dieu les prent en grace'* (chapter 40). This is an echo of

---

* All true Christians, of all estates and conditions, in all places and at all times send up

Saint Paul, Epistle to the Romans viii. 26: 'Likewise the Spirit also helpeth our infirmities: for we know not what we should pray for as we ought: but the Spirit itself maketh intercession for us with groanings which cannot be uttered', and Saint Paul was the most influential authority among scriptural theologians in the Reformation. If we examine some pronouncements linguistically, this scriptural impression is confirmed. Gargantua makes a speech to the prisoners (chapter 50) in an academic style: the first paragraph contains one main clause, with subordinate clauses introduced by *que* or *lorsque*, similes introduced by *comme* and *ainsi*, frequent present and past participles, a rhetorical question and the use of three antitheses in an increasing order of complexity, '*Offrit* ses presens; *ilz* ne feurent receupz ... *Se donna* mancipe ... *ce ne feut* accepté ... *Ceda* ... ses terres et royaulme, *offrant* ... *signée, scellé* et *ratifié* ... ce fut totalement refusé ...'* (The italics are mine.) Here is Gargantua being earnest and believing that speeches which set forth the case are a more worthy form of contest than the war that he has just been waging. The content recalls Erasmus and the whole style is redolent of humanism. This Gargantua is more steadily envisaged than Grandgousier, in fictional terms, but the wars and battles in this book are still grotesque and parodied. When, in the last chapter, he has to say, 'Ce n'est de maintenant que les gens reduictz à la creance Evangelicque sont persecutez; mais bien heureux est celluy qui ne sera scandalizé et qui tousjours tendra au but ...'† it may be that the *invraisemblance* of the whole Abbey of Thélème suggests that it was put together after the *Affaire des Placards*. For on the night of 17 October 1534, placards against the mass were nailed up in several important towns and also in the Chateau d'Amboise where Francis I was in residence and the king was provoked to a sharp retribution. This year marks

their prayers to God, and the Mediatour prayeth and intercedeth for them, and God is gracious to them.

* He offered his presents, they were not received ... he yielded himself voluntarily a servant ... this was not accepted of ... he surrendered ... his whole Countreys and Kingdomes to him, offering ... signed, sealed and ratified ... this was altogether refused ...

† It is not now only (I perceive) that People called to the faith of the Gospel, and convinced with the certainty of Evangelical truths, are persecuted; but happy is that man that shall not be scandalized, but shall alwayes continue to the end ...

the watershed in the royal attitude towards heretics, and from this moment onwards, Rabelais is aware that the persecution of protestants will be intensified. In this sentence we must listen seriously to Gargantua's warning that religious positions are very precarious and to his Christian–Stoic message, which comes out strongly in the last phrase, 'sans par ses affections charnelles estre distraict ny diverty'.* It is certainly syntactically serious and Rabelais has here endowed Gargantua with an academic style in order to express things that he himself felt strongly about. Professor Busson's statement, however, 'qu'il y a plus de christianisme dans une lettre d'Érasme ou de Sadolet que dans tout ce qu'on a appelé le credo des géants'⁴ is rather misleading. On the one side, fictionally, it is of course true. On the fictional level both Grandgousier and Gargantua are presented very well up to a point, but that point is quite important, for it is there that the non-fictional enters. As mouthpieces of the author, Grandgousier and Gargantua *have* to take forgiveness, charity and God seriously. Furthermore, they have to develop certain leitmotifs, such as pacificism and opposition to monasticism, to ceremonies and to the external observances of the church in favour of an inner piety. Rabelais, the real man, is putting forward ideas of his own, transfused with Erasmianism, through the characters he has created. But – and this is quite crucial – it is in a comic work, and one would therefore not expect say, the Eucharist or the nature of the Holy Spirit to be treated theologically or the Confession to be exploited in the way that Erasmus exploits it in his *Naufragium*. The delightful good nature of these giants, their *joie de vivre* and the boisterousness of their character contrast with the sane, enlightened and serious ideas that Erasmus put forth. But we must look at the third giant, Pantagruel, before coming to any final conclusions about the characters of Grandgousier and Gargantua.

The first episode in *Pantagruel* where a mixture of styles occurs is the famous chapter 8. From a narrative point of view we have seen (chapter 4) that the *merveilleux* context contains a serious letter from Gargantua to his son. What we must consider now is

---

* without being distracted or diverted by his carnal affections and depraved nature.

the tone of the letter and thereby try to ascertain whether Gargantua is here a spokesman for Rabelais the real man. Professor Brault while succinctly indicating the essence of the problem, 'The trouble with parody ... is that we are often left uncertain as to the author's true views',[5] nevertheless saw in the letter the 'mock humanism of the muddle-headed old giant'. Whether he is right in this verdict or whether the dominant view, namely that this letter is a hymn to the Renaissance, is right is the question that we must try to answer. We have seen Gargantua's behaviour after the death of his wife Badebec (chapter 3 of *Pantagruel*), where it is conveyed that he is a comic figure both in his *reductio ad absurdum* of scholastic training and in his syntax. For instance, the comic angle of vision is expressed in a paratactic structure: he calls Badebec 'ma mignonne, mamye, mon petit con ... ma tendrette, ma braguette, ma savate, ma pantofle ...'* and when he appeals to God, the religious sentiments mingled with allusions to his old age are assembled in short phrases like, 'Seigneur Dieu, faut-il que je me contriste encores? Cela me fasche; je ne suis plus jeune, je deviens vieulx, le temps est dangereux, je pourray prendre quelque fievre, me voylà affolé. Foy de gentilhomme, il vault mieulx pleurer moins, et boire dadvantaige!'† This is perfectly in keeping with the grotesque and gigantic framework and one views it as a piece of comedy, satirizing rhetorical argumentation. But in chapter 8 Gargantua is writing a letter: and it is again in an academic style. For example, the first two paragraphs make a striking contrast with the style of chapter 3: here, there is no boisterousness, no coarse vocabulary, no juxtaposition of his grief at the death of his wife with subjective impressions of the time he is living in. Instead there is a humanist giving an orthodox view about immortality. Etienne Gilson in 1932[6] said, 'Apprenons la langue de Rabelais avant de le lire ... Pas une d'elles [expressions] qui ne porte et qui ne prouve la survivance d'un théologien fort compétent chez l'auteur de *Pantagruel*', and showed how most of

---

* my minion, my dear heart, my sugar ... my little C ... my tender peggie, my Codpiece darling ... my slipshow-lovie.

† Lord God, must I again contrist my self? This grieves me; I am no longer young, I grow old, the weather is dangerous; I may perhaps take an ague, then shall I be foiled, if not quite undone; by the faith of a Gentleman, it were better to cry lesse, and drink more.

the ideas in this letter were a mixture of Patristic thought, with a
large dose of ancient thought, and of the everyday religious practice of a Franciscan. For example, 'Non doncques sans juste et
equitable cause je rends graces à Dieu' may be compared with
these words from the mass, 'vere dignum et justum est aequum et
salutare, nos tibi semper et ubique gratias agere'. Or another
example taken from Saint Thomas Aquinas (*Summa Theologica*, 1.
75. ad.ii) when Aquinas states that there is no particular substance
that is the *persona*, but it is the unity of body and soul which distinguishes the concept of *persona*. Rabelais exploits this in the
phrase, 'et tel te laisser après ma mort comme un mirouoir repre-
sentant la personne de moy ton pere . . .'* The transitory kind of
physical immortality – which Plato and Cicero had also defined –
is firmly put by Rabelais within a Christian framework, borrowing phrases from the passion of Saint Symphorien as in, 'mon ame
laissera ceste habitation humaine, je ne me reputeray totallement
mourir, ains passer d'un lieu en aultre . . . Hodie vita non tollitur,
sed mutatur in melius. Hodie, nate, ad supernam vitam felici
commutatione migrabis'. This physical immortality participated
in through one's children, by the passing of qualities and virtues
from generation to generation, does not conflict with the doctrine
of individual life after death. But it is a consolation for the fact
that Original Sin deprives Adam's descendants of everlasting life
on earth. This physical immortality is operational until the Last
Judgement, when true immortality in the other world is reached.
Rabelais draws heavily on the New Testament when arguing this:
for instance, 'et ainsi successivement jusques à l'heure du jugement final, quand Jesu-Christ aura rendu à Dieu le pere son
royaulme pacifique . . .' may be compared with Saint Paul, 1 Cor.
xv. 24: 'Then cometh the end when he shall have delivered up the
kingdom to God, even the Father, when he shall have put down
all rule and all authority and power.' He also echoes the language
of scholastic theologians. For example, the phrase 'car alors ces-
seront toutes generations et corruptions' can be compared with
Saint Thomas Aquinas's assertion (*Contra Gentiles* IV. cap. 92) that

* and so to leave thee after my death as a mirrour, representing the person of me thy
  father.

there will be no need for new births as man henceforth is incorruptible and immortal.

There is no suggestion of parody in the religious reasons Gargantua gives for immortality and for his desire to transmit the physical and mental qualities that he himself has developed, through the *persona* of his son. In all this the style is appropriately academic. The first paragraph consists of three hypotactic sentences, the middle one being short; the structure is organized by relative clauses – *desquelles, par laquelle, en laquelle* – and by causal conjunctions like *parce que*; the linking words point the logical progression and the pairing of past participles like *endouayré et aorné* or adjectives like *singuliere et excellente* make the argument clear and precise. The second paragraph starts with a *mais* which makes a clear but not violent contrast with the preceding sentence; the style here is slightly more paratactic, with the argument clarified through conjunctions like *et ains, car alors, et ainsi* which keep the sentence under control. The third paragraph, starting with 'Non doncques sans juste et equitable cause' sums up the point that the argument has reached, and is followed by *car, quand, attendu que*, leading to 'en toy et par toy, je demeure en mon image visible en ce monde, vivant, voyant, et conversant entre gens de honneur et mes amys ...'* After the rather dry religious exposition of the first two and a half paragraphs, the created author now introduces this particular father's desire for physical immortality; the rhythm becomes more striking, the balance between *en toy et par toy*, the triple pattern of *vivant, voyant et conversant*, and the contrast between *gens de honneur* and *mes amys* marks a change from impersonal theological argument to personal aspirations and so makes the personal piety of Gargantua more real. This is made apparent too in the final clause of this third paragraph, 'non sans peché, je le confesse (car nous pechons tous, et continuellement requerons à Dieu qu'il efface noz pechez), mais sans reproche'.† The next three paragraphs contain a

---

* in and by that, I continue in my visible image living in the world, visiting and conversing with people of honour, and other my good friends ...

† not without sin, (because we are all of us trespassers, and therefore ought continually to beseech his divine Majesty to blot our transgressions out of his memory), yet was it by the help and grace of God, without all manner of reproach before men.

mixture of serious theological reasons and a firm personal desire for immortality, expressed once again in a hypotactic sentence structure that marks a contrast with the whole of Gargantua's and Pantagruel's rôle hitherto in this book.

The letter ends on a theological note too. After the saying 'science sans conscience n'est que ruine de l'ame' – knowledge must go hand in hand with conscience – Gargantua moves on to 'il te convient servir, aymer et craindre Dieu, et en luy mettre toutes tes pensées et tout ton espoir; et par foy formee de charité, estre à luy adjoinct, en sorte que jamais n'en soys desamparé par peché'.* This appears to be very like Pantagruel's prayers before battle: for example, in chapter 28 he says, 'toutesfoys je n'espere en ma force ny en mon industrie, mais toute ma fiance est en Dieu, mon protecteur ...'† but without any supporting theological argument of the kind that is appropriate to the letter. The belief that charity and faith together join us to God in such a way that we cannot be disjoined by sin is a scholastic commonplace, and it is thoroughly at home in the scholastic argumentation of the letter.

Thus, so far as the theological ideas in the letter are concerned, there is no justification for following Professor Brault in rejecting the traditional view: the distinctive stylistic character of the letter confirms its serious intent. We have detected the change in tone at the beginning of the chapter where there is a gap between the *merveilleux* tone of the first paragraph and the start of the scholastic argument in 'Très chier filz, Entre les dons, graces et preroga-tives ...'. We can compare the letter to the speeches of Grand-gousier and Gargantua in *Gargantua* where we find the same jerkiness produced by the attempt to fit the grotesque and the serious in the same person. In this chapter as in the earlier ones there are the two attitudes and tones – the first conveyed through a burlesque–epic form of writing outside the letter, the second in the letter itself, a humanist style – which we have called Rabelais's academic style.

* it behooveth thee to serve, to love, to feare God, and on him to cast all thy thoughts and all thy hope, and by faith formed in charity to cleave unto him, so that thou mayest never be separated from him by thy sins.
† I do nevertheless trust neither in my force not in mine industry, but all my confidence is in God my Protectour.

But there remains the more famous part of the letter and this poses the crucial problem: how can a gigantic programme which is idealized still make sense as non-parody? Rabelais traces the progress of literature. By this time, 1532, the whole contrast between Gothic darkness and Renaissance light is commonplace amongst humanist writers. The Italian humanists from Petrarch in the fourteenth century onwards and their sixteenth-century French successors employed the image of winter and spring again and again. In fact the dark middle ages had become a 'myth' projected by the Renaissance writers as part of a cyclical view of history in which antiquity had been the Golden Age, the middle ages were marked by darkness and superstition and the Renaissance was represented as bursting with light and life. Whether this myth had any valid factual basis is too large a question to be tackled here, but the self-consciousness and self-awareness of the period must be taken seriously as one of the beliefs men living and participating in it certainly held. We can see the 'real' Rabelais's view of it in the Latin letter that he wrote to his friend Tiraqueau on 3 June 1532 (*Œuvres complètes*, vol. II, p. 481). His observation in this letter on the reflorescence of culture in France confirms the seriousness of this theme in *Pantagruel*, chapter 8 – a seriousness which one would otherwise be tempted not to impute to such a comic book as the story of a giant. The picture of the ideal educated man here corresponds very closely to the views expounded by such different writers as Leonardo da Vinci and Du Bellay: man should be a polymath, a walking encyclopaedia.

Syntactically, the pedagogical part of the letter belongs to the same register as the religious part, but it is not so drily expressed, and there appears to be more emotional feeling conveyed in these clear firm statements. One paragraph here will suffice to illustrate how this works: 'Que diray je? Les femmes et filles ont aspiré à ceste louange et manne celeste de bonne doctrine. Tant y a que en l'eage où je suis, j'ay esté contrainct de apprendre les lettres Grecques ...'* Syntactically, this is rather looser than the religious

---

* What shall I say? the very women and children have aspired to this praise and celestial Manna of good learning: yet so it is, that in the age I am now of, I have been constrained to learn the Greek tongue ...

paragraphs; but it is still hypotactic. Since Gargantua is now not speaking as the mouthpiece of Rabelais but of what he himself knows, the structural organization of his sentences is more relaxed. The educational programme is of course gigantic, and Gargantua makes one or two arrogant claims about his own scholarly prowess: for instance, 'à difficulté seroys je receu en la premiere classe des petitz grimaulx, qui, en mon eage virile, estoys (non à tord) reputé le plus sçavant dudict siecle',* where the humour is perfectly in keeping with a letter from father to son in school. Finally the letter is sent from Utopia – proof that it is indeed a gigantic ideal. But as for the parody, irony and ambiguity, it is difficult to detect anything of these in the letter at all.

Much of the narrative in *Pantagruel* has to be seen from the Olympian perspective and the reader's relationship to this giant is the same as towards Gargantua. The similes alone show us how the reader is meant to judge: for instance in the trial episode, chapter 13, after hearing the two sides of the case from Humesvene and Baisecul, Pantagruel walks solemnly to and fro, 'pensant bien profundement, comme l'on povoit estimer, car il gehaignoyt comme un asne qu'on sangle trop fort . . .'† Pantagruel is here being used as a mouthpiece for satire on law courts, and the speech in which he delivers his judgement is interesting precisely because of the character of the parody that the giant is given: its vocabulary is a mixture of Latinized jargon and coarse French, and syntactically it is a parody of the long, involved and meticulously explanatory sentences that a court judgement would normally have. For instance: 'Que, considérée l'orripilation de la ratepenade declinent bravement du solstice estival pour mugueter les billesvesées qui ont eu mat du pyon par les males vexations des lucifuges qui sont au climat dia Rhomès . . .'‡ The style is similar

---

* that now hardly should I be admitted unto the first forme of the little Grammar schoolboyes: I say, I, who in my youthful days was, (and that justly) reputed the most learned of that age . . .

† for he did groan like an Asse, whilest they girth him too hard, with the very intensiveness of considering how he was bound in conscience to do right to both parties . . .

‡ That in regard of the sudden quaking, shivering and hoarinesse of the flickermouse, bravely declining from the estival soltice, to attempt by private means the surprisal of toyish trifles in those, who are a little unwell for having taken a draught too much,

to the chapters by Humesvene and Baisecul; the syntax is muddled and there is a whole series of *non sequiturs*. The reader cannot make sense of this *coq-à-l'asne*, nor is he meant to.

The Olympian author gives his comment on Pantagruel's marvellous judgement at the beginning of chapter 14: 'Le jugement de Pantagruel feut incontinent sceu et entendu de tout le monde, et imprimé à force, et redigé es archives du palays, en sorte que le monde commença à dire: "Salomon ... ne montra tel chief d'œuvre de prudence comme a faict le bon Pantagruel." '* Once again the Menippean satirist is at work here, inviting his readers to laugh with him at the law. Throughout the book the only things that bring Pantagruel alive are his good nature, his benevolence and his *joie de vivre* – his first reaction to good news or success is to feast everybody. The only time that he seems to be serious is in chapter 29. We must look at this section more closely, in particular his address to God before the battle with LoupGarou. He begins, 'Seigneur Dieu, qui tousjours as esté mon protecteur et mon servateur, tu vois la destresse en laquelle je suis maintenant.'† No hint of irony or parody here: the terms in which God is addressed, as '*protecteur*' and '*servateur*' are conventional, and the syntax is clear. In the next sentence we find 'rien ... sinon ... ainsi comme ... en cas que ... qui'; *car* at the beginning of the following sentence emphasizes the logical connection and another *car* introduces a complex structure *qui ... ou ... plus ... duquel ... comme*. The next sentence starts with a *doncques*, again pointing the logical direction of the paragraph, and an elaborate structure which is conditional: 'comme ... que ... tant que ... ou ... si que ... qui'. The hypotactic style again. And the content of the speech is highly scriptural: the only just war is in defence of one-

---

through the lewd demeanour and vexation of the beetles, that inhabit the diarodal climate of an hypocritical Ape on horseback ...

* The great wit and judgement of Pantagruel, was immediately after this made known unto all the world, by setting forth his praises in print, and putting upon record this late wonderful proof he hath given thereof amongst the Rolls of the Crown, and Registers of the Palace, in such sort, that every body began to say, that Solomon, who by a probable guess only ... shewed never in his time such a Masterpiece of wisdom, as the good Pantagruel hath done ...

† O thou Lord God, who hast alwayes been my Protectour, and my Saviour, thou seest the distresse wherein I am at this time ...

self and one's country; one's faith and religious matters in general are God's concern in which no other man has the right to interfere. For, 'tu ne veulx coadjuteur, sinon de confession catholicque et service de ta parolle ...'* God wants only 'adjuvantes' (St Paul, 2 Cor. vi. 1), people who share in God's work by preaching and ministering the word by example and suffering. The only vow that men can make is, 'je feray prescher ton sainct Evangile purement, simplement et entierement ...'† The tone of the reformers is clearly heard here. The dedication is to the ministry of the word, to the task of preaching the Gospel purely, simply and entirely. No mention of the administering of the sacraments, which is an essential part of the catholic concept of the sacerdotal ministry. And furthermore Pantagruel goes on to promise God that 'les abus d'un tas de papelars et faulx prophetes, qui ont par constitutions humaines et inventions depravees envenimé tout le monde, seront d'entour moy exterminez'.‡ This last phrase seems like Rabelais's real voice breaking the framework of the fiction that he is creating: hypocrites and false prophets are precisely the Christian leitmotifs that he has used through the whole work, and one could compare him to Erasmus or Marguerite de Navarre in her *Heptaméron*. Her satire on the monks and friars is a humanist topic but it is also directly linked, for instance in the twenty-third story, with that hope and faith in God which the monks were not teaching. That such remarks were dangerous later on, when events in France had reached crisis point, is indicated by the fact that in the second edition of the *Heptaméron* in 1559, the editor, Claude Gruget, has toned down many of the author's attacks on the Franciscans, suppressed many of the Pauline and Johannine quotations and often gives orthodox answers to problems where a specifically scriptural position had been adopted by Marguerite de Navarre. The stance now taken by Rabelais was possible during Erasmus's lifetime and shortly after; but it died with the Wars of Religion and the Council of Trent. In the twen-

---

* thou wilt have no coadjutors, only a Catholick Confession and service of thy Word ...
† I will cause thy holy Gospel to be purely, simply and entirely preached ...
‡ the abuses of a rabble of hypocrites and false prophets, who by humane constitutions, and depraved inventions, have impoisened all the world, shall be quite exterminated from about me.

tieth century we are lured into believing that religious divisions were hard and fast: the Reformation, and in particular Calvin in France, destroyed the humanist belief that the inner unity of faith and religion was to be achieved by peace. Rabelais's kind of humanism remains flexible and supple and is not weighed down by zealotry or radicalism of any kind.

In answer to this very scriptural prayer to God by Pantagruel there comes a voice from heaven saying *Hoc fac et vinces*. This might be a conflation of Christ's *hoc fac et vives* with Constantine's *in hoc signo vinces* which were the words that appeared on the cross in the sky at the time of his conversion. But the conscious artist is deliberately employing parody to lead his readers away from the purely religious argumentation. Indeed it seems to be true in general that whenever a specifically religious allusion or argument is elaborated in the serious academic style it is deliberately interrupted or followed by parody or by Pantagruel's natural style in order that the distinctly topical note should not take over the style completely.

In the first book Pantagruel is seen on two planes: as a gigantic companion to Panurge and as the serious expounder of ideas that were current in 1532. Whenever he is depicted in the first of these rôles the tone is that of the natural, boisterous, humorous and rustic giant who expresses himself mainly in dialogue and in a paratactic style. In his serious rôle, he employs a hypotactic sentence structure very like Grandgousier or Gargantua in their academic style. In the first two books, all the comments of the giants are *évangéliques* – the formulas at the end of letters, the content of the letters, the prayers to God before battle, the anti-monastic satire, the attitude to the saints and to the Virgin Mary, the satire against the theological orthodoxy of the Sorbonne, the pacifist pleas and the views on pilgrimages. They are not bitter or virulent but are merely the commonplace ideas that almost any Christian humanist would have held in 1532–4. Part of the giants' character has been injected into them by Rabelais the man from the loftier realms of scriptural and Stoic thought. Their jerkiness as fictional characters is due to the fact that this particular element has not been coordinated to form a unified whole in which the readers can believe. In *Pantagruel* and *Gargantua* the giants are quite earnest when talking about war or about religion, and they tend to take it for granted that words are unblinkable realities; Pantagruel's benevolence is visible in his face and this one trait makes him come alive on a fictional level.

After this first book, we meet Pantagruel again in the *Tiers Livre*. He has now grown up and there are few of the hilarious gigantic jokes that were used previously to show the discrepancy between reality and the marvellous. As a fictional character he is set firmly within the gigantic framework of the beginning and end of the *Tiers Livre*. In one sense he has developed into an adult – Stoic and scriptural – he is the leader of the company. But the Stoic aspects do not make him into a tragic figure. When we look at another Stoic literary hero, Vergil's Aeneas, we can clearly see a development from the resigned servant of Fate in the early books to the willing collaborator with Providence, the purposeful leader of his people in the latter part of the poem. 'We see the increasing load of responsibility that lies on a leader's shoulders, the self-control that responsibility demands, the sacrifices and the anguish of decision that it imposes, the flaws in Aeneas' character that it discovers.'[7]

There is nowhere in the whole *Tiers Livre* a crisis which calls for an anguished decision on the part of Pantagruel; his own marriage is an affair totally outside his control; to a Stoic, marriage is externally without value, and when Gargantua is brought in from the dead to speak against marriages contracted without the consent of parents, Pantagruel seems almost in a hurry as he says 'I leave it to you, father.' Nowhere are there sacrifices to be made; and the self-control which is in the character of Pantagruel is perfect as a norm in comedy. However, to see Pantagruel as a norm for a delightfully riotous and grotesque comedy is one thing; to see him as a dramatically conceived character is another. And it is not in Pantagruel's power to become the latter. In the chapter on the *Tiers Livre* (chapter 6) we saw the two threads of character running through the whole book, not alternating in any chosen pattern but with the serious one always playing the more dominant rôle. There was an element of schematization in Pantagruel which made him rather an abstraction, so far as his ideas were concerned. As a norm in a comedy it was the intellectual skeleton of the character that was important. Take the counterpoint of Panurge and Pantagruel. Through the detached eyes of Pantagruel the antics of Panurge appear extremely comic. This is where the Stoic values in fact become relevant to the basis of the comic; for it is precisely because Pantagruel does not assign great importance to the things that are outside his control and directed by Destiny or Fate that he is able to be detached.

But in syntactic terms he is much better orientated in the *Tiers Livre* than he was in the first book, and a brief glance at the style of his speeches and their content will prove instructive. Take his first speech in chapter 2: at the end of Panurge's *bled en herbe* discourse Pantagruel gives an answer in the form of an example taken from the Roman emperors. Every time he uses examples from either Greek or Latin antiquity he adopts the academic style. Thus in chapter 5 too his discourse on the subject of borrowing money is bound tightly together by the careful use of adverbs, relative and adverbial clauses. In chapter 6 there is a dialogue between Pantagruel and Panurge and his interruptions again exhibit a hypotactic structure: for instance, he gives his view of the law of Moses in sentences which start with 'c'estoit affin que ... ainsi pour le moins ... aussi que ... pour mieulx ... seulement', where the multiple subordinate clauses convey a general impression of weight and immobility. In chapter 7 he presents the Stoic position on the neutrality of external things like clothes, and here again the structure is complex: 'Chascun abonde en son sens, mesmement en choses foraines, externes et indifferentes, lesquelles ... pource qu'elles ... qui est ...: bien, si bonne est ...; mal, si ...' This one sentence is divided up by a colon and two semi-colons, but relative and conditional clauses carry the structure along. The vocabulary is Latinized: for example, the Pauline original *Unusquisque in suo sensu abundet* (Rom. xiv. 5) reveals that '*abonde*' is subjunctive not indicative, *l'esprit munde* is used in the sense of *clean from filth* which it had in Latin, and '*indifferentes*' is a recent loan word from Latin into French. (See Calvin's use of it in the 1541 edition of the *Institution*.) Thus one can see reflected in stylistic terms the development of Pantagruel into a more mature and serious character.

Pantagruel is committed to expounding things allegorically, because of the rhetoric. In the first place, the ability to argue a case one way while Panurge by similar methods argues the opposite is the very basis of the comic counterpoint between them, and rhetoric can produce the elaboration of simple points into vast complicated correspondences. Secondly, while he uses allegory one way and Panurge another, the reader, without even following the arguments of either, knows that Pantagruel is bound to be right, since we have already seen that he is the norm for the comedy. Thus, when Pantagruel expounds the sibylline pronouncements solemnly but with his tongue in his cheek we have Panurge saying, 'Vous exposez allegoricquement ce lieu, et l'interpretez à larrecin et furt. Je loue l'exposition, l'allegorie me plaist, mais non à vostre sens'* (chapter 18). Or in chapter 12, we find a parody of allegorical exegesis in Pantagruel's exposition of the Vergilian line

Nec Deus hunc mensa, Dea nec dignata cubili est.

Panurge's quest is gratuitous: and Pantagruel knows that in his companion he has a perfect example of someone who will take all the advice at one level only. Thus, to prove that Minerva is the goddess from whom Panurge will provoke unfavourable reactions Pantagruel says, 'Plus vous diray, et le prendrez comme extraict de haulte mythologie.'† One can savour Pantagruel's tongue-in-cheek attitude here by seeing Panurge's reaction to it, 'Ventre guoy ... seroys je bien Vulcan, duquel parle le poëte?'‡ The staple of most comedy is incongruity; here one has two people, both drawing out the thread of their verbosities on the unexpected way that concepts, modes of experience, and behaviour can be linked together. Panurge is always imperturbably

---

* You expound this Passage allegorically, and interpret it to Theft and Larceny. I love the Exposition, and the Allegory pleaseth me; but not according to the Sense whereto you stretch it.
† Moreover, I will tell you, and you may take it as extracted out of the profoundest Mysteries of Mythology ...
‡ By the Belly of St. Buff ... should I be Vulcan, whom the Poet blazons?

serious; Pantagruel is always tolerant. Moreover, in the same chapter he has a joke against Panurge, saying that Panurge has more courage and bravery than he thought but after all ' "c'est ce que l'on dict, que le Jan en vaulx deux, et Hercules seul n'auza contre deux combattre". "Je suys Jan?" dist Panurge. "Rien, rien," respondit Pantagruel. "Je pensois au jeu de l'ourche et tricquet-rac." '* The joke about cuckolds is lost on Panurge precisely because he can only see one side of the question. This links with language: Pantagruel and Panurge are poles apart on the very concept of the origin of communication. In chapter 19 Pantagruel asserts that language is not natural (a distinctly anti-Stoic belief as the Stoics thought that all words correspond to something in the physical world) but rather a system of coding worked out according to the convenience of peoples: 'C'est abus, dire que ayons languaige naturel. Les languaiges sont par institutions arbitraires et convenences des peuples; les voix (comme disent les dialecticiens), ne signifient naturellement, mais à plaisir.'† This means that one can convert one thing into another by verbal substitution and so exploit rhetoric and satire to demonstrate that words are merely words, with no hidden meaning or hermetic secret. Pantagruel believes in *conventional* language – this is the modern view, and one could find plenty of support for it from Dante to Du Bellay. It is important for the norm in the comedy: Rabelais is saying what would be approved as commonplace by his contemporaries. Panurge, on the other hand, believes in *natural* language: that is, words correspond directly to reality. If he learns to ask the right questions, if he learns how to extract the hidden meaning in any linguistic communication – then words will lead to truth. But this is to impose on language an entirely arbitrary use of words

* nor is it strange; for the Jan is worth two, and two in fight against Hercules are too too strong. Am I a Jan? quoth Panurge. No, no, (answer'd Pantagruel) my mind was only running upon the lurch and tricktrack.

† It is a meer abusing of our Understandings to give Credit to the words of those, who say that there is any such thing as a Natural Language. All Speeches have had their primary Origin from the Arbitrary Institutions, Accords and Agreements of Nations in their respective Condescendments to what should be noted and betokened by them. An Articulate Voice (according to the Dialecticians) hath naturally no signification at all; for that the sence and meaning thereof did totally depend upon the good will and pleasure of the first Deviser and Imposer of it.

and ultimately to make language the unconscious store of his own sexual desires.

But if we were expected always to react favourably to Pantagruel and unfavourably to Panurge, that would imply that we should accept the truth of all Pantagruel's explanations of the world. But the comedy depends on the perspective provided by the Olympian author and so we view the two contestants and their rhetoric impartially. The Olympian author is supremely self-conscious: he suppresses all explicit moral judgements and it is up to the reader to catch the moral hints. To quote Northrop Fry, 'Rhetorical value-judgements are closely related to social values, and are usually cleared through a customs-house of moral metaphors: sincerity, economy, subtlety, simplicity and the like'.[8] Through the perspective he himself constitutes, and the little hints he provides throughout the text, Rabelais creates in Pantagruel a character who may at times be expressing ideas that he accepted, but at other times can be seen as contradicting what he actually believed. It is in the *Tiers Livre* that Rabelais's irony reaches its fullest development. The reader is shown the paradoxical nature of everything – attitudes, characters, religious views, metaphysical ideas – and cannot adopt a steady and consistent view.

There is about the characterization of Pantagruel in the *Tiers Livre* very much of the technique of *collage*: the glueing of pieces of string, strips of paper, corks or boxes of matches to canvas and the application of ink, oil paint or gouache to them. For Rabelais has taken hints of characters from the old chronicles, the *chansons de geste*, epic and romance, and created out of them a new character Pantagruel, who is to be partly a spokesman for Rabelais's own ideas, partly the norm for comedy, partly the leader of a company in a world where the two main principles are *joie de vivre* and human tolerance. As in our reaction to *papiers collés*, evaluation depends on our response to the new form of art, with its own idiom, vocabulary and syntax, and on the degree to which these combine successfully with Rabelais's linguistic skill and transform his Menippean satire into comedy.

A few further observations can be made about Pantagruel in the

Quart Livre. Between the two versions his rôle altered. In the 1548 (partial) edition he is a member of the company; but by 1552 he has acquired all the traits of a leader of the company. For example, in chapter 3 of the 1548 version he stands with frere Jan on board ship and Panurge 'dist secretement à Pantagruel et à frere Jan' to stand on one side and watch the fun. In the 1552 version Epistemon takes Pantagruel's place next to frere Jan and thus Pantagruel is not in on the joke that Panurge is planning to play on Dindenault. Again, in chapter 6 of the 1548 version Pantagruel acts as a member of the ship's crew in asking after one Chiquanous who has just been beaten, while in the 1552 version (chapter 16) the *nous* technique takes over the more trivial rôle at this point, 'Pantagruel estoit resté en sa nauf et ja faisoit sonner la retraicte. Nous, doubtans qu'elles feussent . . .'* Numerous other alterations of this kind between the 1548 and the 1552 version make it clear that Pantagruel has passed beyond a purely trivial and comic narrative rôle and has surpassed all the other characters in the degree of schematization and abstraction that he exhibits. Moreover, not only is Pantagruel now the leader, but the framework of the *merveilleux* is as firmly established in the *Quart Livre* as it was in *Pantagruel* or *Gargantua*.

That Rabelais has not developed Pantagruel any further as spokesman of a religious point of view can be illustrated from the episode of the storm at sea (chapters 18–24). Here a number of key scriptural and Calvinian words like *praedestiné, evertuer, scandale* and *cooperer* are used, but with some ambiguity. On the one hand Rabelais is consciously playing with words which by this time have dangerous connotations; and on the other, there is a serious condemnation of the fundamental tenets of a non-religious attitude. This second point is the really important one, and it is clearly illustrated in the opposition between the active collaborators with God's will and the passive instruments like Panurge, who do nothing but weep, wail and ridicule the whole company. For both these points, we can again usefully compare the two versions. For example, in the whole of chapter 19 the

---

* Pantagruel had kept on board, and already had caus'd a Retreat to be sounded ... We ask'd them ...

second version makes only one addition to Pantagruel's rôle. And that is, he is described as 'prealablement avoir imploré l'ayde du grand Dieu Servateur et faicte oraison publicque en fervente devotion...'* This is in keeping with his rôle in the first chapter (in both versions): as leader of the company, he there holds a public religious service, prays and then leads the congregation in singing Marot's translation of the psalm *Quand Israel hors d'Aegypte sortit*. This is the only addition to Pantagruel's rôle in the whole chapter; he fades out as the burlesque between frere Jan and Panurge is spotlighted. One has only to glance at Erasmus's *Naufragium* (which Rabelais certainly knew and imitated in this episode) to see the vast differences in treatment. Erasmus has the captain of the ship coming up at this point to say, 'Friends ... I'm no longer master of my ship; the winds have won. The only thing left to do is to put our hope in God and each one prepare himself for the end.'[9] Later on he comes up again and says, 'Friends ... the hour warns each of us to commend himself to God and prepare for death.' This is indeed a pessimistic verdict on saving the ship, and its bearing on the satire is quite clear: Erasmus gives us this speech *before* the satiric description of the sailors singing *Salve Regina* and calling on the Virgin *Stella Maris*, as queen of the sky and ruler of the world. The norm is provided by Adolph, the character telling the story; the themes and incidents satirize humanity's behaviour during a crisis; there is an echo throughout of Saint Paul's adventures as related in Acts, chapters 27 and 28. Our framework in Rabelais is the heightened fantasy of Panurge and the burlesque dialogue that he carries on with frere Jan. This is the angle of vision that we have when reading the episode.

The next intervention of the pilot and Pantagruel is only found in the 1552 version. Pantagruel declares 'En sommes nous là ... Le bon Dieu servateur nous soyt en ayde' and the captain Jamet Brahier replies, 'Chascun pense de son ame, et se mette en devotion, n'esperans ayde que par miracle des Cieulx!'† The only other

---

* having first implor'd the help of the Great and Almighty Deliverer, and pray'd publickly with fervent Devotion ...
† Is it come to that, said Pantagruel, our good Saviour then help us ... To Prayers, to Prayers, let all think on their Souls, and fall to Prayers; nor hope to scape but by a Miracle.

serious intervention by Pantagruel while the storm is raging is in
the next chapter – another remark that is added in the 1552
version, 'Seigneur Dieu, saulve nous; nous perissons. Non
toutesfoys advieigne scelon nos affections, mais ta saincte volunté
soit faicte'.* There is a similarity between the voice from heaven
in *Pantagruel*, chapter 29, *Alors fut ouye une voix*, and the beginning
of the cry here *Alors feut ouye une piteuse exclamation* . . ., and the
words also allude to a passage in the Gospels, Matt. viii. 25,
where during a storm at sea Christ was awakened by his disciples
with the cry 'Domine, salva nos, perimus'. Similarly the second half
of the passage echoes Christ's words during the Agony in the
Garden 'Verumtamen non sicut ego volo, sed sicut te'. (Matt. xxvi.
40; cf. Luke xxii. 42: 'Verumtamen non mea voluntas, sed tua
fiat', and Mark xiv. 36: 'Sed non quod ego volo, sed quod tu'.)
These emotively charged allusions underline that this is a serious
intervention on Pantagruel's part, and the 1552 version has certainly come closer to Erasmus. Nevertheless, the differences between
Rabelais and Erasmus are still vast. At a number of points they
agree: they coincide as regards prayer, and the activity of each
member during the height of the storm, the hostility to monks, to
auricular confession and to the superstitious cults connected with
the Virgin Mary. But, much more important than these – which
had all been present already in the 1532 publication of *Pantagruel* –
are the serious aspects of religion that Erasmus introduced into his
Naufragium: the silent prayer to God by the woman in the story,
the captain's cry, which emphasizes the preparation of each
member on board for death, Adolph's condemnation of his own
injustices in his confession to God, his appeal to God for mercy
and his own sense of conscience. These are things which Erasmus
felt strongly about and they are brought to the fore in this
colloquy. In Rabelais's handling of the storm at sea there is by
contrast only one positive point about religion: and that is the
importance of prayer and activity. This has sustained his giants
all through the three previous books and it is one point in which
the *Quart Livre* shows a clear continuity with them. One must

* Lord save us, we perish: Yet not as we would have it, but thy holy Will be done.

conclude in fact that these three additions in the 1552 version are not in themselves sufficient evidence for Pantagruel's religious ideas; they merely show that he is as religious as his father and grandfather.

The next chapter (chapter 22 in the 1552 version) starts with Pantagruel sighting land. He speaks in the boisterous style that is now familiar to us, 'Terre, terre ... je voy terre! Enfans, couraige de brebis! Nous ne sommes pas loing de port.'* And later on in the chapter he says things that would strike us as discordant if we were not already familiar with the fabulous giant's trick of using a mock-epic name like Ucalegon (from Vergil's *Aeneid* and particularly from Juvenal, Satire 3), 'Mais qui est cetuy Ucalegon là bas qui ainsi crie et se desconforte? Ne tenoys je l'arbre sceurement des mains, et plus droict que ne feroient deux cens gumenes?'† What we have here is an abrupt shift of angle in our view of Pantagruel, and throughout the *Quart Livre* we are kept conscious of the irregular line that his fictional life is following. A couple of examples will be sufficient to indicate that Pantagruel is once more a fabulous giant.

The group of chapters around Quaresmeprenant (chapters 29–35) clearly show that we are meant to admire Pantagruel *qua* giant; in chapter 34 it is the Olympian author's voice that is heard when we read 'Vous dictes, et est escript que' or 'Vous nous racontez aussi d'un archier Indian' and we are meant to be astonished that, 'Le noble Pantagruel en l'art de jecter et darder estoit sans comparaison plus admirable.'‡ The Olympian author uses the same devices as he had in the first two books to suggest the *merveilleux* qualities of his giants: for example, the giant's measurements are compared to bridges and he is depicted vanquishing the Physetere single-handed.

As a fictional character Pantagruel does not develop much in

---

* Shoar, shoar ... land to, my Friends, I see Land, pluck up a good Spirit Boys, 'tis within a kenning, so we are not far from a Port ...

† But who is this Ucalegon below, that cries and makes such a sad moan? Were it not that I hold the Mast firmly with both my Hands, and kept it streighter than two hundred Tacklings ... [Motteux keeps the present tense *I hold* as in the 1548 version instead of the imperfect *tenoys* in the 1552 version.]

‡ The noble Pantagruel was without Comparison, more admirable yet in the Art of Shooting and Darting.

the fourth book. We can observe a growing irritability in his reaction to some of the jokes. Thus in chapter 9 after one of Panurge's quips, 'Le bon Pantagruel tout voyoit, et escouttoit; mais à ces propous, il cuyda perdre contenance', or in chapter 16 after Panurge's tale of the seigneur Basché, he says, 'Ceste narration ... sembleroit joyeuse, ne feust que davant nos œilz fault la craincte de Dieu continuellement avoir.'* In chapter 50 he is nearly sick at one of frere Jan's jokes and in chapter 60 he is moved to downright anger. In every case Pantagruel's reaction has a serious religious motivation: for example, in response to frere Jan's joke in chapter 50, 'Quand ... telz contes vous nous ferez, soyez records d'apporter un bassin. Peu s'en fault que ne rende ma guorge. User ainsi du sacre nom de Dieu en choses tant hordes et abhominables! Fy, j'en diz fy! Si dedans vostre moynerie est tel abus de parolles en usaige, laissez le là; ne le transportez hors les cloistres.'† If one recalls that Gargantua was brought into the *Tiers Livre* for the primary purpose of lashing out at clandestine marriages and canon law, then the fact that Pantagruel even in his 'natural' style has such earnest reasons for disliking the jokes of frere Jan and Panurge suggests a schematic line of seriousness in the giants running through the third and fourth books. But this breaks down sharply as soon as the Olympian author comes in, and one last example, the Death of Pan story (chapters 26–8), will show that the giants cannot be neatly summed up in this way. After the storm at sea the company comes to the isles of the Macreons where both the old Macrobe and Pantagruel hold the floor with their speeches. First of all, the context is firmly gigantic and unreal: from the welcome the people give them and the provisions they exchange to the Ionic language in which the old Macrobian talks, everything has to be taken with the usual pinch of salt. Furthermore Pantagruel takes seriously the episode that they have

* This Story would seem pleasant enough ... were we not to have always the Fear of God before our Eyes.

† Pray, said Pantagruel, when you are for telling us some such nauseous Tale, be so kind as not to forget to provide a Bason, Fryar Jhon; I'll assure you, I had much ado to forbear bringing up my Breakfast: Fy, I wonder a Man of your Coat is not asham'd to use thus the Sacred Name of God, in speaking of things so filthy and abominable. Fy, I say: If among your Monking Tribes such an abuse of Words is allow'd, I beseech you leave it there, and do not let it come out of the Cloysters.

just passed through – the storm at sea, whereas the other characters are more ambiguous in their attitude. Finally, Pantagruel takes
up the topical note, the death of Guillaume du Bellay, links it with
exempla from antiquity and makes the distinction between secular
heroes and the one God Pan, who is Christ.[10] Here Pantagruel
speaks for Rabelais the real man once more: he cites the Stoics but
does not diminish Christ to the scale of a classical hero; rather he
presents him clearly as the God of the Christian faith. When he
uses *tout* he is moving towards a Christian and indeed specifically
Pauline climax, 'tout ce que sommes, tout ce que vivons, tout ce
que avons, tout ce que esperons, est luy, en luy, de luy, par luy'.*
The speech is in an academic style and our intellectual sympathy
with its contents is engaged. But at the end the Olympian author
returns again with 'nous veismes les larmes decouller de ses œilz
grosses comme œufz de austruche. Je me donne à Dieu, si j'en mens
d'un seul mot'.† We are left, then, on the fictional level with the
two Pantagruels that we met in the first book. But fictional
characters have within them a large reservation: does one ever
really believe in them? Are they not part of the suspension of
disbelief which carries the reader through the story until the book
is closed, when the reader no longer has to accept them as real
human beings? With the giants there never was a suspension of
disbelief, for all the time we were conscious of the fact that the
merveilleux and the real, the fantasy and the grotesque, the
bouffonnerie and the serious, the robot and the human were
included together. The reader always found it impossible to
believe in them as fictional characters. Where the other characters
like Dindenault, Picrochole, Panurge, Homenaz and frere Jan
were all mirrors in which Rabelais could offer the reader images
of himself and his situation as a writer, with the giants Rabelais
represented norms of behaviour in a fantastic and gigantic world.
The core of his giants is health; and in some senses, that is more
important than the intellectual schematization that they undergo

---

* for all that we are, all that we live, all that we have, all that we hope, is Him, by Him'
from Him, and in Him (cf. Acts xvii. 25–8).
† we saw the Tears flow out of his eyes as big as Ostridge's Eggs. God take me presently,
if I tell you one single syllable of a Lye in the Matter.

during the development of his art. Contagious laughter, the belly quake, is a primitive, an instinctive, a childlike humour that Hugo saw in Rabelais's works:

> Rabelais, que nul ne comprit:
> Il berce Adam pour qu'il s'endorme,
> Et son éclat de rire énorme
> Est un des gouffres de l'esprit.

And it is this humour, which dislocates the balance between body and soul, which is transmitted by the giants. Furthermore, there is the suggestion that nature, health and morals are intimately linked: what is morally desirable is physically attractive and living according to nature is living a good life. One might compare the Stoic paradox that only the morally good are free, since no man can wish to be bad, with the theme of excluding the ugly, botched and lame from the Abbey of Thélème or with the fact that all the characters possess healthy, vigorous bodies. One might see a similarity between non-commitment to any external affair in Montaigne with Rabelais's Stoic indifference: but in both the result is not a moral stance but an aesthetic one. For Rabelais, the suspension of judgement and the need to act as if terrestrial matters are not important became a fit theory for comedy. In Pantagruel we find health, an irrepressible overflow of energy mingled with human tolerance and hatred of inhumanity and cruelty.

There is no sense of sin at all in Rabelais; death is not a metaphysical problem; his heroes are devoid of mental anxiety or metaphysical crises; religion is taken for granted as something good. He writes above all a comic work: the grotesque frame of the books excludes any feeling of high tragedy. With the distance and detachment of the Olympian author we, as readers, are constantly disconcerted: our customary attitudes cease and pure metaphor starts at the same point as pure comedy; suspension of old ways of looking at the world and the creation of new ones. This is the last thing we have to look at before coming back to the Pantagruelism which sums up Rabelais's work.

POETIC PROSE

Poetry is a *disinterested* use of words: that is, words are not used in their current everyday context as a means to an end – the imparting of a practical communication. They are used free from the weight of utility and free too of the death that total comprehension brings. Poetry and literary prose are an art 'de contraindre continûment le langage à intéresser l'oreille' and an art which constantly moves in opposition to the 'penchant prosaïque du lecteur'. When Zola said, in his letter of 22 March 1885, to Henri Céard, 'Vous n'êtes pas stupéfait, comme les autres, de trouver en moi un poète ... J'agrandis, cela est certain ... J'ai l'hypertrophie du détail, le saut dans les étoiles sur le tremplin de l'observation exacte ...' he implied that his creation of a surrealist world, showing the interpenetration of phenomena and immense personalized forces playing on depersonalized men who are but puppets in a black and white universe, was poetic. Aesthetic and symbolical elements are so fused that, for instance, the last paragraph of *Germinal* is intensely satisfying to the reader, suggesting through the sound of pickaxes and the smell of a flowering spring a new kind of life within a cycle of birth and death.

Rabelais would have agreed with Zola on the qualities needed in a poet and would have made the same claim for his own fantastical and magnified world, quickened by humour and thick with detail, but he might have added that the listener/speaker conspiracy heightened the effect of surrealist poetry in his work. For, from his prologues onwards, Rabelais has made out a large contract between author and reader; and in his choice of the type of fiction he is writing – Menippean satire – he has emphasized that he asks of the reader a certain kind of attention and promises him something in return. Rabelais's ebullient creativeness in linguistic formulation demands from his reader not only suppleness of mind and imaginative sympathy but also a certain degree of self-discipline. The sheer delight the author has in creating something new from the raw materials of syllables or words; the thesaurus of words from Greek, Latin, dialects, jargon and slang which he exploits; the associations and semantic overtones he has recourse to and the different patterns speech itself embarks on – all this means that the reading of his work is at first rather slow. Moreover, for the whole of this chapter, one must leave Urquhart's interpretation, brilliant as it is, and concentrate solely on the French which Rabelais wrote.

To enter this complex fabric of words I am going to take the famous example of a sentence in English and follow the analysis made of it by Professor Gleason in his *Introduction to descriptive linguistics* (New York, 1961, p. 150): *The iggle squiggs trazed wombly in the harlish goop.* The syntactic structure is clear: the marker -*s* suggests the plural of a noun; -*ed* suggests a past tense of a verb; -*ly* which is normally the termination of an adverb and -*ish* is normally an adjectival form; the phrase *the iggle squiggs* is familiar to the reader through other constructions like it in English, and he identifies it as a definite article followed by an adjective and a noun; he infers that *trazed wombly* is a verb plus an adverb and the last part of the sentence – *in the harlish goop* – easily fits in as a prepositional phrase. The appeal to word-order, one of the fundamental structural markers in any language which we already know, is natural and justified, and the whole sentence satisfies our criteria of grammatical congruence. But the meaning is obscure: the only words that we recognize are *the, in* and *the;* dictionaries do not help us; we seek to work out a sense or several senses by analogy; we look for its context – but it is an isolated sentence. We conclude that it is a probable grammatical structure, but until we are given a clue as to the meanings of the words, it has to be classified as nonsense. This excursion into unreality could only be stimulating if it were either given a context or a lexicon. It might be a line of a poem where the semantic implications of other words in other lines would serve as pointers to the meaning of *iggle squiggs;* or it might be a line of a play where the character would be identifiable by other means.

Now compare this sentence with one of the languages which Panurge speaks at his first entry on stage:

Al barildim gotfano dech min brin alabo dordin falbroth ringuam albaras. Nin porthzadilkin almucathim milko prin al elmim enthoth dal heben ensouim; kuthim al dum alkatim nim broth dechoth porth min michais im endoth, pruch dal maisoulum hol moth dansrilrim lupaldas im voldemoth.

This has no clear structure markers such as Gleason's example showed; it is not a grammatical structure in a language that we already know; one guesses that it is an Indo-European language; one tries it out as a parody of Spanish with Arabic thrown in; but one does not really know of what language it is a deformation. If we read it aloud, the sound, the alliteration and the near-rhymes – '*broth dechoth porth* ... *indoth*' – strike us, and we conclude that it is a piece of alliterative non-sense. However, the context might help in interpreting the passage. This scene is the *coup de foudre* between Panurge and Pantagruel: on the one hand we know that Panurge is a pitiful figure and on the other hand Pantagruel 'falls for him' and misreads his features as an aristo-cratic mien. Panurge launches forth into languages that neither Pantagruel nor we his readers can understand. To Panurge, language is the stuff of magic rather than an instrument of reason; he is given the rôle of showing the duplicity of language; the world as articulated by Panurge is not the real world but a world turned upside down; the world as articulated by Pantagruel is the real world governed by commonsense. Panurge prefers words to things, the imaginary to the real and his only suppleness is verbal. He is perpetually in motion, an effervescent knave who has words at his command: whether existent or non-existent is immaterial to him and it is part of his 'placing' in *Pantagruel*. This is an inaugural comic scene with poetic implications. For, while Panurge is paraphrasing in different languages the fact that he is ravenously hungry and thirsty, the semantic, morphological and syntactic units of language produce an exoticism which dazzles Pantagruel, his henchmen, and us to blindness. Panurge is a figure who, by his very inexhaustibility, opts for the magic world of words rather than the sensible world of things. He already announces a surrealist world which by its absurdity disrupts our normal world.

This element of surrealism in Rabelais is akin to that of Joyce's. Out of the vast erudition come rushing forth words, sounds, assonances and alliteration like the famous thunderclap on the first page of *Finnegans Wake*, 'The fall (bababadalgharaghtakkinarronnkonnbronntonnerronntuonnthunntrovarrhounawnskawntoohoohoordenenthurnuk!)'. Joyce's thunder could be analysed into its 'morphemes' but it is the onomatopoeic effect which makes audible the voice of God's wrath causing man to fall in the Garden of Eden. Readers of both Joyce and Rabelais who catch the alliteration and enjoy the pleasure of sounds and polysyllables being embedded in new contexts, are caught up in the ebullience and form-creating energy they both exhibit. It is a two-way process between reader and author. As Professor Donald Davie said in his book, *Articulate Energy*,[1] 'The reader undertakes not to tear a word from its context and scrutinise it in isolation. The poet reserves the right to use at any point a word that may seem, by its appearance, to have little or no meaning; he engages, in return to give it meaning in the context of the whole.' The reader has to agree to let some words in a passage remain obscure at a first reading, in the expectation that the whole context will give them a meaning. This process is exciting but difficult, and can only be understood by an audience which is activated by a desire to discover for itself what Joyce and Rabelais meant. Neither of them subscribes to the fallacy that everything in literature is meant to be easily understood, but Joyce was always looking for expressions that were multi-layered so that the reader is mesmerized by the semantic barrage of words and in the end tires of *Finnegans Wake* and its narrative of man's tragicomic destiny. Rabelais has the conscious understanding that to push words too far away from a meaning is non-communicative.

Indeed, as a proof of his self-consciousness in communicating, Rabelais wrote the *Briefve Declaration* after he had finished the *Quart Livre* in which he explains some of the obscurities and difficulties that his readers might have come across. For example; '*Bringuenarilles*, nom faict à plaisir comme grand nombre d'aultres en cestuy livre', or '*Nargues et Zargues*, noms faicts à plaisir', or '*Decretalictonez*, meurtriers des Decretales. C'est une diction monstrueuse, composée d'un mot Latin et d'un autre Grec.' He consciously took the technique of neologism and word-coinage as an essential element of his comic, fantastic and burlesque book. So that the last example is the telescoping of a Latin with a Greek word and is *monstrueuse*, while another example, '*Comme Sainct Jan de la Palisse*, maniere de parler vulgaire par syncope, en lieu de l'Apocalypse; comme Idolatre pour Idololatre', is consciously copying the vulgar way of pronouncing the word Apocalypse. Queneau, in *Zazie dans le métro*, is doing precisely the same when he says, 'Skeutadittaleur (Ce que tu as dit à l'heure)', but in the poem *Si tu t'imagines*, he goes further than merely putting down what everyone hears,

> Si tu t'imagines
> si tu t'imagines
> fillette fillette
> si tu t'imagines
> xa va xa va xa
> va durer toujours
> la saison des za
> la saison des za
> saison des amours ...

Here we have gone beyond the literal transcription of demotic idiom, beyond the familiar virtuoso patter of words to a stage where literary tradition, rhythms, assonance, astonishment and aesthetic delight combine to make it a battle of wits between the author and his reader. For instance, the basic irony on which this renewal of Ronsard's *Mignonne, allons voir si la rose* rests, depends on a reader who is aware of certain trends in tradition, and of styles in communication. Joyce, Queneau and Rabelais are masters of encyclopaedic erudition and all three play with styles, with tones, with ironic levels and with the sound of the spoken word.

In the sixteenth century, style entailed ornateness. Erasmus, in his *De duplici copia* runs through all the devices a writer ought to be aware of, from the formulation of words for different occasions to figures of speech, with examples from classical literature. There are at least two ways in which any writer can train himself in language: either by deliberately restricting and refining his language (as in seventeenth-century France) or by extending the horizon of one language through borrowing from other languages. The sixteenth century chose the latter (as did, for instance, Laforgue, Apollinaire and Éluard). It is well known that most of the books of humanist rhetoric (that is, *before* French vernacular criticism had really started) concentrated to a high degree on copiousness or plentifulness – on having a rich array of words, and then being able to choose the best words for a particular occasion. When we see Rabelais in this context we understand how the processs of imitation was vital to him. For instance in words which are *sordida* (e.g. kitchen and bathroom terms) he had not only the whole medieval French tradition to imitate but also Petronius or Seneca in his *Apocolocyntosis*. For their latinity was far removed from what is now called classical Latin: it was literary Latin mingled with colloquial Latin, slang of the less highly educated, vulgarisms in pronunciation and grammar, old dialects, the jargon of soldiers, provincialisms, the hybrid language based on a mixture of Greek and Latin and rampant diminutives parodying poetic Latin. Erasmus saw as invaluable for humour and irony words which are *prisca* or obsolete and combinations of Greek and Latin words which *non mediocrem addunt gratiam*. Erasmus's ideal, and Rabelais's too, was that a writer should be in total command of every different note in the scale of words, of every semi-tone and tone in building a melody. This demanded a self-conscious presence of the author in the composition in the same way as Baudelaire, quoting Gautier, said, '*l'écrivain qui ne savait pas tout dire*, celui qu'une idée si étrange, si subtile qu'on la supposât, si imprévue, tombant comme une pierre de la lune, *prenait au dépourvu et sans matériel pour lui donner corps, n'était pas un écrivain*'.[2] But Erasmus did not write in his mother tongue. Rabelais did. The humanist Rabelais wrote in Latin; the artist Rabelais chose his mother tongue. And this choice freed him from his past and enabled him to use French as a poetic language by the very fact of its being *other*; the otherness which Montaigne opted for too.

We saw in the last chapter that in the giants' ways of writing letters, of making serious speeches and of long discourses we find what we called his 'academic' style. And in this conscious taking-up of Cicero there is a certain diffuseness and lack of conciseness, and even of judgement and taste, which remind one of Quintilian's dislike of the excesses of Asianic style in Book 8. 3.56, where words are 'et tumida et pusilla et praedulcia et abundantia et arcessita et exultantia ...' This is partly due to the bi-focal attitude to culture: reading Cicero or Seneca for their content inevitably affects one's native or vernacular style. (For example, classical scholars of the present age tend to have symmetry, the balance of phrases, the use of antithesis unconsciously instilled into them and so their English style tends to be more close to that of Gibbon than to that of Dr Leavis.) Partly too, the translation of aspects like Latin compounds meant that one had a style that was less concise than the original. And partly the awakening of languages in the Renaissance meant that writers became intensely aware of the poverty of their own vernacular and were drawn towards the grand style in prose and poetry. Valéry stated a truism after translating the *Eclogues* into French,

> La langue latine est, en général, plus dense que la nôtre. Elle n'use pas d'articles; elle fait l'économie des auxiliaires ... elle est avare de prépositions; elle peut dire les mêmes choses en moins de mots, elle dispose d'ailleurs des arrangements de ceux-ci avec une liberté qui nous est presque entièrement refusée, et qui fait notre envie. Cette latitude est des plus favorables à la poésie ...[3]

One is not surpised to find Rabelais less ebullient in imitating literary Latin than he is in the mixture of styles and in the transformation and recreation of Ciceronian periods into something quite exciting, which we shall see later.

Yet, paradoxically, it is the presence of Latin language and literature that starts Rabelais off on the path of reality to reach fantasy in that idiolect of French and Latin tongues. Take the simple example of Saint Victor's library (*Pantagruel*, chapter 7): the coupling of authors' names to fantastic titles was originally a popular technique, used through the middle ages. But very soon Rabelais leaves off satirizing the theological, symbolical and allegorical interpretations and starts to play with letters, with syllables, with their deformation and their alliteration. From *Barbouilamenta Scoti* he reaches 'La Pelletiere des Tyrelupins, extraicte de la *Bote fauve* incornifistibulée en *la Somme Angelicque*' where there is a juxtaposition of the '*Summa*' of Saint Thomas Aquinas with the coined French word '*incornifistibulée*'. It is an

artificial process by a detached author who can rely on his readers
to respond to every device of vulgarizing language, of mocking
allegorical titles and of playing with the French and Latin tongues.
In addition, the content of most of the titles is 'low': eating,
drinking, swearing, copulating, farting, urinating, so that in the
title of a book like, 'M. N. Rostocostojambedanesse, "De Mous-
tarda post prandium servienda, lib. quatuordecim, apostilati per
M. Vaurrillonis" ', the joke for the reader lies in realizing that the
first word can be 'parsed' in various ways; for instance, '*Rosto-
costo*' is the Italian for *côte rôtie*, and the following phrase may
either be a '*jambe d'anesse*', or if read another way the whole word
may be construed as 'Rostocostojam Bedanesse'. That would turn
it into a satirical shaft at Beda, the theologian par excellence of
the Sorbonne in the 1520s and the 1530s who was celebrated for
his gluttony. And the author's name is directly followed by a
Latin title, treating a culinary topic with enormous solemnity.
Another example is the list of cooks in the *Quart Livre*, chapter
40 – where the pleasure for the reader is firstly in its inexhaustibility and secondly in the word-coinages. Some names are
derived from culinary operations such as Marmitige, Paillefrite
or Guasteroust, others suggest the traditional foolishness of cooks,
as in Visedecaché (a nit-wit) or Badelory (a fool); others are taken
from the food eaten, like Cressonardiere, Escargotandiere or
Boudinanderie. This medieval way of exploiting kitchen humour
might remain on a flat prose level were it not animated in
Rabelais by the movement, the rhythm, the symmetry and the
alliteration within his prose. The encyclopædic erudition is fused
with the comic here, in the same way as Joyce's three-page kyrielle
of names attached to Anna Livia Plurabelle.

The ebullience and form-creating energy in these lists, word-
coinages and foreign words produce almost a ritual dance with
language, sometimes losing sight of meaning altogether, where
the main delight to the reader is in making new words. It is a
fermented language which operates in the four books; yet Rabelais is so far from being a disordered prose writer that one realizes
that his universe was as complex as Joyce's. The denseness and the
excessive concreteness of sixteenth-century vocabulary derive

partly from the fact that authors like Rabelais were extending its range. For Rabelais is not only aware that neologisms would increase the richness of the French language but he sees also that the principle of word-coinage can be used for comic and parodic purposes. He starts from the basic structure of French (syntax being the most heritable quality in any civilization, and a quality that Rabelais, unlike Joyce, valued) and he can add to this either Latin, Greek or purely invented elements so that the coinage is halfway between the recognizably intelligible and the purely fantastic. For example, he often adds Latin suffixes to non-Latin words, as in 'l'Escossais docteur Decrelalipotent' or suffixes like *-fluus* in 'la suavité melliflue de vos discretes parolles' or *-vagus* in *deux filopendoles coelivages*. The extreme delight with which one can read 'Antipericatametanapareugedamphicribationes merdicantium' arises from our knowledge that he has juxtaposed the Greek prepositions *anti, peri, kata, meta, ana, para* with a noun *cribationes* which looks like a Latin word. When we consult Latin dictionaries, we find there is a late Latin word *cribratura* which means 'the act of sifting', another one *cribratio* with the same meaning, and a number of similar words with meanings related to 'sieving', 'sifting' – what is now called a semantic field. But there is no noun *cribationes*. Rabelais has made up a noun not far removed from his contemporaries' knowledge of Latin and linked it with Greek prepositions; the result is a gallop through the Greek, the joke of the non-existent Latin and burlesque laughter when the reader expects *mendicantium* and to his surprise finds *merdicantium*.

To Rabelais's humanist friends, whole sentences in Janotus de Bragmardo's speech (*Gargantua*, chapter 19) would be comic like the following: 'pour la substantificque [note this adjective and link it to the *sustantificque mouelle* in the prologue to *Gargantua*] qualité de la complexion elementaire que est intronificquée en la terresterité de leur nature quidditative ...' This makes us laugh as a parody of pomposity, much as we laugh at the pompous cliché-ridden language of a businessman today who commences his discourse with an over-tired metaphor, proceeds to his divisions and subdivisions and terminates with a cliché citation. When we find the basic technique of word coinage allied with Latin and Greek formations informing a whole episode, as in the consultation with Her Trippa (*Tiers Livre*, chapter 25) we realize that comic lyricism is combined with the impressive sound of unfamiliar technicalities. Listen to the name of all the sciences that Her Trippa talks about, 'catoptromantie ... coscinomantie ... alphitomantie ... tyromantie ... gyromantie ... sternomantie ... libanomantie ... gastromantie ... ceromantie ... capnomantie ...' and read the whole passage constructed around these words. It satisfies our sense of hearing; the series of syllables ending on -*mantie* by repetition lulls our ears in an almost magic way; the symmetry of the words gives them a certain exotic charm; and the basic enumeration continues exhaustively. When we read it for the second time we see that the absurdly grotesque and comic Her Trippa is intoxicated by the effect of words and the illusion of encyclopaedic learning. Thus, for instance, the alliteration, the assonance and the near-rhyme scheme of the words reinforces the rhetoric, and it is heightened to such a peak that it reaches bathos, 'Par sycomantie? O art divine en feueille de figuier! ... Voulez vous en sçavoir par l'art de aruspicine? par extispicine? par augure prins du vol des oizeaulx, du chant des oscines, du bal solistime des canes?' The meaning of the words is comic: for example, *coscinomantie* means divination by means of sieves; *astragalomantie*, divination by means of little bones; *cephaleonomantie*, divination by means of an ass's head. While Her Trippa sings of his sciences, Panurge adopts the rôle that he took in the debate with Dindenault and makes short, sharp replies; Panurge responds on a prosaic level while Her Trippa expatiates on a poetic level. Her Trippa takes the readers along the track from reality to fantasy, while Panurge remains in reality. Her Trippa is dancing while Panurge is walking – to use Valéry's famous definition of the difference between poetry and non-literary prose.

At other times Panurge is dancing while Pantagruel or Epistemon are walking. Words are musicalized, in that the meaning, the sound, the alliteration become the primary incentive for using them. *Gargantua*, chapter 24, is a good example of the musicalization of words. A fast succession of assonances gives the impression of a rhythm hammered out, 'alloient veoir les lapidaires, orfevres et tailleurs de pierreries, ou les alchymistes et monoyeurs, ou les haultelissiers, les tissotiers, les velotiers, les horologiers, miralliers...' Repetitions, enumerations and the rhythm of the sentence bowl one along and one's attention is directed to the effects rather than to the meaning of each single word. Words are both keys to the conventional understanding of ideas and also something in their own right as musical entities. Words, sometimes deprived of rational connotations, produce a sound pattern which is suggestive of what Rabelais wants to talk about. Take, for instance, the Olympian author's description of Gargantua's codpiece (*Gargantua*, chapter 8). It is a Priapic description starting with a comparison between the *corne d'abondance* and Gargantua's *braguette;* then he elaborates on the physical magnificence of the codpiece, with the ordinary lexical meaning of the words suggesting that it is the finest in the world. But the patterning, the alliterative use of *s* and *r* make it into something more poetic, 'tousjours gualante, succulente, resudante, tousjours fructifiante, plene d'humeurs, plene de fleurs, plene de fruictz, plene de toutes delices'. The interweaving of sounds, the assonances, the rhyming nature of the present participle, the way that Rabelais repeats '*tousjours*' twice, following it with a four-fold repetition of '*plene de*', the concrete nature of the visualization – all reinforce the suggestion that Gargantua's codpiece is the finest, most succulent and most fruity in the whole world.

There are numerous examples where the sound actually dominates the meaning. A good instance is in the prologue to the *Tiers Livre* where there is a picture of Diogenes working to roll out his barrel. All the verbs are in the imperfect so that the sound *-oit* provides the key motif; one has the crackling of words ending in *-toit*, the whistling of words ending in *-soit*, the stuttering of words in *-poit*, and the sonorous orgy ends with *caparassonnoit*. The disorder of this listing is merely apparent, as is shown in the excellent analysis of it by Professor Tétel:[4] he says 'il lui faut un arrangement des verbes produisant des jeux sonores plus variés', and one would add that the sound and the rhythm supply an alternative form of structure from the syntax here.

le tournoit, viroit, brouilloit, barbouilloit,
hersoit, versoit, renversoit,
nattoit, grattoit, flattoit,
barattoit, bastoit, boutoit, butoit, tabustoit, cullebutoit,
trepoit, trempoit, tapoit, timpoit,
estouppoit, destouppoit, detraquoit,
triquotoit, tripotoit, chapotoit,
croulloit, elançoit, chamailloit,
bransloit, esbransloit, levoit, lavoit, clavoit, entravoit,
bracquoit, bricquoit, blocquoit,
tracassoit, ramassoit, clabossoit,
afestoit, affustoit,
baffouoit, enclouoit, amadouoit, goildronnoit, mittonnoit, tastonnoit,
bimbelotoit, clabossoit, terrassoit,
bistorioit, vreloppoit, chaluppoit,
charmoit, armoit, gizarmoit,
enharnachoit, empennachoit, caparassonnoit.

By classifying them and printing them almost in the shape of a free verse poem, Professor Tétel makes his point that our attention is directed by the sound-pattern of these enumerations. Moreover the arrangement of type in his analysis corresponds to an arrangement of rhythms. The apparent spontaneity of the list is belied by the variants made in the different editions of the *Tiers Livre* during Rabelais's lifetime, where he adds further words to an already apparently inexhaustible list. And the unselfconscious effect is belied by our awareness that Rabelais was consciously playing with the French language. The *sorcellerie évocatoire*, which is at the basis of every man's success as a literary writer, entails communication and intelligibility, And when we come across monstrosities of word-coinage like 'morrambouzevezengouzequoque-morguatasacbacguevezinemaffressé' the pleasure palls and we almost throw the book away. But it is precisely at this point that style enters and the battle of wits, in which the reader has a part to play, takes over.

In the creation of a macro–microcosm where everything is seen as if it were in a Chagall canvas it is the illogical stamp of most of Rabelais's images that we find comic. For instance, in *Pantagruel*, chapter 1, we have the comparison between the swelling nose and, 'la fleute d'un alambic, tout diapré, tout estincelé de bubeletes, pullulant, purpuré, à pompettes, tout esmaillé, tout boutonné et brodé de gueules ...' The two terms of comparison are so wide apart that the simile collapses; one forgets about the spigot of a winestill and concentrates on the one term, the nose, which is embroidered in the rest of the sentence. A feature of rhetorical style is its tendency to degrade metaphor. Poetry often reverses this degradation of language by restoring to a phrase which has become hackneyed its original imaginative content. Most of our language consists of dead metaphors, where we never think of the literal meaning. Language becomes an algebraic convention or a notation no longer evoking the images imprisoned in the words. Rabelais is always restoring health into the French language by the concreteness of his metaphors. Hardly ever does he affect emotional feelings, and hardly ever does he indulge in abstractions. The easiest way to concretize an image is to give it its proper sense so that the figurative sense enters in a comic way. For example, the list of activities of Gargantua's childhood (*Gargantua*, chapter 11). Beginning with the physical things that Gargantua did (e.g. *pissoit sus ses souliers*), he is soon using proverbs like *retournoit à ses moutons*, literally the first sense is 'going back to our sheep' while the second meaning is 'getting back to the point'. Or *mettoyt la charrette devant les beufz* ('putting the cart before the horse') which was an old proverb where readers do not expect the literal sense to be evoked. When it is, there is both an element of surprise and of comedy there. Later on Rabelais enjoys things like *Saultoyt du coq à l'asne* because by bringing in both the literal and the figurative senses ('to hop from one subject to another') he is poking fun at the literary genre *coqs à l'asne* and producing laughter from his readers. Rabelais chooses to qualify with fresh epithets, with unexpected adverbs, and to introduce one feature that is new not simply for the sake of its being new (although that too would delight him) but because the phrase or proverb is so old that it has ceased to convey a physical thing and has become an abstract counter. Thus for instance in the *Quart Livre* chapter 32 his description of Quaresmeprenant's sleep, 'Corybantioit dormant, dormoit corybantiant, les œilz ouvers comme font les lievres de Champaigne ...' forces us to think of the common expression *dormir les yeux ouverts* by adding two new details – '*corybantier*', which he explains in the *Briefve Declaration* was to sleep with one's eyes open, and the comparison with '*les lievres de Champaigne*'. Rabelais's imagination is obviously one that can make abstract things concrete: for example of Quaresmeprenant it is said, 's'il souspiroit, c'estoient langues de boeuf fumées', or 's'il rottoit, c'estoient huytres en escalle'. Or again in the *Quart Livre*, instead of accumulating evidence about Gaster's inventions Rabelais personifies Gaster and materializes every thought, desire and accomplishment so that the whole discussion shifts from the abstract to the concrete. But the excessive precision in physiological terms, when he describes Quaresmeprenant, takes the reader away from the visual to the non-visual. The details are more unreal, more shocking to commonsense and so cannot be perceived by the eye of the reader. Each line is based on a visual similitude, for instance: 'Les membranes, comme la coqueluche d'un moine', or 'L'entonnoir, comme un oiseau de masson', or 'La voulte, comme un gouimphe', and so long as one is concentrating simply on one line Rabelais's imagination is excellent. He is accurate on tiny details, but once one has asked 'What does Quaresmeprenant look like?' all the details fade away and one is left with almost an abstraction like 'comically repelling' or 'fantastic but unvisualizable'. There are so many concretions that they pile one on top of the other, and cancel each other out; one sees just a gigantic mass of flesh with very little to qualify it.

Where the linguistic comedy is based not on single words but whole sentences like, 'copieux, landores, malotrus, dendins, baugears, tezez, gaubregeux, gogueluz, claquedans, boyers d'etrons, bergiers de merde ...' (*Gargantua*, chapter 25), the opulence of the vocabulary seems effortless and unlimited, each item springing forward from the other. This list is comic, but another might start by being satirical and end by being fantastic, like the famous one 'Sorbillans, Sorbonagres, Sorbonigenes, Sorbonicoles, Sorboniformes, Sorbonisequens, Norborisans, Borsonisans, Saniborsans'. By playing with the order of letters in a word, by adding Latin suffixes like *-colus*, *-genus*, *-formus*, *-sequens* Rabelais can take his reader far enough away from the topical digs at the Sorbonne into a world of fantasy and unreality where the reader's whole delight is in looking at the way Rabelais is creative in language.

The creation of fantastic worlds on each island in the *Quart Livre* depends largely on this linguistic skill. Thus, for example, in chapter 9 in the *Isle des Alliances* Rabelais elaborates gratuitously with wit, verve and obscenity the terms of endearment used by the couples there: 'En pareille alliance, l'un appelloit une sienne: mon homelaicte, elle le nommoit mon oeuf; et estoient alliez comme une homelaicte d'oeufz.' This is only one of a long list of friendship terms where wit and ingenuity lie in perceiving the unexpected relationship between two different things, so that he can split something originally figurative into two literal halves. One is aware throughout this episode how schoolboy punning, lavatory humour and something as poetic as the *bled en herbe* passage (*Tiers Livre*, chapter 2) are thrown into the mixture until the words come spinning out like a succession of catherine wheels in a firework display. In another episode, chapter 43 of *Quart Livre*, the simple announcement from Alcofribas 'Ils ne vivent que de vent' gives the bias, and from there on the whole episode is one huge elaboration. The people eat, drink and live on wind; their houses are weather-cocks, 'Ilz ne fiantent, ilz ne pissent, ilz ne crachent en ceste isle. En recompense, ilz vesnent, ilz pedent, ilz rottent copieusement.' Out of a mass of words, sounds, metaphors, obscenity, crudity and erudition comes the fantastic world that Rabelais is creating.

The accumulation of synonyms – whether verbs, nouns, past participles, present participles, adjectives or adverbs – the repetition of words, sounds, of meanings and semantic resemblances is part of the exuberance of Rabelais's prose. The other part is in the rhythm and movement created by the words themselves. This, one could call a crescendo brought about by style. And in this kind of crescendo, one is conscious of symmetry, of asymmetry, of chiasmus, of antithesis all coming from the Latin side of Rabelais's reading and imitation, but not combining into a Ciceronian style. Take chapter 2 of *Pantagruel* and the description of the aridity and heat of that season when the giant was born:

Les herbes estoient sans verdure/,les rivieres taries/,les
   fontaines à sec/;
les pauvres poissons/,delaissez de leurs propres elemens/,
vagans et crians par la terre horriblement/;
les oyseaux tumbans de l'air par faulte de rosée/;
les loups/,les regnars/,cerfz/,sangliers/,dains/,lievres/,connilz/,
belettes/,foynes/,blereaux et aultres bestes/
l'on trouvoit par les champs mortes,
la gueulle baye.

When read aloud there is harmony and sonority as well as a forceful
rhythm here: a triple clause starts it off, perfect in its cadences;
the next rhythmic structure is still triple, but the position of the
adverb *'horriblement'* destroys the Ciceronian-ness of the period;
the next rhythmic group is one phrase followed by an accumulation of nouns where one reads more quickly and is carried along
both by the word-associations and by the sound. The last piece tails
away instead of being brought to a climax as Cicero would have
done. This is a totally different rhythm, which takes us along a
linear path, rather than the elaboration of a symmetrical structure.

   This is a transformation of the Ciceronian period, and Rabelais
often exploits it. In this example, the rhythmic expectancy is
destroyed and a new comic one takes its place: from *'loups'* onwards one is caught up in the inexhaustibility of the listing. There
is a combination of vigour and symmetry in this style which
points to the underlying *joie de vivre* that Rabelais has in linguistic
formulation: *Vivez joyeulx, esbaudissez vous, mes amours* seems
to be his constant advice to readers. Another example will show
that even with parallelisms of construction there is nothing here
like Latin structure:

De quoy se complaignant ... entendit que mieulx luy vauldroit rien *n'aprendre*
que *telz* livres soubz *telz* precepteurs *aprendre*, car leur *sçavoir* n'estoit que *besterie*
et leur *sapience* n'estoit que *moufles, abastardisant* les bons et nobles *esperitz* et
corrompent toute fleur de *jeunesse* ... quelle difference y a entre le sçavoir de voz
resveurs mateologiens du temps jadis et les *jeunes gens* de maintenant.

                         (*Gargantua*, chapter 15; my italics)

The repetition, grotesque rhythms, alliteration, echo rhyme,
grotesque word with a pejorative prefix ('*mateologiens*') – all poke
fun at scholastic learning. Or take 'Ilz *feurent folz* comme poëtes,

et resveurs comme *philosophes*; autant pleins de *f*ine *f*ollie, comme estoit leur *phi*losophie' (*Tiers Livre*, chapter 18), where the parallelism, the alliterative patterning which leads to the thought that '*philosophie*' is a '*f*ine *f*ollie': these are what catch the reader's ear.

It is a commonplace to remark on the speed and movement in Rabelais's dialogue. The whole quest of the *Tiers Livre* is a linguistic game where the author can make correspondences around the two words *coqu* and *mariage*. I am going to take one scene in that book – the consultation of Trouillogan by Panurge in chapter 36 – and explore its implications both for the comic and for movement. The ground base is Panurge's narcissism, his egoism, his *philautia;* he is the person who does not know that he does not know anything. There is added to these traits a comic loss of temper. (Cf. Alceste in Molière or indeed Panurge's consultations with Raminagrobis or Her Trippa.) Trouillogan is also risible, with his total lack of understanding and his inability to communicate anything – itself a comment on Pyrrhonian philosophy.

P. ... me doibs-je *marier*?

TR. Il y a de l'apparence.

P. Et si je *ne marie poinct*?

TR. Je n'y *voy* inconvenient aulcun.

P. Vous n'y en *voyez* poinct?

TR. Nul, ou la *veue* me deçoit.

P. Je y en trouve plus de *cinq cens*.

TR. Comptez les.

P. Je diz improprement parlant, et prenent nombre certain pour incertain; determiné, pour indeterminé, c'est à dire beaucoup.

TR. J'escoute.

P. Je ne peuz me passer de femme, de par tous les diables.

TR. Houstez ces villaines bestes.

P. De par Dieu soit! Car mes Salmiguondinoys disent coucher seul ou sans femme estre vie brutale, et telle la disoit Dido en ses lamentations.

TR. A vostre commandement.

P. Pe lé quau De! j'en suis bien. Doncques, me *marieray je*?

TR. Par adventure.

P. M'en trouveray je bien?

TR. Scelon la rencontre.

P. Aussi, si je *rencontre* bien, comme j'espoire, seray je heureux?

TR. Assez.

P. Tournons à contre poil. Et si *rencontre* mal?

TR. Je m'en excuse.

P. Mais conseillez moy, de grace. Que doibs je faire?

TR. Ce que vouldrez.

P. *Tarabin tarabas.*

TR. Ne invocquez rien, je vous prie.

P. On nom de Dieu soit! Je ne veulx sinon ce que me conseillerez. Que m'en conseillez vous?

TR. Rien.

P. Me mariray je?

TR. Je n'y estois pas.

P. Je ne me mariray doncques poinct?

TR. Je n'en peu mais.

P. Si je ne suis marié, je ne seray jamais coqu?

TR. Je y pensois.

P. Mettons le cas que je sois marié.

TR. Où le mettrons-nous?   (The italics are mine.)

And so the two go on and on. It is clear that Panurge is asking the same questions as the ones we have met throughout the book, and Trouillogan is not even answering them. But here Panurge's earlier speechifying is compressed and speeded to such an extent that his questions are cut off, his obscurity is heightened and his temper gets frayed almost from the beginning. His first question is like a lash of the whip that sets the top spinning again; Trouillogan's answer is not an answer to Panurge's question; Panurge's second question is the first one put into the negative and it receives the same sort of response from Trouillogan. Panurge's third question takes up the '*voir*' of Trouillogan – who in turn takes the question absolutely literally – he is thinking of the act of perceiving while Panurge is talking of the act of understanding. Panurge's comment that he can *see* 500 inconveniences to getting married gets the answer 'Count the 500'. And so Panurge has to explain why he had chosen to express 'many' as a specific large number. The dialogue so far has moved at an incredible pace with the couplets of disappointment alternating with the literal sense of Trouillogan. At this point Panurge invokes all the devils and again Trouillogan takes it quite literally – get rid of such foul beasts around you! Panurge, the reader notices, gets irritated, nay angry and indignant, and the created author brings in all the leit-motifs of his excessive lust: swearing, racy language, the wenches of Salmigondin juxtaposed with the speech of Dido on her death and we realize that the fool is letting all the aspects of his temperament run riot. The final oath '*Pe lé quau De*' ends this little dance. And he starts from scratch again, with '*Doncques*' should I get married or not? The second dance is exactly like the first but with slight variations and inversions, the fixed point being '*rencontre*'. One feels Panurge's temper rising with phrases like '*de grace*', '*tarabin tarabas*', until he bursts forth in anger, 'On nom de Dieu soit! Je ne veulx sinon ce que me conseillerez'. The tone is raised and shouting takes the place of talking. He has ended the dance on a high pitch of frenzy. And again he starts from the beginning, tracing again the steps of the previous movements. The alternation between Trouillogan's obtuse literalism and the comic automatism of the fool is exactly the same as in the two previous dances, so that the reader laughs at both, ' "Mettons le cas que je sois marié." "Où le mettrons-nous?" '

In this slice of dialogue the dramatic and comic rhythm depends almost entirely on the reader's ear not on his eye. The grammatical resources of both are contrasted: those of Trouillogan being short, sharp, logical and detached, while those of Panurge are a mixture of emotive words and longer words which in the dialogue make a nonsensical statement. For example, Trouillogan's '*Comptez les*' and '*J'escoute*' frames the muddled language of, 'Je diz improprement parlant, et prenant nombre certain pour incertain; determiné, pour indeterminé, c'est à dire beaucoup.' The personalized and contrasting grammatical style of the two characters dramatizes the sequence of topics and determines the whole dance of the conversation. Furthermore the tones of the dialogue also contrast: it is like a bizarre duet, in which Trouillogan singing throughout in time and tune, sets off the shrill and cracked voice of Panurge. The gap between the voices makes it clear that there is something breathless and something uncontrollable about the vicissitudes of the world; Panurge feels that if he could only get an answer *now* from Trouillogan he would be saved from personal disaster. He finally bursts out, 'Par la chair, je renie; par le sang, je renague; par le corps je renonce. Il m'eschappe.' And the dialogue is at an end.

This dialogue is a comic masterpiece and its excellence is due to Rabelais's aural skill and his dramatic inventiveness. The last two examples that I want to take are a contrast to each other: in the one, the context demands that the rhythm is slow and dignified. It is the famous passage on the Stoic attitude of Pantagruel in the *Tiers Livre*, chapter 2; 'Car tous les biens que le ciel couvre et que la terre contient en toutes ses dimensions: haulteur, profondité, longitude, et latitude, ne sont dignes d'esmouvoir nos affections et troubler nos sens et espritz.' The simple predication has recursive phrases and clauses embedded between subject and verb; the main verb comes two-thirds of the way through but is carefully prepared for by the noun '*biens*' which is the fourth word. The beginning is the forceful word '*car*', which draws our attention to the fact that this sentence gives reasons why Pantagruel should not be *scandalizé*. There are two short subordinate clauses introduced by *que*, there is an enumeration of the '*dimensions*' and finally there is a reduplication of verbs and nouns which bring the sentence to an almost Ciceronian close. The rhythm is unhurried, and majestic. But the movement is not at all the same as the next example, where the Olympian author describes the '*enfleure tres horrible*' in chapter 1 of *Pantagruel*:

Les aultres enfloyent par les espaules,/
et tant estoyent bossus
   qu'on les appelloit *montiferes*,/
      comme *porte montaignes*,
dont vous en voyez encores par le monde en
divers sexes et dignités,/
et de ceste race yssit Esopet,/
duquel vous avez les beaulx faictz et dictz par escript./
Les aultres enfloyent en longueur par le membre,
qu'on nomme le laboureur de nature,/
en sorte qu'ilz le avoyent merveilleusement long,
     grand, gras, gros, vert et
        acresté à la mode antique,/
si bien qu'ilz s'en servoyent de ceinture,
le redoublans à cinq ou six foys par le corps:/
et s'il advenoit,/
   qu'il feust en poinct et eust vent en pouppe,/
à les veoir eussiez dict que c'estoyent gens qui eussent

leurs lances en l'arrest/
   pour jouster à la quintaine.
Et d'iceulx est perdue la race,/
  ainsi comme disent les femmes,
  car elles lamentent
        continuellement qu'
  Il n'en est plus de ces gros, etc.
vous sçavez le reste de la chanson.

Where the Ciceronian sentence in the previous example could be silently read and savoured this passage has to be read aloud before one gets the flavour of its rhythm and relishes the variety of tones in the rhetoric. The presentation of information which is fantastic, the alternation between past and present tenses and the semi-symmetry of each part make each enlargement twist and turn through the very movement of style. The long sentence in the second 'stanza' is mingled with hypotactic *'en sorte que, si bien que'* sentences and paratactic *'et et et'* ones. The verbal action is comic; the rhythm is sometimes running, sometimes tripping, and sometimes comes to a complete halt; and the long sentences are not *containing*, that is, there is no explicit sign of balance, of clauses forming a pattern, but rather they are *dislocating*: they make us aware of the created author rather than of the content of what is being said. They make us aware of the author's imagination: the fantastical basted with burlesque and grotesque. Rabelais is here playing the rôle of *l'Abstracteur de quintessence*, the alchemist of words and rhythms. The qualities of *nouveauté*, and *dépaysement* are predominant and he energizes them through the power of his rhythm. Unlike imagery, rhythm is essential to our conception of poetic prose and it is here that Rabelais may be called a poet. Valéry's statement, 'Le tempérament national devenu de plus en plus prosaïque depuis le XVIe siècle ...' could be fruitfully applied to both Rabelais and Montaigne. The grand style, admired by the sixteenth century, became in the hands of these two great writers something totally different from a Ciceronian style. Montaigne said; 'Quand j'entreprendroy de suyvre cet autre stile [i.e. that of Cicero] aequable, uny et ordonné, je n'y sçaurois advenir ...' (II.17) and Rabelais could have said the same.

For the movement that he transfuses through his style is not Cicero's but his own.

If we now try looking at the famous Pantagruelism we find this *mot bouffon de ce bouffon* (Dupuyherbault) rather puzzling. The word *pantagrueliste* does not appear at all in the 1532 edition of *Pantagruel*: the first time that we meet it is in *Gargantua*, chapter 1, where it is simply a term of address to the readers, 'en Pantagruel-isant, c'est-à-dire beuvans à gré et lisans les gestes horrificques de Pantagruel',* where Rabelais takes the trouble to give a spoof explanation. The second time is in chapter 3 – 'Messieurs les anciens Pantagruelistes ont conformé ...' where the Olympian author is being satirical about historians and chroniclers. In the same book (chapter 48) he uses the corresponding derivative from Gargantua merely to distinguish the followers of Gargantua in the battle from those on the other side. Near the end of the *Tiers Livre*, in chapter 50, he uses the term *pantagruelistes* to mean scholars or those who busy themselves about *pantagruelion: Quelques pantagruelistes modernes ....* So in one sense, Pantagruel-ism in the books themselves does not mean anything more than is required and made clear by each context in which it occurs. It is a comic coinage and we are not meant to take it seriously.

But these words also occur in the prologues and are sometimes actually an addition in a later edition, as for example, chapter 34 of *Pantagruel* where the author says, 'si desirez estre bons Panta-gruelistes (c'est à dire vivre en paix, joy, santé, faisans tousjours grande chere) ne vous fiez jamais en gens qui regardent par un pertuys'.† This links up with the *joie de vivre*, both intellectual and physical, that is the prevailing attitude of the whole work. The themes of good health, good eating and drinking are connected with laughter. And this is what he expects his readers to be: people who enjoy laughing, with an internal serenity that comes from a certain attitude to war, religion and indeed everything in

---

* in your pantagruelising, that is to say, in drinking stiffly to your own hearts desire; and reading the dreadful and horrifick acts of Pantagruel.

† and if you desire to be good Pantagruelists (that is to say, to live in peace, joy, health, making your selves alwayes merry) never trust those men that always peep out at one hole.

life. The same term and the same evaluation of it occurs in the
prologue to *Gargantua*: his readers are represented as *en toutes
bonnes compaignies de Pantagruelistes*. Thus in the first two books the
emphasis is certainly on *bons viveurs*, but *bon viveurs* who will read
these books with the tolerance, sense of humour and delight in
playing with language that they demand.

In the prologue to the *Tiers Livre* there is a different definition
of Pantagruelism (quoted in chapter 3, p. 38) which stresses above
all tolerance and a good heart: it is still of a piece with the author–
reader conspiracy, and so once again will comprise 'all those who
read my books'. The last and by far the fullest definition offers a
synoptic view of the concept. It is given in the prologue to the
Quart Livre: 'Je suys, moiennant un peu de Pantagruelisme (vous
entendez que c'est certaine gayeté d'esprit conficte en mespris des
choses fortuites), sain et degourt ...'* The essential Stoicism of
this statement is borrowed from the title of Budé's *De contemptu
rerum fortuitarum*, published in 1521; but the Stoicism of that work
hardly corresponds to the one that Rabelais defines here, and one
is led to think that he is gently parodying the humanist scholars of
the time. On the other hand, the detachment and the delight that
one finds in the prologues, the Stoic indifference to external affairs,
with the giants, like corks in the sea, constantly bobbing to the
surface of adversity, is certainly there but it is not the whole
picture. For when we include all the other characters as well, we
find many other qualities held up for our admiration – tolerance,
a sense of fun, a tranquil attitude to life combined with the
determination to live it to the full, and of course physical bravery.
So there are in a sense two overlapping circles (see p. 227).

Flaubert said laughter could be defined as 'le dédain et la compré-
hension mêlés, et en somme la plus haute manière de voir la vie'
and Rabelais's books on the giants certainly endorses this. As a
Menippean satirist who took giants as mouthpieces of his own
ideas but who endowed them with *joie de vivre* and tolerance in a
world quickened by wit and laughter, Rabelais takes the ideas,
attitudes and values of the real world, which is Erasmian in its

---

* By the means of a little Pantagruelism, (which you know is a certain Jollity of Mind
pickled in the scorn of Fortune) you see me now Hale, and Cheery ...

orientation, and transmutes that world into the fictional world. In the end, he does not create truth and reality around his giants, but around the whole universe that he has created in his work.

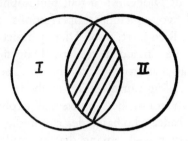

I	II
health	laughter
joie de vivre	comic detachment
praise of the body	Stoic indifference
nature – the harmonious working of the whole world	nature in all its senses accepted
emotional attitude	intellectual attitude

Montaigne calls the books of Rabelais *simplement plaisans* (*Essais*, II.10) and aligns them with modern books such as Boccaccio's *Decameron* or ancient ones such as Vergil's *Georgics*. This aesthetic judgement is significant. For Montaigne has two ways of reading: either an involvement with the pattern, the experience and the poetry of any work, or learning from books how to live well and how to die well. On the same register, he has two different kinds of books: those that give pleasure and those that are fit both to *plaire* and *instruire*. And he puts Rabelais in the first category. He rejects implicitly the didactic, the *moraliste*, the scholarly and the pedantic aspects that critics see in Rabelais's works and recognizes that the man was not moralizing or preaching. If we take Rabelais's prologues now as epilogues of his work, there are two permanent features we can comment on. First, his unbounded admiration for Socrates: Socrates' motto 'I know that I know nothing', the denial that he had any positive doctrines to impart; his assertion that man's soul was immortal; his serenity and confidence in facing death – these were the features which made him the prince of philosophers to men like Erasmus, Montaigne and Rabelais. Allied to him in the prologues is Diogenes; and in the prologue to the *Tiers Livre* we find Rabelais's final position in life expressed through his appreciation of Diogenes: 'il feut philosophe rare et joyeux entre mille. S'il avoit quelques imperfections, aussi avez vous, aussi avons nous. Rien n'est, sinon Dieu, perfaict'. He includes in this judgement his intended readers, Diogenes and himself. Secondly, Rabelais is an ironic writer, but not a sophisticated one: he is constantly calling our attention to the fact that he is being ironical. But as an ironist, he suppresses all explicit moral judgements – it is the reader who has to detect it in the work. He deprecates himself constantly, knowing that his readers will not read him on only one level. His mockery of allegorical method, 'Croyez vous en vostre foy qu'oncques Homere, escrivant l'*Iliade* et *Odyssée*, pensast es allegories lesquelles de luy ont calfreté Plutarche, Heraclides Ponticq, Eustatie, Phornute, et ce que d'iceulx Politian a desrobé?' is new in modern Western European literature. Rabelais rejected the Stoic and the Christian attitude towards literature – moral effusions to help man in his progress through the world. The *sustantificque mouelle* involves us not in finding a decent allegorical meaning which is not incompatible with Christianity but in savouring, and in aesthetically relishing the rich substance of his writing. In Bacon's statement, 'Some books are to be tasted, others to be swallowed, and some few to be chewed and digested: that is, some books are to be read only in parts; others to be read, but not curiously; and some few to be read wholly, and with diligence and attention', the last category can be applied to Rabelais's work.

Judgement and taste may at times be lacking, jokes or puns carry on too long, fantasy become monstrous, cruelty and obscenity jar on a modern reader, and the artistic self-indulgence pall, but one accepts these 'faults' in Rabelais just as one accepts other 'faults' in Balzac, Dickens or Shakespeare. Whether one admits or not the term Menippean satire to characterize his whole work is less important than seeing closely into the fictional and non-fictional worlds of Rabelais. The distance, detachment and tranquillity are there, but so are the *joie de vivre* and the ebullience. The author can move outside his fictional world and mock that world. Where both Cervantes and Rabelais start with a parody, Cervantes takes the reader deeper into the truth and reality of the world through his characters, whilst Rabelais takes the world and transforms that into something entirely different from what we as readers are used to. As a Renaissance doctor and as a Renaissance humanist he offers laughter to the world; and that laughter he clearly defined in the poem at the beginning of his work – *Amis lecteurs, qui ce livre lisez*. We can recognize ourselves as his readers: the conspiracy between author and reader, without whose relationship there would be no comedy; a social phenomenon transmuted to a literary one; the reminder that there is no room for pity or sympathy in his comic work, that moral reactions are as irrelevant as emotional ones, that laughter distracts one's attention from judging moral issues but not from moral meditation. The balance between his work and his audience entails a certain level of intelligence, a certain sophistication and above all the readiness to participate in his linguistic fun. This, in fact, completes the circle of our study: everything, from the introduction of a conspiracy in the prologues to the awareness of the poetic prose of the last chapter, is dependent on the conditional *if*: *if* we are prepared to sign that contract and open the door to the two-way making of fiction.

NOTES

CHAPTER I. INTRODUCTION

1 In the first extant edition (Lyons, 1535) and the second edition (Paris, 1537), the text of chapter 5 followed immediately after chapter 4, without the chapter heading of later editions, *Les propos des bien yvres. Chapitre V.*

2 Significantly, this was missing in the first extant edition of *Gargantua*, but was added in the François Juste edition of 1537.

CHAPTER 2. ORIENTATIONS: 'ARTFUL RAB'LAIS'

1 T. S. Eliot, *Selected Essays* (London, 1953), p. 14.

2 French translation in *Œuvres complètes*, vol. 2, p. 485.

3 For a discussion of the relevant Stoic doctrines, see E. Vernon Arnold, *Roman Stoicism* (Cambridge, 1911), especially, pp. 281–3 and pp. 291–300.

4 Erasmus seems to have provided the Latin for Rabelais to translate in this passage. See his *Hyperaspistes*, quoted by H. Busson, *Le rationalisme dans la littérature française de la Renaissance* (Paris, 1922), p. 173.

5 See Arnold, *Roman Stoicism*, p. 290, footnote 121.

6 H. Busson, 'Les églises contre Rabelais', *THR, ER* VII (1967), 2–81, esp. 74 and 75.

7 *Ibid.* p. 75.

CHAPTER 3. THE PROLOGUES

1 Translated by John Wilson in 1668 (Michigan, 1963), p. 3.

2 The special number of the *THR* devoted to *Rabelais, IVe. centenaire de sa mort* (1953), contains a number of articles which use this phrase *sustantificque mouelle* to unravel the religious thought, the political and social ideas that can be extracted from below the bark of Rabelais's work. For a critique of this book, see Leo Spitzer, 'Rabelais et les "rabelaisants"', *Studi francesi* (1960), 401–23, and 'Ancora sul prologo al Gargantua ...', *Studi francesi* (1965), 423–34.

3 *Praise of Folly*, p. 3.

4 *A True History*, I (Loeb Classical Library), vol. 1, p. 253.

5 *Le Maccheronee*, ed. A. Luzio (Bari, 1928), vol. 2, p. 284.

6 Margaret Mann Phillips, *The Adages of Erasmus* (Cambridge, 1964), p. 269.

7 *Ibid.* pp. 275–6.

8 See the excellent article by Floyd Gray, 'Structure and Meaning in the Prologue to the *Tiers Livre*', *L'Esprit créateur* (1963), 57–62.

9 See J. Bompaire, *Lucien Écrivain. Imitation et Création* (Paris, 1958), p. 288. *Dionysus* (in Loeb edition), vol. 1, p. 55.

10 *Étude sur le comique de Rabelais* (Florence, 1964), p. 103.

11 Phillips, *Adages of Erasmus*, p. 271.

12 Bompaire, *Lucien Écrivain*, p. 288.

13 The material used in this chapter appeared first in an article for *The Modern Language Review* LXII (1967), 407–19. I am grateful to the editors of that journal for permission to re-use this material in a modified form.

CHAPTER 4. THE OLYMPIAN AUTHOR

1 *L'ère du soupçon* (Paris, 1956), p. 76.

2 'Mallarmé et la critique biographique', *Comparative Literature Studies* IV (1967), 34.

3 A new translation by J. M. Cohen in Penguin Classics (London, 1950), p. 75.

4 *Ibid.* p. 355.

5 We shall be discussing this in the next chapter.

6 *A True Story*, 1 (Loeb Classical Library), vol. 1, pp. 249–51.

7 *Mimesis* (London, 1956), p. 237.

8 E. Gilson, *Les idées et les lettres* (Paris, 1932), pp. 197–241. A more detailed analysis will be made in chapter 8.

9 Professor Gerard J. Brault in his article ' "Ung Abysme de Science": on the interpretation of Gargantua's letter to Pantagruel', *BHR* XXVIII (1966), 615–32, makes his whole argument stand on the parody entailed by the whole chapter. This, as we shall see when we discuss the characters of the giants below, chapter 8, is stylistically unsound, but Professor Brault makes the valuable point that there are humorous similes in the framework to this chapter on education.

10 There are several examples of stories like this one in antiquity and in the middle ages but Lucian's story of the whale in his *True Story*, 1, vol. 1, pp. 287–302 was perhaps the most famous one in the Renaissance.

11 *Aspects of Rabelais's Christian Comedy* (London, 1968), pp. 9–10.

12 See M. A. Screech, 'Some Reflexions on the Abbey of Thelema', *THR*, *ER* VIII (1969), 109–14. By taking a closer look at the narrative technique and frere Jan's rôle Professor Screech quite convincingly suggests that the Abbey of Thélème was not 'conceived in one single burst of creative activity' but rather the parts were juxtaposed unrealistically – frere Jan is really not an appropriate abbot for Thélème and chapters 54 and 58 are pessimistic while the other chapters are optimistic. This leads Professor Screech to hazard the hypothesis that *Gargantua*, as we have it today, must have been written after the *Affaire des Placards* and not before it, as was previously thought.

13 For the convenience of English readers I have used 'scriptural' instead of 'evangelical', the more obvious rendering of *évangélique* which is normally used to describe the group of pre-Reformation Biblical scholars in France. For the latter term has too specific an Anglican connotation, being normally used of the theological movement which grew up in the late eighteenth and nineteenth centuries and brought into the church of England a new emphasis on the sole authority of Scripture and the Ministry of the Word, at the same time minimizing the importance of liturgical worship. The split between the evangelicals like William Wilberforce and his successors on the one hand and the high church party on the other was a minor echo of the much more fundamental divorce between the protestant reformers and the Roman church in the sixteenth century. The wider sense of 'evangelical' applied more generally to the protestant churches would, of course, add further confusion in the context of Erasmus's and Rabelais's pre-Reformation ideas.

14 References to the partial edition will be to Jean Plattard, *Le Quart Livre de Pantagruel* (*Édition dite partielle, Lyon, 1548*) (Paris, 1910).

15 N. Friedman, 'Point of View in Fiction: The development of a Critical Concept', *Publications of the Modern Language Association of America* (1955), 1160.

CHAPTER 5. THE CHOICE OF FORM

1 Abraham C. Keller, *The Telling of Tales in Rabelais. Aspects of his Narrative Art.* [*Analecta Romanica* 12 (Frankfurt am Main, 1963).]

2 Miriam Allott, *Novelists on the Novel* (London, 1959), p. 227, a quotation from Fielding's review of Charlotte Lennox's *The Female Quixote*.

3 *The Life and Opinions of Tristram Shandy*, I. xxii.

4 This will be dealt with more fully in chapter 6.

5 Princeton, 1957, p. 304.

6 *Les Saturnales*, ed. Henri Bornecque (Classiques Garnier), vol. I, p. 106.

7 *Satyre Ménippée*, ed. Ch. Read (Paris, n.d.), pp. 11–13. The phrase in italics is so Rabelaisian that it is difficult not to see Passerat's hand in the writing of it.
8 *Les Œuvres du P. Rapin* (Amsterdam, 1709), vol. II, pp. 204–5. Justus Lipsius had published in 1581 a *Satyra Menippea, sive Somnium*, and likes Petronius because 'nuda illa nequitia ... nihil offendor: ioci me delectant, urbanitas capit ...'. The whole genre of Menippean satire in the sixteenth century needs examination for it seems to be strangely neglected. It would enlighten our ideas on many aspects of the polemic around religion as well as the literary problems of 'imitation'.
9 This title is argued very convincingly by J. P. Sullivan in *The Satyricon of Petronius* (London, 1968), p. 89, as being a more accurate translation of *Apocolocyntosis* than the usual *The Pumpkinification of Claudius*.
10 Loeb edition, 1930, with an English translation by W. H. D. Rouse, p. 371.
11 See the facsimile reprint of the 1532 edition: Notice par Pierre Champion (Paris, 1925), pp. 1–2.
12 *Histoire Maccaronique de Merlin Coccaie. Prototype de Rabelais* (Paris, 1606), vol. II, p. 414.
13 *The Aeneid of Virgil*, translated by C. Day Lewis (London, 1952), book II, lines 701–8.
14 'L'énigme du Pantagruelion', *THR, ER* I (1956), 46–72.
15 See J. Plattard, *L'invention et la composition dans l'œuvre de Rabelais* (Paris, 1909); Tétel, *Étude*, and R. C. Flowers, *Voltaire's Stylistic Transformation of Rabelaisian Satirical Devices* (Washington, D.C., 1951).

CHAPTER 6. THE 'TIERS LIVRE'

1 This is Abel Lefranc's thesis which can be found in the introduction to the *Tiers Livre* in his edition of the *Œuvres complètes*, or in his book, *Rabelais. Études sur Gargantua, Pantagruel, Le Tiers Livre* (Paris, 1953).
2 This is Professor Screech's thesis and can be found in *The Rabelaisian Marriage* (London, 1958), his edition of the *Tiers Livre* (Geneva–Paris, 1964), his *Aspects of Rabelais's Christian Comedy*, or in the article, 'Aspects du rôle de la médecine dans la philosophie comique de Rabelais', in *Invention et Imitation. Études sur la littérature du seizième siècle*, ed. J. A. G. Tans (The Hague, 1968), pp. 39–48.
3 *Bladum suum en vert* occurs frequently in the sermons of the time but each time the context is totally different from this one in Rabelais.
4 For a full account of the satirical eulogy in the Renaissance, see C. A. Mayer, 'Rabelais' Satirical Eulogy: The Praise of Borrowing', *THR* VII (1953), 147–55.
5 *Ibid.*
6 The term 'comic romance' will be defined in the next chapter.
7 *The Rabelaisian Marriage*, pp. 84–103.
8 For a wider discussion of the Stoic elements here, see M. A. Screech 'Some Stoic Elements in Rabelais's Religious Thought', in *THR, ER* I (1956), 73–97, and also 'Further Precision on the Stoic-Evangelical Crux: *chascun abonde en son sens*', in *BHR* XXII (1960), 549–51.
9 For fuller discussion, see chapter 8.
10 *Aeneid*, trans. Day Lewis, p. 119.
11 One might also remember Saint Paul's dictum forbidding Christians to indulge in *stultiloquium* and *scurrilitas* (Eph. v. 4).

CHAPTER 7. CHARACTERS

1 *Anatomy of Criticism*, pp. 223–39.
2 Charles F. Hockett, *A course in modern linguistics* (New York, 1958), p. 564.
3 The *paratactic* structure is the simple sentence with the connecting link between successive sentences being provided, if at all, by such words as the conjunctions *and* or *but* or *so*. The *hypotactic* structure is more complex: a number of subordinate

clauses are linked to a main clause by *comme, ainsi, non seulement mais aussi* and a network of participles. The same development from paratactic to hypotactic in French can be seen in Latin from Plautus to Livy or in English between Anglo-Saxon and modern English.

4 *Étude*, p. 56.
5 *Aspects of the Novel* (London, 1947), chapter 4.
6 *Ibid.*
7 Everyman edition, pp. xvii–xviii.
8 References made to the 1548 version are to Jean Plattard, *Le Quart Livre*.

CHAPTER 8. THE GIANTS

1 For a definition of hypotactic and paratactic styles, see chapter 7, note 3.
2 Phillips, *Adages of Erasmus*, pp. 348–9.
3 Incidentally, it is this same herb that Epistemon seriously suggests to cure Panurge in the *Tiers Livre*, chapter 24.
4 H. Busson, 'La Morale des Thélémites', *THR, ER* VI (1965), 23–50.
5 ' "Ung Abysme de Science" ', p. 617.
6 *Les idées et les lettres*, p. 231.
7 K. Quinn, *Virgil's Aeneid: a critical description* (London, 1968), p. 71.
8 *Anatomy of Criticism*, p. 21.
9 Craig Thompson's translation of *The Colloquies of Erasmus* (Chicago and London, 1965), p. 140.
10 For a full discussion of the whole episode, see M. A. Screech, 'The Death of Pan and Heroes in Rabelais. A study in Syncretism', *BHR* XVII (1955), 36–55.

CHAPTER 9. POETIC PROSE

1 London, 1955, p. 104.
2 Baudelaire, *Œuvres complètes*, ed. Y.-G. Le Dantec (Pléiade edition, Paris, 1954), pp. 1,025–6.
3 Valéry, *Œuvres*, ed. Jean Hytier (Pléiade edition, Paris, 1957), vol. I, p. 207.
4 *Étude*, pp. 103–4.

CHRONOLOGY

This brief chronology is presented in three sections: the facts of Rabelais's biography; classical literature – ancient and modern – and vernacular literature. It is not in any way meant to be complete but provides a skeleton of phenomena related to this book.

Rabelais's life

1494(?) Assumed birth of François Rabelais at La Devinière, near Chinon.

1520 Letter (non-extant) to Budé mentioned by Rabelais in a second letter to Budé.

1521 The second letter to Budé in Latin sent from the Franciscan monastery, Fontenay-le-Comte.

1523–4 Difficulties with his superiors at Fontenay-le-Comte over his Greek studies.

1524–5 Rabelais has the authority of Pope Clement VII to pass to the Benedictine Order at Maillezais.

1530 François Rabelais on matriculation register of Medical Faculty of Montpellier.

1532 Letter to Tiraqueau sent from Lyons.
Publishes his first scholarly works in Latin: for example, the *Aphorisms* of Hippocrates.
Letter to Erasmus sent from Lyons in November.
Presumed publication of *Pantagruel* and the *Pantagrueline Prognostication*. Both works signed by the pseudonym Alcofrybas Nasier.

1533 Condemnation of *Pantagruel* by the Sorbonne (an undated letter of Calvin).

1534 In Italy from February to April as Medical Secretary to Jean du Bellay.
Published, on return to Lyons, an edition of Marliani's *Topographia antiquae Romae* with a preface–epistle to Jean du Bellay dated 31 August 1534.

17–18 October *Affaire des Placards.*
Gargantua. First edition is undated.

1535 Second voyage to Rome with Jean du Bellay. Letters written from Rome to his patron, Geoffroy d'Estissac, Archbishop of Maillezais.

1536 Pope Paul III grants him the regularization of his monkish state and allows him to practise medicine.
Becomes a monk at Saint-Maur-des-Fossés.

1537 Present at a banquet offered to Étienne Dolet.
Receives his Doctorate of Medicine at Montpellier.

1537–8	Lectures and demonstrates at Montpellier.
1538	At Aigues-Mortes and then in Lyons.
1540	At Turin with Guillaume du Bellay, seigneur de Langey.
1542	Definitive edition of *Pantagruel* and *Gargantua* published by François Juste at Lyons.
1543	Both *Pantagruel* and *Gargantua* figure among books censored by the Sorbonne.
1546	Publication of the *Tiers Livre*, with a dedication to Marguerite de Navarre and a *privilège* from Francis I.
1546–7	At Metz.
1548	Partial edition of the *Quart Livre*.
1549	At Rome with Jean du Bellay. Description of a *Sciomachia* given by Jean du Bellay.
	Dupuyherbault attacks him in his *Theotimus*.
1550	Calvin attacks him in the *Traité des Scandales*.
1551	Obtains the benefice of Meudon.
1552	The complete *Quart Livre* published with a dedication to Cardinal Odet de Châtillon.
1553	In January resigns from Meudon.
	On 9 April his presumed death.
1554	Epitaph of Rabelais by Tahureau.
1562	Publication of *L'Isle Sonnante*, the first sixteen chapters of the *Cinquiesme Livre* attributed to Rabelais.
1564	The complete *Cinquiesme Livre* published.

Latin and Greek literature

1469	Apuleius, *Metamorphoseon*, in 11 books. First edition.
	Aulus Gellius, *Noctes Atticae*, in 20 books. First edition.
1482	*Scriptores Panegyrici Latini*, containing: (1) Pliny the Younger's *Panegyricus;* (2) ten other panegyrics by various authors on diverse emperors; (3) The *Agricola* of Tacitus; (4) *Petronii arbitri satyrici fragmenta: quae extant.*
1496	Lucian, 82 separate writings, mostly in the form of dialogues.
1500	Erasmus, *Adagia*. First edition.
1503	First Aldine edition of Lucian. Inferior ms., but served as a basis for all sixteenth-century editions.
	Maillard, *Sermones de Adventu, Quadragesimales*.
1506	Erasmus's translation into Latin of 18 short dialogues and 10 longer ones of Lucian. (Editions of Lucian were very frequent in the first half of the sixteenth century: between 1496 and 1550 there were 85 editions of his complete works or of parts of them.)
1511	Erasmus, *Moriae Encomium*.
1512	Erasmus, *De duplici copia verborum ac rerum commentarii duo*.

1513 *Lucii Annaei Senecae in morte Claudii Cesaris Ludus nuper repertus.* First edition.

1514 Jean Raulin, *Sermones de penitentia.*

1515 Jean Raulin, *Opus sermonum quadragesimalium.*
Epistolae obscurorum virorum.
New edition of Erasmus's *Adagia*, now containing 3,411 adages and including for the first time *Sileni Alcibiadis.*

1516 More, *Utopia.*
Erasmus, *Institutio Principis Christiani.*

1517 Folengo (Merlin Coccaius), *Opus macaronicorum.*

1518 Erasmus, *Colloquia* (first authorized edition).

1519 Guillaume Pépin, *Sermones dominicales.*

1520 Pomponazzi, *De fato.*
A Paris edition of Petronius' *Satyricon.*

1522 New enlarged edition of Erasmus's *Colloquia.*

1524 Erasmus, *De libero arbitrio.*

1525 Luther, *De servo arbitrio.*

1528 Erasmus, *Ciceronianus.*

1535 Dolet, *De imitatione ciceroniana,* directed against Erasmus.

1536 Calvin, *Institutio religionis christianae.*

1537 Bonaventure des Périers, *Cymbalum mundi.*

Vernacular literature

1476 *Chronique de Turpin* (prosified).

1478 *Melusine* (prosified).

1480 *Les quatre fils Aymon* (prosified).

1486 *Fierabras* (prosified).

1489 *Tristan* (prosified).

1493 *Le petit Artus de Bretagne* (prosified).

1496 *Robert le Diable* (prosified).

1498 *Merlin avec les Propheties* (prosified).
Ogier le Danois (prosified).
Lancelot du Lac (prosified).

1513 *Huon de Bordeaux* (prosified).

1516 Gringore, *Mère Sotte.*

1517 Folengo, *Baldus.*

1518 *Guérin de Monglave* (prosified).

1525 Menot, *Carême de Tours.*
Geoffrey à la grant dent (prosified).
Jehan de Paris (prosified).

1526 Menot, *Carêmes de Paris.*

1528 *Perceforest* (prosified).

1530 Lefèvre d'Étaples, *La Sainte Bible.*

Giglan, fils de Gauvain et Geoffrey de Mayence (prosified).

Geoffrey Tory, *Champfleury.*

1532   Marot, *L'Adolescence Clementine.*

1538   Clément Marot, *Œuvres.*

1540   *Amadis de Gaule* (book 1 published in French).

1541   Calvin's translation into French of his *Institutio.*

       Marot translated some psalms.

1544   Dolet translated dialogues of Plato.

       Scève, *Délie.*

1545   Pernette du Guillet, *Œuvres.*

1549   Du Bellay, *Defense et illustration de la langue française,* and *Olive.*

1550   Ronsard, *Odes.*

       Calvin, *Traité des Scandales.*

SELECT BIBLIOGRAPHY

Editions

Œuvres complètes, ed. A. Lefranc *et al.* Vols 1–6, Paris–Geneva, 1912–55 (incomplete; stops at chapter 17 of the *Quart Livre*).
Œuvres complètes, ed. P. Jourda. 2 vols, Paris, 1962.
Le Tiers Livre, ed. M. A. Screech. Geneva–Paris, 1964.
Le Quart Livre, ed. R. Marichal. Geneva–Lille, 1947.
Le Quart Livre de Pantagruel (Édition dite partielle, Lyon, 1548), ed. Jean Plattard, Paris, 1910.

General criticism

Booth, W. C. *The Rhetoric of Fiction*, Chicago, 1961.
Frye, Northrop. *Anatomy of Criticism*, Princeton, 1957.

Studies on the language

Huguet, E. *Étude sur la syntaxe de Rabelais*. Paris, 1894.
Sainéan, L. *La langue de Rabelais*. Paris, 1922.

Rabelais criticism

Febvre, L. *Le problème de l'incroyance au XVIe siècle. La religion de Rabelais.* Paris, 1942; reprinted, 1962.
Krailsheimer, A. J. *Rabelais and the Franciscans.* Oxford, 1963.
Lefranc, A. *Rabelais*, Paris, 1953.
Plattard, J. *L'invention et la composition dans l'œuvre de Rabelais.* Paris, 1909.
Screech, M. A. *The Rabelaisian Marriage.* London, 1958.
L'Évangélisme de Rabelais (THR xxxii; *ER* ii) Geneva, 1959.
Tétel, M. *Étude sur le comique de Rabelais.* Florence, 1964.

INDEX